IMAGES
of America

FORTUNA AND THE EEL RIVER VALLEY

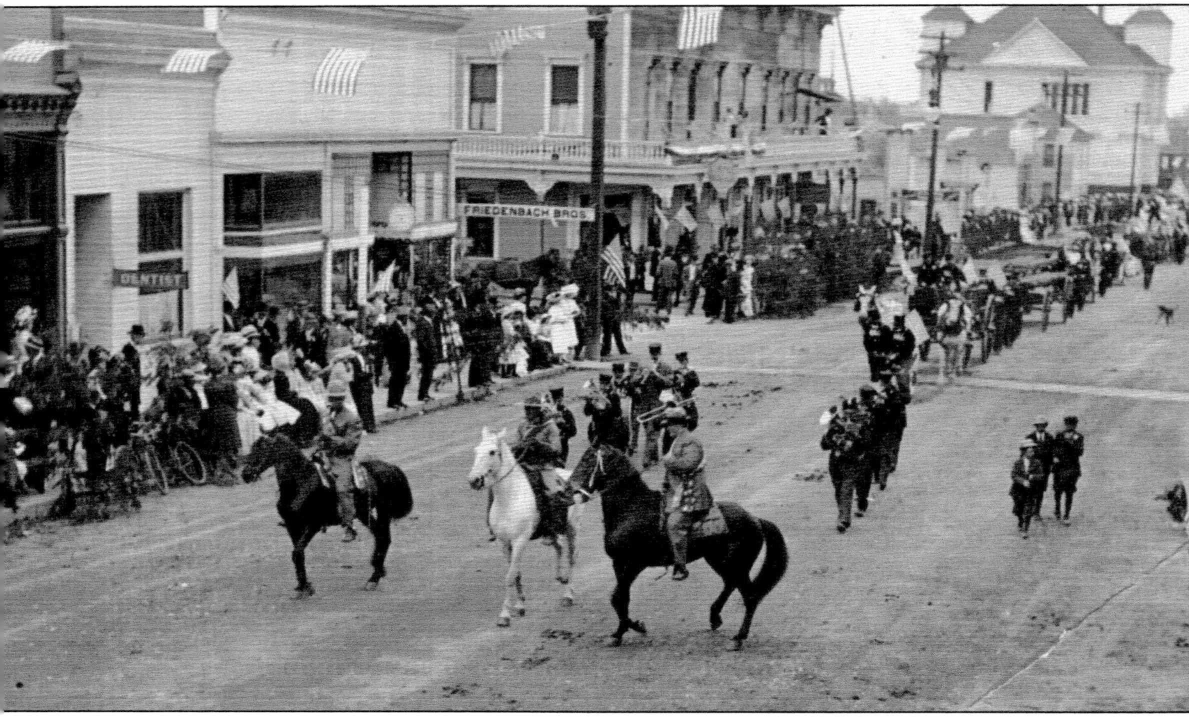

In 1911, completion of the Northwestern Pacific Railroad was imminent, Fortuna High School was well attended, the mills were in high production, and the future seemed assured. A destructive downtown fire in June could not dampen spirits, and Fortuna celebrated its prosperity with a large Fourth of July parade. Dentist W.S. O'Connor was parade marshal. Also seen in the Main Street parade are the town's band and fire department. (Courtesy of Fortuna Depot Museum.)

On the Cover: Since formation in 1904, the Fortuna Volunteer Fire Department (FVFD) has been an integral part of the community. The department has been active in both fire protection and civic improvements. The cover illustrates the hook and ladder and hose companies, including their mascot dogs and Fire Chief L.L. Bryan (kneeling behind the dog on the left), in the early 1900s. (Courtesy of Fortuna Volunteer Fire Department.)

IMAGES
of America

FORTUNA AND THE EEL RIVER VALLEY

Fortuna Depot Museum
Alex Service
Susan O'Hara

ARCADIA
PUBLISHING

ISBN 978-0-7385-7522-3

Published by Arcadia Publishing
Charleston, South Carolina

Printed in the United States of America

Library of Congress Control Number: 2011921760

For all general information, please contact Arcadia Publishing:
Telephone 843-853-2070
Fax 843-853-0044
E-mail sales@arcadiapublishing.com
For customer service and orders:
Toll-Free 1-888-313-2665

Visit us on the Internet at www.arcadiapublishing.com

The authors dedicate this book to the Fortuna Depot Museum and those who have served on the Fortuna Historical Commission for their ongoing efforts to preserve and interpret the history of the Eel River Valley. We would like to thank past and present Fortuna City Councils for their support and vision in creating the museum.

Contents

ACKNOWLEDGMENTS

The authors would like to thank John Crotty, director of Fortuna Parks and Recreation, and the Fortuna Historical Commission for their support of this project. They would like to thank Bob Lutz, Shannon McWhorter, Marguerita Nichols, Doug and Marilyn Strehl, the Bear River Band of the Rohnerville Rancheria, the Clarke Historical Museum in Eureka, Clendenen's Cider Works, the Fortuna Volunteer Fire Department, and the Humboldt County Office of Education for research assistance and for sharing images used in this book. They would also like to thank Beth Rundell for having the vision to create the Depot Museum, and those who have served as curators, commissioners, and volunteers, furthering the museum's mission of preserving the history of Fortuna and the Eel River Valley.

The artifacts found in the museum have helped in the research for this book. One particularly useful collection was the Fortuna High School *Megaphone* yearbook, of which the museum has a complete collection from 1906 to the present. The authors extensively utilized photograph collections donated by the Brown, Combs, Conant, Daggett, Davidson, Elliott, Gillard, Hellard, Roberts, Rohner, Towne, and Umland families. Two additional important sources of information were the May 30, 1896, *Eel River Valley Advance* and the pictorial edition of the *Humboldt Beacon* of January 17, 1913. Finally, the authors would like to thank the community for their ongoing support of the museum and its mission. The authors are donating their royalties to support the Depot Museum.

Unless otherwise noted, the images used in this book come from the Depot Museum photograph collection.

INTRODUCTION

While not an exhaustive account of the Eel River Valley in California's Humboldt County, this pictorial history seeks to capture the essence of this valley and the towns that are found along the east side of the Eel River. The time period covered is from the 1860s, when photographs became widely available, to the opening of the Fortuna Depot Museum in 1976. The authors have chosen a thematic rather than chronological approach in selecting photographs to tell the story of the valley. They have also included in the book images from the junction of the two main forks of the Eel River at Dyerville to near the mouth of the river, as the Eel River has provided an important element in the history of the region.

Prior to the Gold Rush in 1849, the Eel River Valley was inhabited by members of the Wiyot, Nongatl, and Sinkyone tribes. These Native Americans relied on the river for salmon and the lamprey eel for which the Josiah Gregg party named the river. They had semipermanent villages along the river and would travel to the hills during the summer.

Their way of life was irrevocably altered in 1850 with the arrival of the *Laura Virginia* in Humboldt Bay. Euro-American settlers quickly spread out from the bay to seek homesteads. In addition to finding rich farmland along the alluvial flats of the Eel River, settlers also discovered the "red gold" of the redwood trees. Lumber mills and farms soon coexisted along the river.

The first settlement on the east side of the river was Rohnerville, closely followed by Hydesville and Rio Dell. Near the river, some five miles from Rohnerville, a small community began with the creation of the Springville Mill in 1874. The area was originally called Slide because of a nearby troubling landslide. The eponymous slide site is still visible near the north end of town. This name was later changed to Springville for the many springs in the surrounding hills. However, when residents sought a post office, the name was refused since there was already a Springville, California. The town was again named Slide, and it got a post office. In the 1880s, the name was changed again, this time to Fortuna, after a petition from residents. The city of Fortuna was incorporated in 1906.

Fortuna, now the largest of the communities along the river, was described in Fortuna High School's 1911 yearbook, the *Megaphone*, as being

> Situated in the midst of green fields and rolling hills covered with tall timber . . . Although it is only one of the many busy country towns in Humboldt, yet it is one [that] is rapidly forging ahead and one destined to have a more varied history than its contemporaries.
>
> Huge logging trains, indicating the chief industry of the vicinity, enter every few minutes, and in almost every direction there is a hazy outline in the sky caused by some industrious mill. Fortuna is directly connected with the largest mills in the county, notably Newburg mill, Scotia mill, Fortuna moulding mill, Robinson's mill, and Newell and McIntyre's mill at Alton. These mills all help to swell the trade of Fortuna.
>
> Next but not least is dairying, which occupies an important role in the resources of southern Humboldt. Thousands of dollars' worth of butter is annually shipped from

Fortuna and its neighborhood to San Francisco and the bay cities, where it finds a ready consumption. Humboldt butter is famed far and wide for its excellence and has won first prize this year in a state dairy contest.

Farming and the raising of fruit trees, especially apples, are an important adjunct to the county products. A person residing in Fortuna in fall time will find an abundance of ripe, juicy apples. Enough fruits and apples are grown to supply a drying and canning establishment during six months of the year.

South of Fortuna and near to the high school building is the sometimes turbulent Eel River. In winter, it is a roaring torrent carrying everything in its resistless grasp, but in summer its banks are a paradise for camping parties and the angler. Eel River furnishes another source of wealth to Humboldt County during the fishing season. Hundreds of boxes of huge salmon are daily shipped from Fortuna, although a part of the catch is canned here.

Altogether Fortuna, with its straight, clean streets and rows of white houses, presents an inviting appearance, attractive alike to the tourist or settler.

The school system is unusually excellent for a small town. The high school, supported by Fortuna School District alone, suggests an unwonted appreciation of educational advantages by the inhabitants. This year has witnessed the gathering of more laurels for Fortuna High than any other year since its initial entrance into the Athletic League. We attribute this directly to the splendid school spirit and perseverance [that have] prevailed among the students this year.

With the advent of the railroad connecting with San Francisco, Fortuna, by virtue of its climate and location, will become one of the largest cities on the Pacific coast.

The railroad was completed in 1914 and the Redwood Highway a few years later. Road construction was important, as it led more people to the region and allowed for easier travel within the county. Bridges replaced the various ferries that had allowed for crossing of the river. These changes, along with technological advances in both the lumber industry and in everyday life, greatly impacted the valley and its residents. Another influence on the river communities and the residents of the valley was periodic flooding of the Eel River, including the devastating flood of 1964. Fires ravaged wooden structures of towns and mills, frequently changing cityscapes.

Throughout the decades, another common element in the Eel River Valley has been the communities' celebrations and the many organizations and volunteer associations that help to sponsor these events, which include annual sports, such as baseball and basketball and an annual rodeo that started in 1921. The local high school and various grammar schools are also central to community daily life. Fortuna was the third town in Humboldt County to have a high school. Fortuna High opened its doors in 1903 with 32 students. In 1905, the first graduating class consisted of only two students.

The lumber industry has faded in importance in the Eel River Valley, as has the agriculture industry that once flourished along the river's banks. The train that was so important in 1911 no longer runs. However, the images in this book provide glimpses of a past that still influences the present. The communities along the Eel are still growing and changing in response to historical forces that shaped the region.

One

People and Places of the Eel River Valley

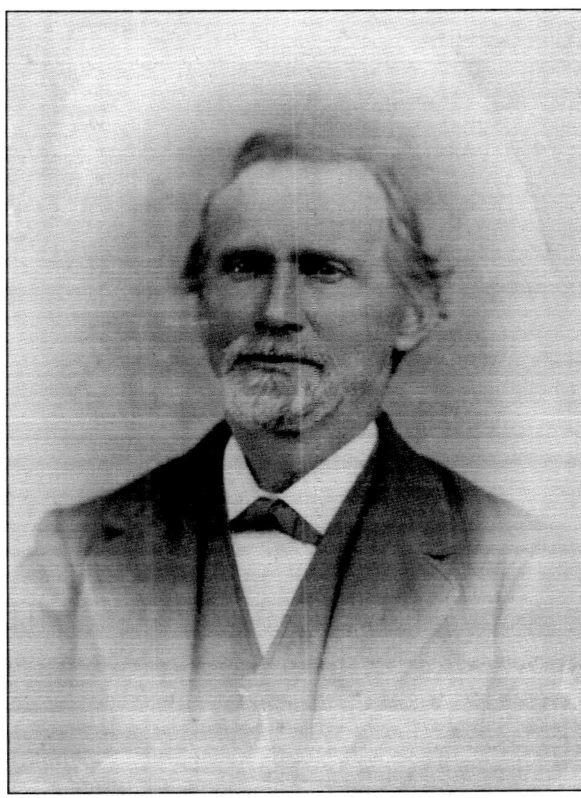

Henry Rohner emigrated from Switzerland at the age of 17 and joined the California Gold Rush. Instead of gold, his eventual fortune came from commerce, timber, and real estate. Around 1859, he opened the first store in the area that became Rohnerville, and in 1874, his Springville Mill was the first business in the future Fortuna. By the time he died in 1900, he was known as the founding father of both Rohnerville and Fortuna.

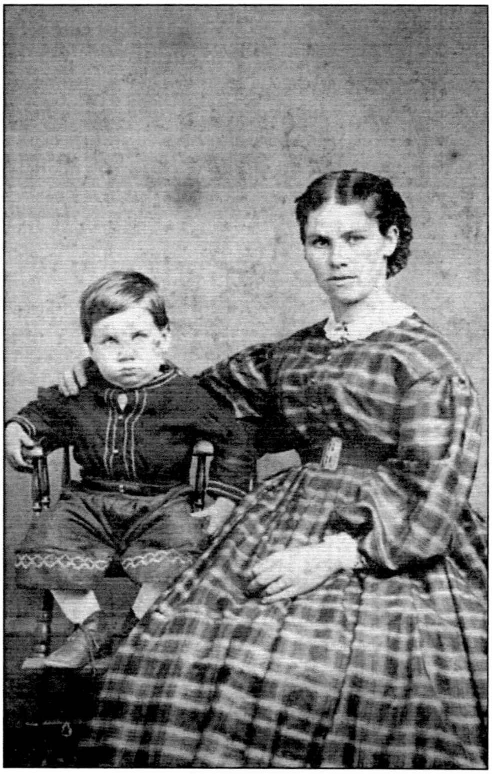

Mary Bulkeley was born in Pennsylvania. Her family moved west to Wisconsin, and in 1854, when she was nine years old, they journeyed to California by covered wagon. The family settled at Table Bluff. When she was 16, she married 32-year-old Henry Rohner, the storekeeper at Rohnerville. She is shown here with Henry Rohner Jr., the second of the couple's seven children.

Henry Rohner built this mansion on Main Street to replace the home that appears at the beginning of chapter two. The mansion was torn down in the early 1940s, to the dismay of the pioneers' teenage grandson Frank Rohner. He raced into the building to salvage a newel post as a souvenir minutes before bulldozers went to work. In the early 21st century, a Chinese restaurant stands on this site.

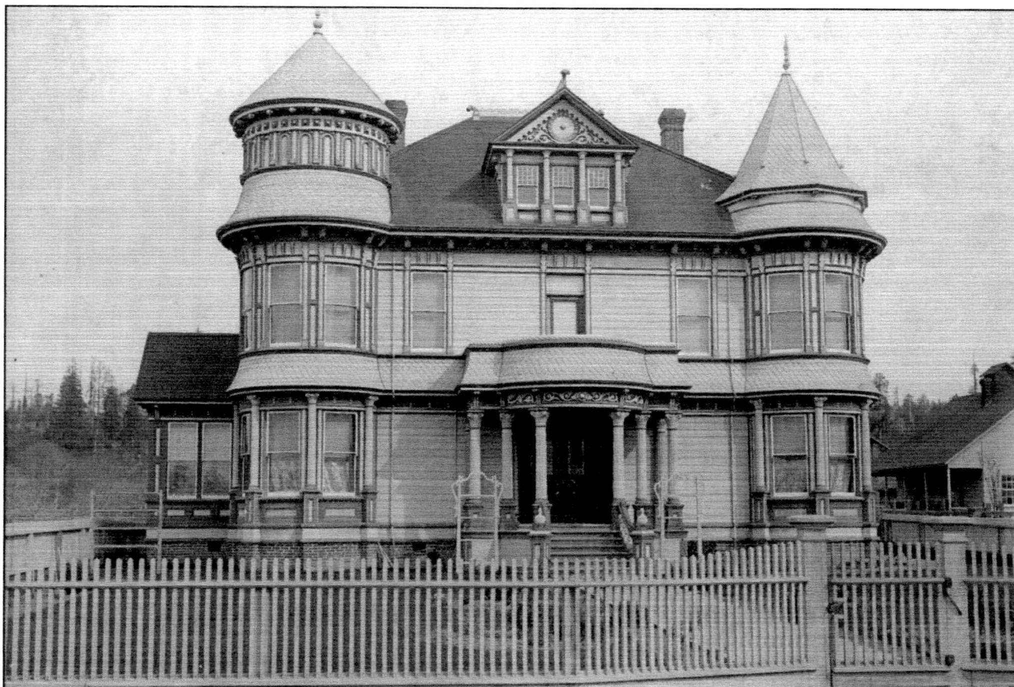

Minnie Brown was granddaughter of famed abolitionist John Brown. She was about one year old when she traveled west with her grandmother, parents, and some of her aunts and uncles to seek a new start after John Brown's execution. The family settled in Rohnerville. Minnie Brown married Thomas Burns in 1883, became the mother of three children, and died at 39, probably of cancer. She is buried in the Old Rohnerville Cemetery.

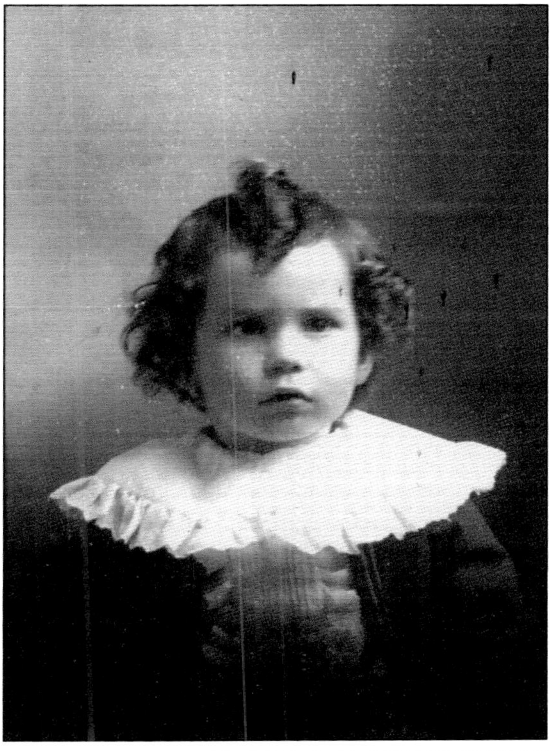

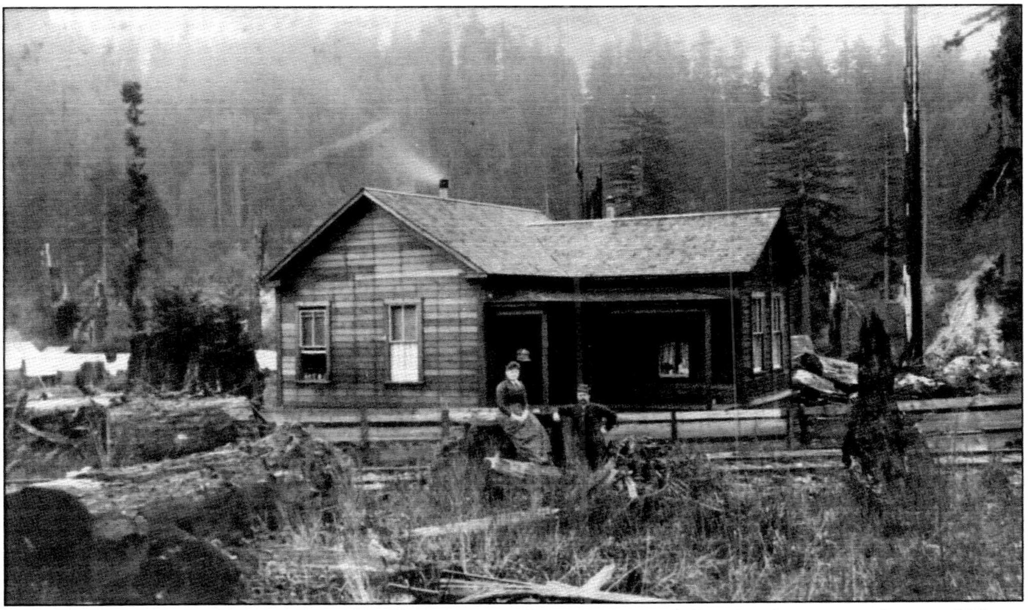

The Pacific Lumber Company's mill town was Scotia, named for the large numbers of Nova Scotians working there. Mill worker Kimball Hatch came from Maine and his wife, Emma Cootey, from Vermont. According to voter registration records from 1884 and 1890, more of Humboldt County's citizens hailed from Maine than from any other state. This photograph is thought to have been taken outside their Scotia home shortly after the couple's marriage in 1890.

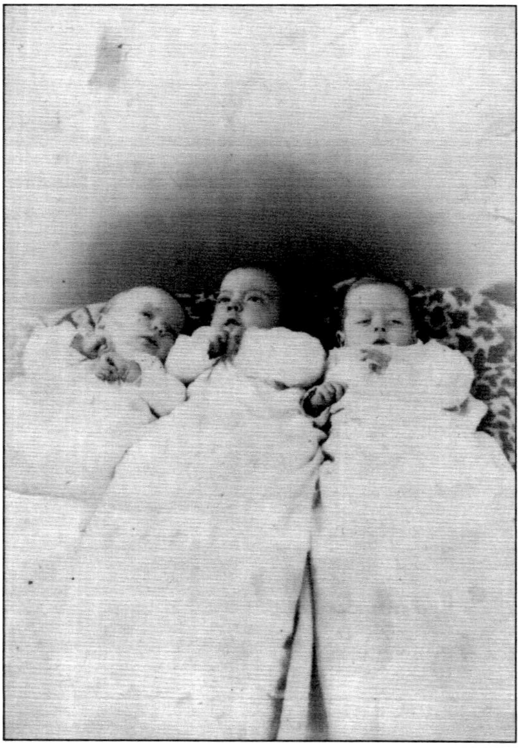

Humboldt's first triplets were Daisy, Louisa, and Harry Natwick, born in June 1892 in Hydesville. This and similar souvenir photographs were sold at the County Fair in Rohnerville, where the triplets were displayed at about two months old. Their father, Henry, was from Norway, and their mother, Cordelia, was from Nevada. Henry Natwick was a machinist at the Newburg Mill, an officer of the Woodmen of the World, and president of the Fortuna Building and Loan Association.

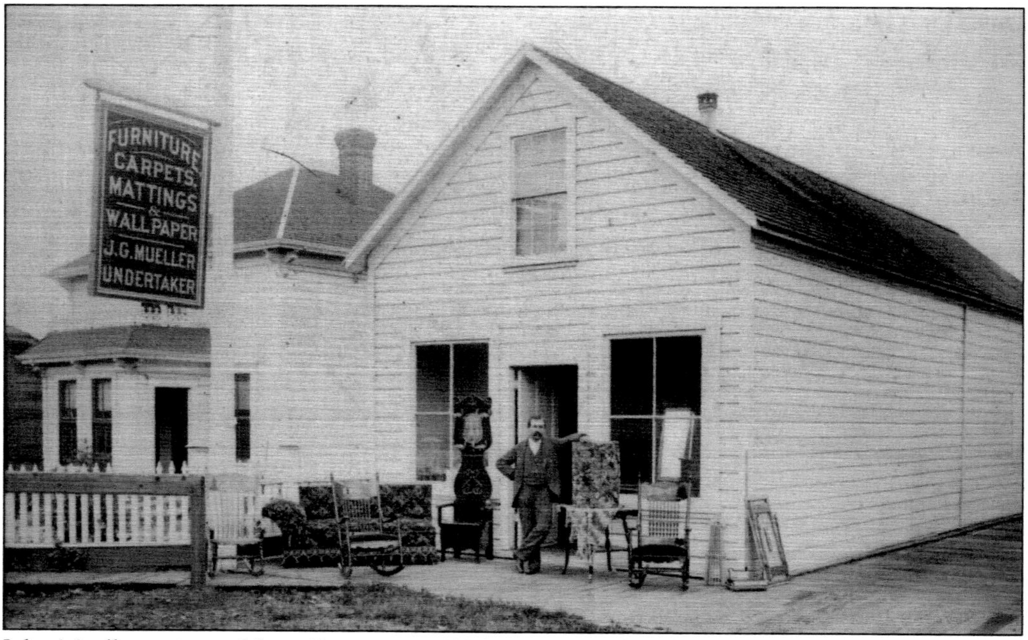

John Mueller emigrated from Germany in 1886 at age 18 and ran his furniture business in Loleta for over 30 years. His wife, Ida Buttle, was born in California, the child of immigrants from England. She was a charter member of the Loleta's Los Amegos Civic Club formed in 1906 "to promise acquaintanceship, good fellowship, and cooperation among the women of this village."

According to the *Eel River Advance* in 1896, Virginian William J. Swortzel "knows no such word as fail, and consequently has no time to parley with reverses or halt in his onward business career." When this photograph captured the family home around 1895, Swortzel had risen from clerk in the Springville Mill to co-owner of the Swortzel and Williams mill and founder of the Fortuna Merchandising Company, as well as having served as postmaster, school trustee, and county supervisor.

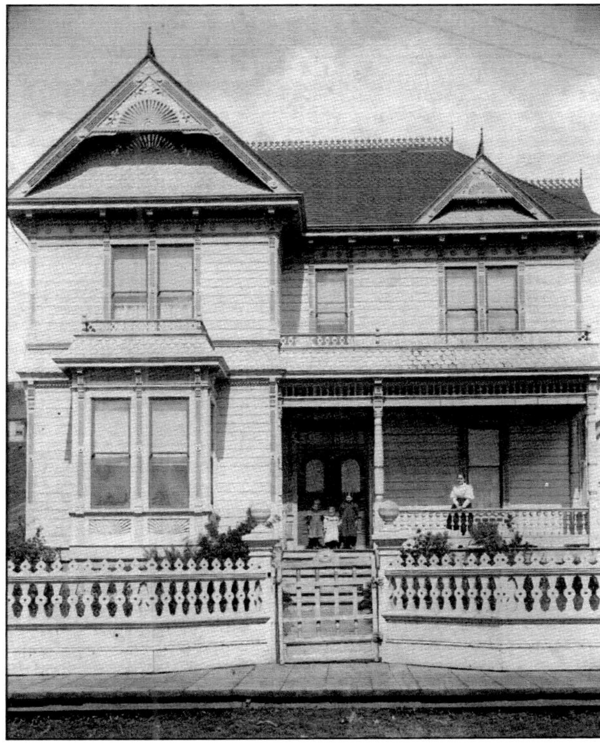

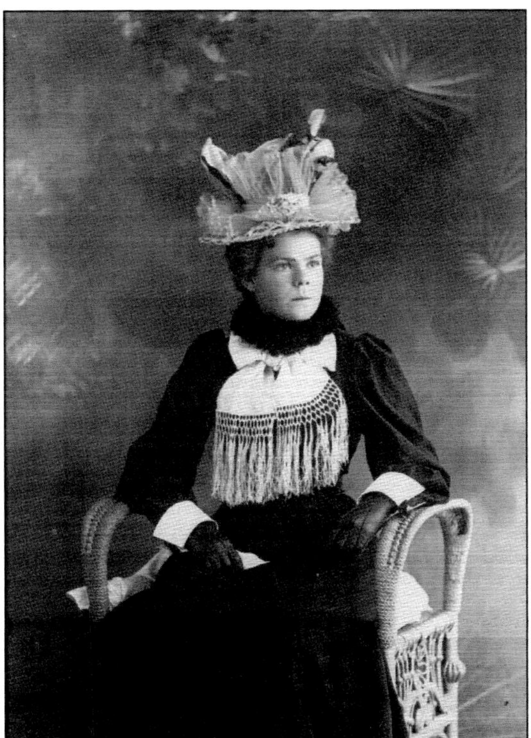

Swedish emigrant Hansine Ingebor Erickson came to America in 1883 at age five. This portrait was taken in 1904 when she lodged with the Fell family on Fortuna's Sandy Prairie Road (later renamed Twelfth Street). In May of that year, she married West Virginian John Brissey, who, throughout his career, was a teacher, a lumber worker, a bridge carpenter, a canning company employee, and a mailman.

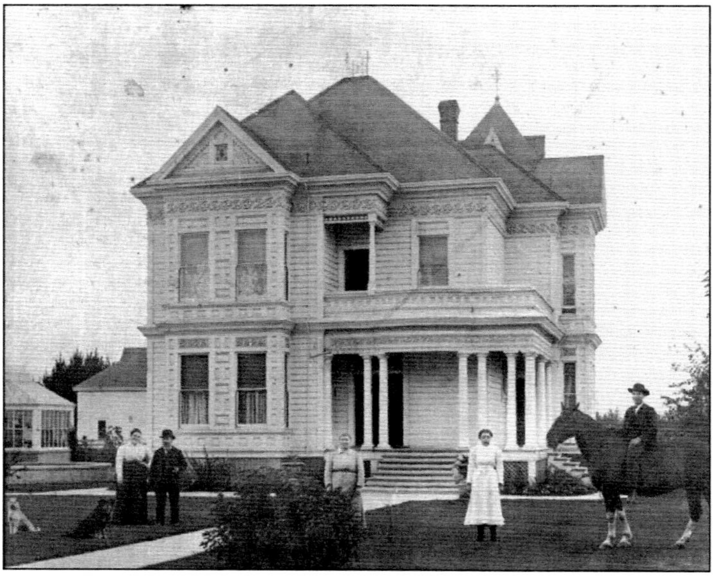

Finnish Tekla Dahl immigrated when she was 18, joining an uncle in Alaska. There she married Scottish emigrant Archibald Campbell, a mine superintendant. The couple prospered, and in 1896, they came to Rohnerville, where they built this house on Rohnerville Road. The Campbells sent for her family to join them. Pictured from left to right are Tekla and Archibald Campbell with Tekla's mother, Wilhelmina Dahl, sister Vera, and brother Otto.

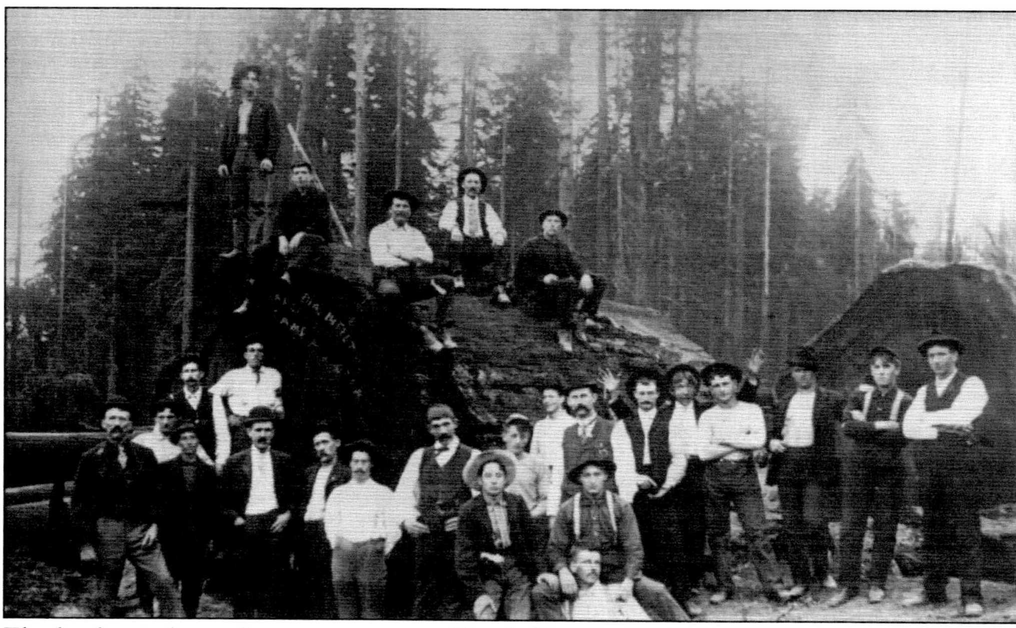

The lumber industry drew newcomers to Humboldt County from across America and Europe. The most common places of origin in Humboldt's 1890 voter registration records were California, Maine, New York, Ohio, Canada, Ireland, England, Germany, Denmark, and Sweden. Lumberman Les Spinney recalled, "The hardy and long-working crews were of Scandinavian descent . . . quite a few Irishmen . . . Polish . . . a few Italians, and some stubborn Englishmen."

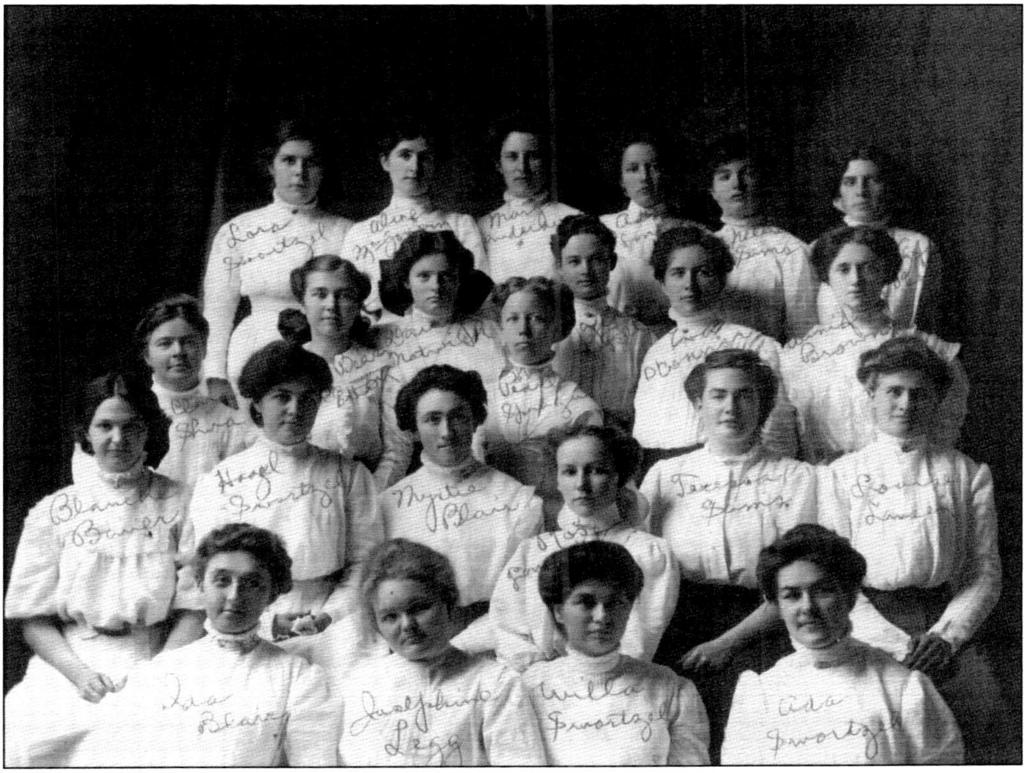

This c. 1910 photograph shows the Loyal Daughters, the young women's group at Fortuna's First Christian Church. There was also a Loyal Sons group for the congregation's young men. Most of the women pictured here were born in California, but their parents hailed from Illinois, Iowa, Maine, Massachusetts, Missouri, Nevada, Ohio, Pennsylvania, and Virginia, as well as England, Canada, Germany, and Norway.

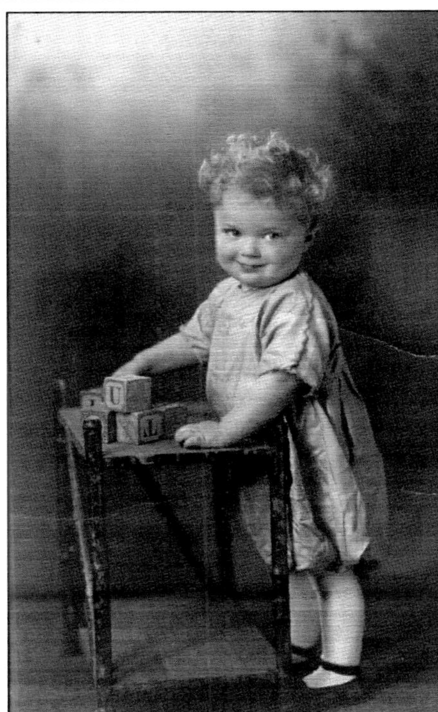

The Ephraim Goble family traveled west from Illinois in 1869 and settled near Ferndale. Garvin Goble, born in Fortuna in 1916, was one of many great-grandchildren of the pioneers. As Dr. Goble, he practiced here for 37 years, following his return from the US Army Medical Corps in 1946.

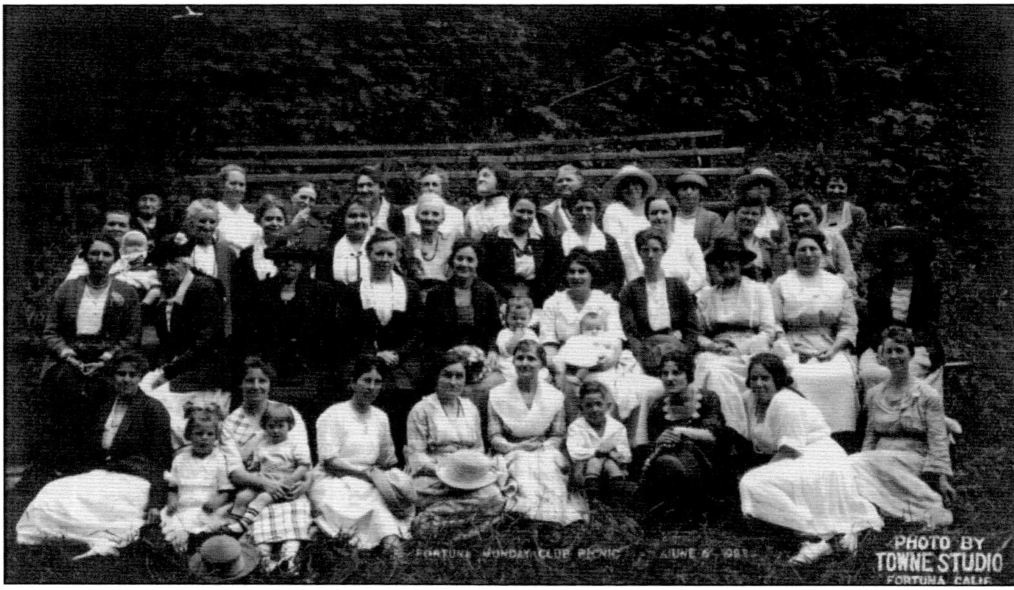

The Monday Club was a women's literary study group. One of its founders was Bertie White McNulty Hansen (third row, third from the right). Hansen was the first woman to hold the office of postmaster in Fortuna. The daughter of pioneers, she was the first child to be born along Yager Creek. She was also the first Fortuna woman to register to vote when California's women won suffrage in 1911.

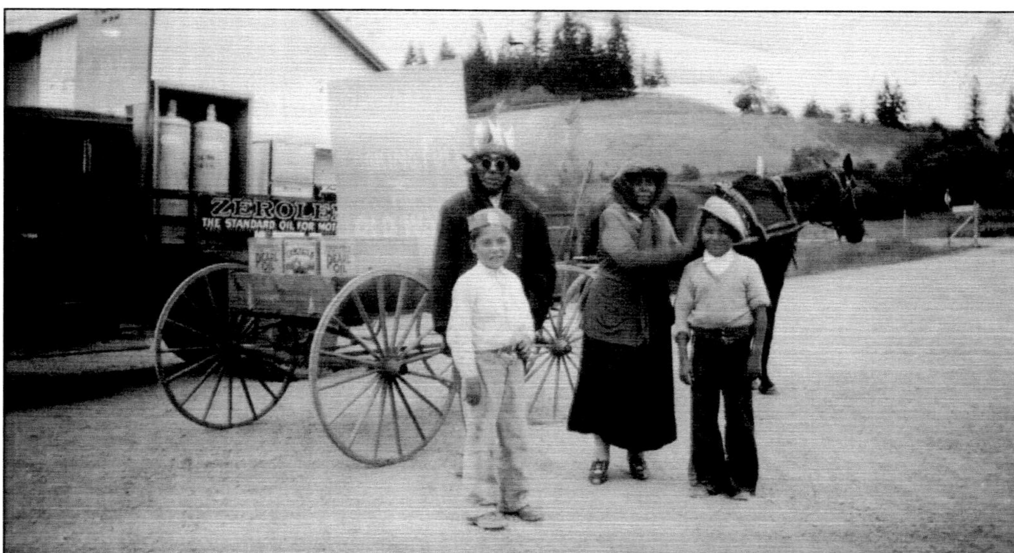

This couple is believed to be George and Susie Burt, Native American community leaders in the area. George Burt, a Sinkyone, was forcibly relocated to the Smith River Reservation as a child. In adulthood, he managed to return to his birthplace, obtaining a homestead near Bull Creek. The Burts moved to Fortuna in their old age. They gave up their land in order to pay for burial plots for their family in Newburg Cemetery.

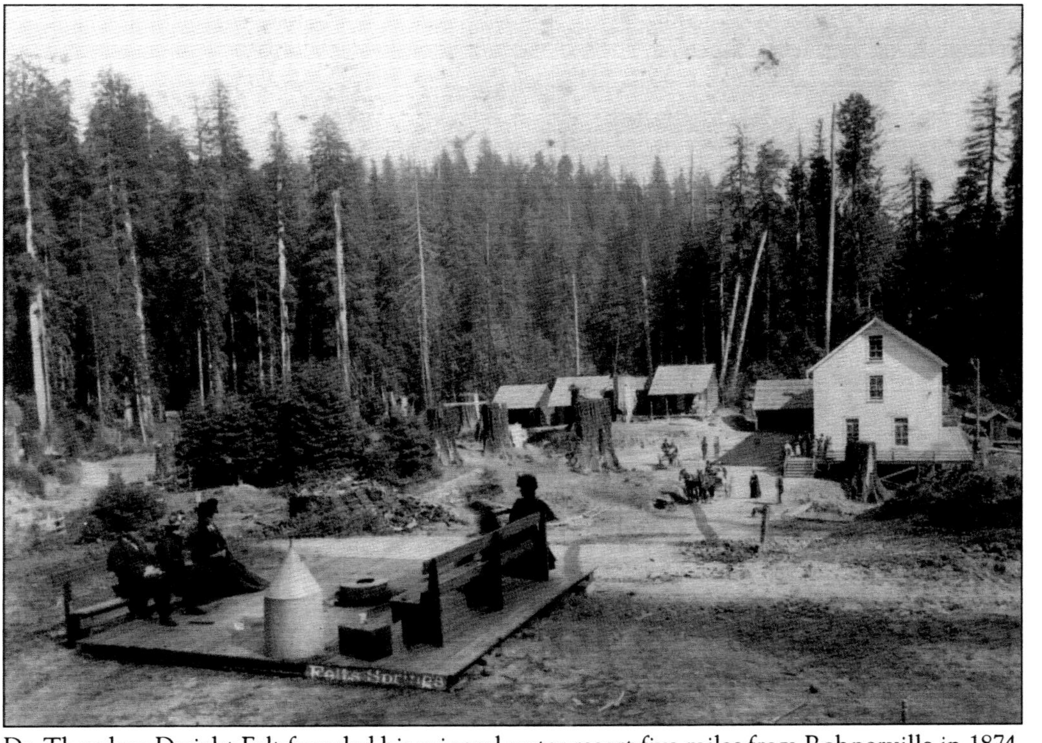

Dr. Theodore Dwight Felt founded his mineral-water resort five miles from Rohnerville in 1874, advertising "the finest and best mineral springs at present known in the state of California." Fire twice destroyed Felt's hotel in the resort's early years, but the 1890 Humboldt County directory stated that "the hotel and cottages at the spring provide accommodation for 50 to 60 guests. . . . This is one of the gem retreats of California for recreation and rest."

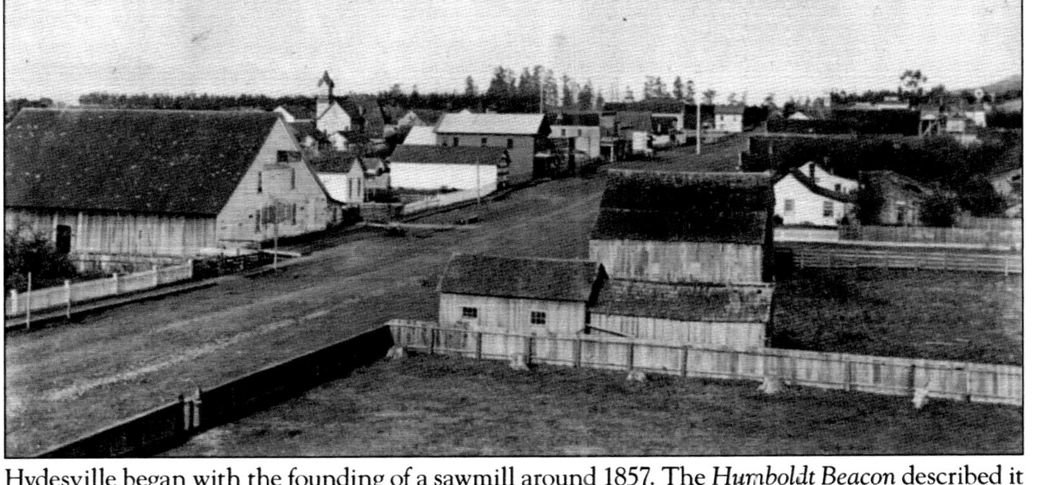

Hydesville began with the founding of a sawmill around 1857. The *Humboldt Beacon* described it in 1913 as "ideally located on the broad tableland which, rising above the valley of the Van Duzen, stretches northward to the timbered hills." The newspaper read, "Soil and climatic conditions [are] ideal for the Hydesville [straw]berry farmer, he but awaits the completion of the overland railroad to more extensively engage in the growing of this luscious berry."

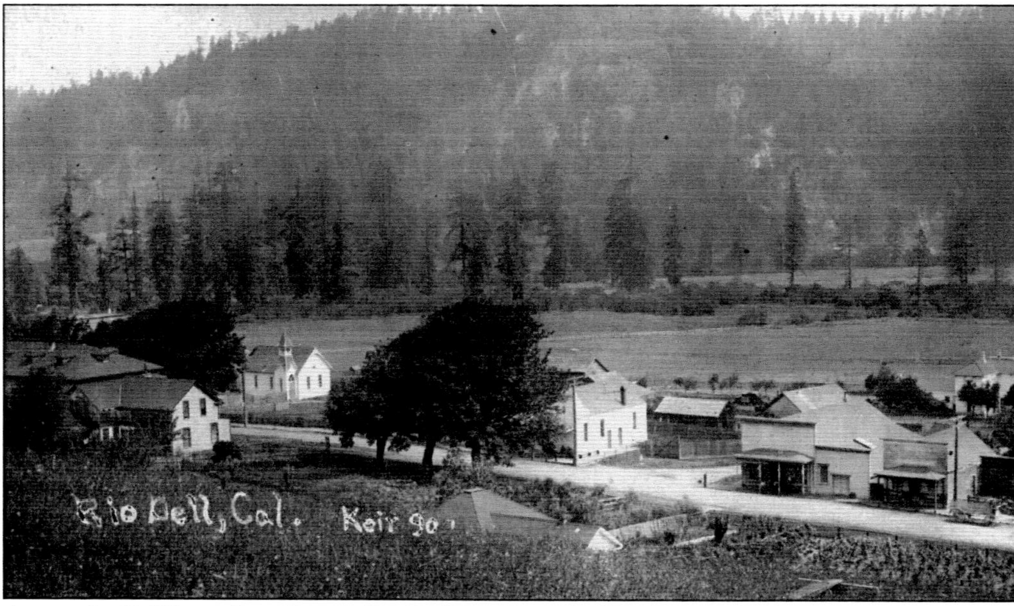

Across the Eel River from Scotia, Rio Dell was described by the *Humboldt Beacon* in 1913 as the most picturesquely situated town in Humboldt County. Visible here is the business district, which in 1885 included two hotels, a drugstore, livery stable, school, blacksmith shop, and saloon. The 1885–1886 Humboldt business directory called Rio Dell "a summer resort of considerable note." (Courtesy of Bob Lutz.)

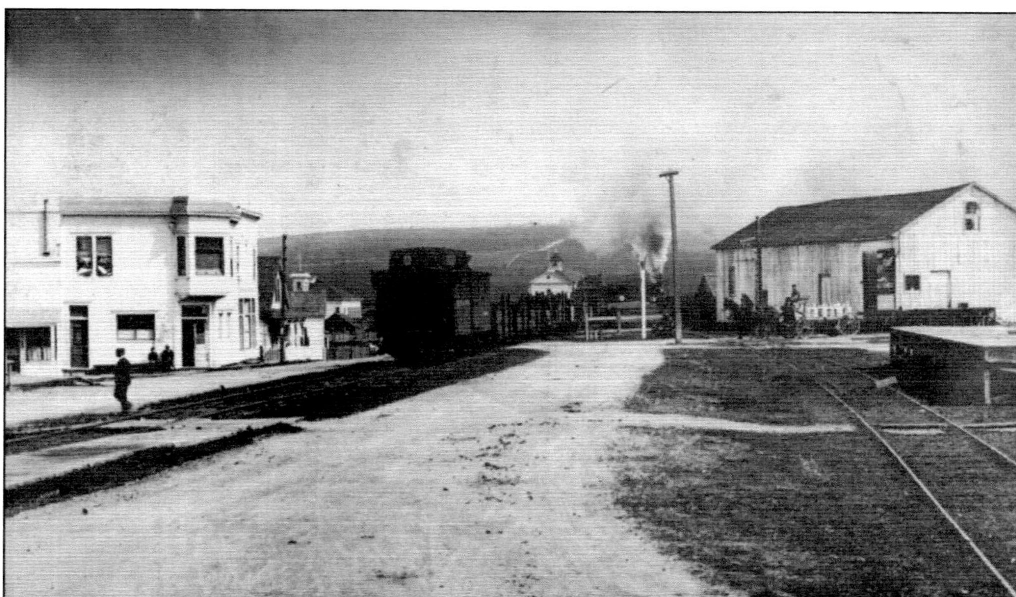

The *Humboldt Beacon* of January 17, 1913, read, "Loleta, a live bustling town on the Northwestern Pacific Railroad . . . owes its prosperity to the rich farming and dairying land surrounding it." The description continued, "The town has a splendid water system and, what a great many towns larger than Loleta are without, a sewer system."

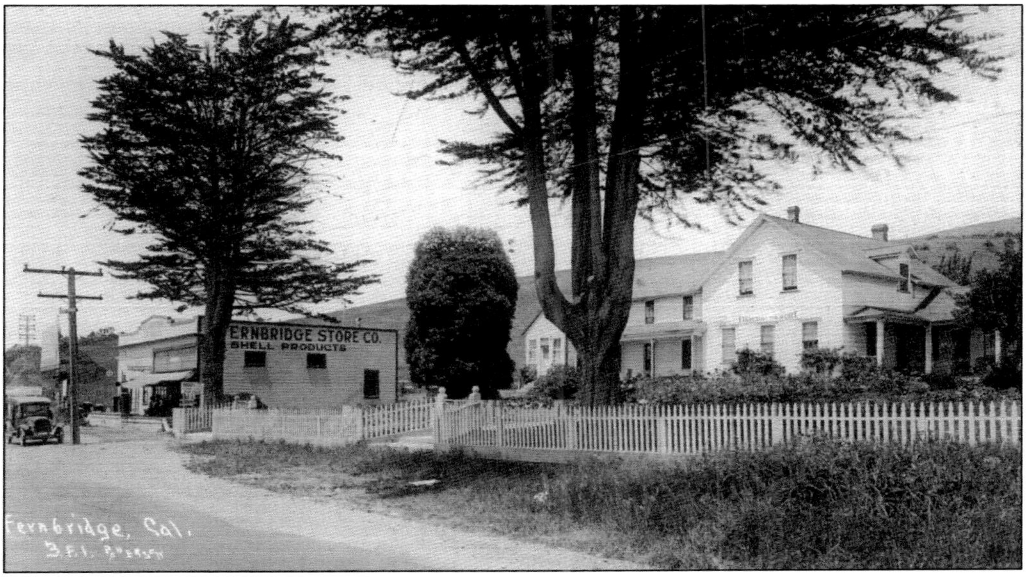

Originating as a railroad stop, Fernbridge has been known by many names, including Weeott, Ferndale Junction, and Singley. The name Fernbridge was selected with the construction of the eponymous bridge in 1911. The community was also referred to as Greig's Resort after the fishing resort founded by Fortuna livery stable owner T.G. Greig. In 1913, the resort was operated by S.H. Goe. According to the *Humboldt Beacon*, Goe "made life worth living while you were a guest." (Courtesy of Marguerita Nichols.)

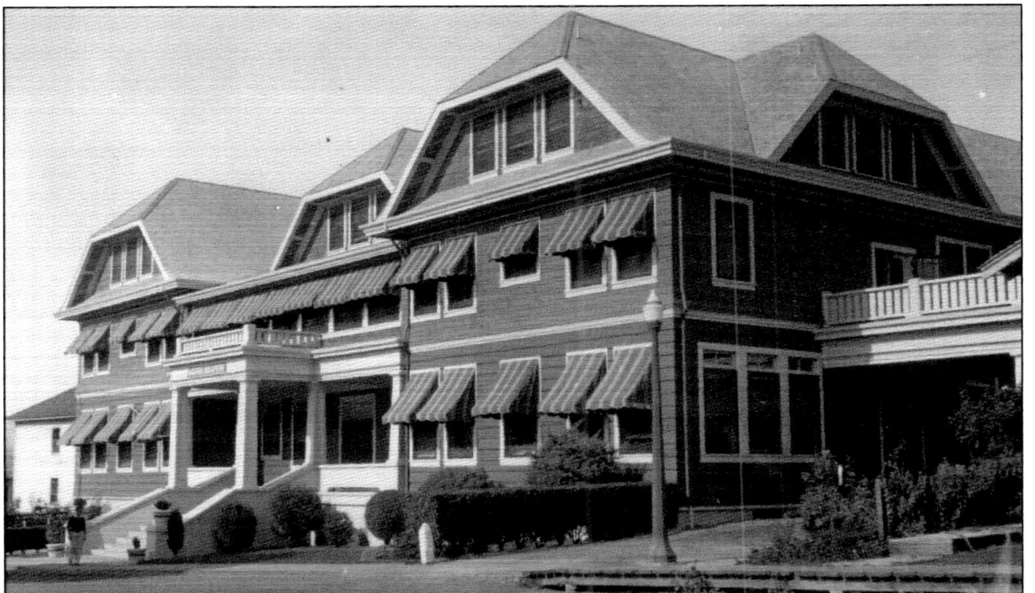

Scotia Hospital served the Eel River Valley from the early 20th century until it closed in 1957 with the opening of Fortuna's Redwood Memorial Hospital. This Scotia Hospital building was constructed in 1925, the same year this photograph was taken. The Pacific Lumber Company's 1920s civic improvements also included the Scotia Inn, the Winema Theater, and the neoclassical Bank of Scotia, all showcasing redwood construction.

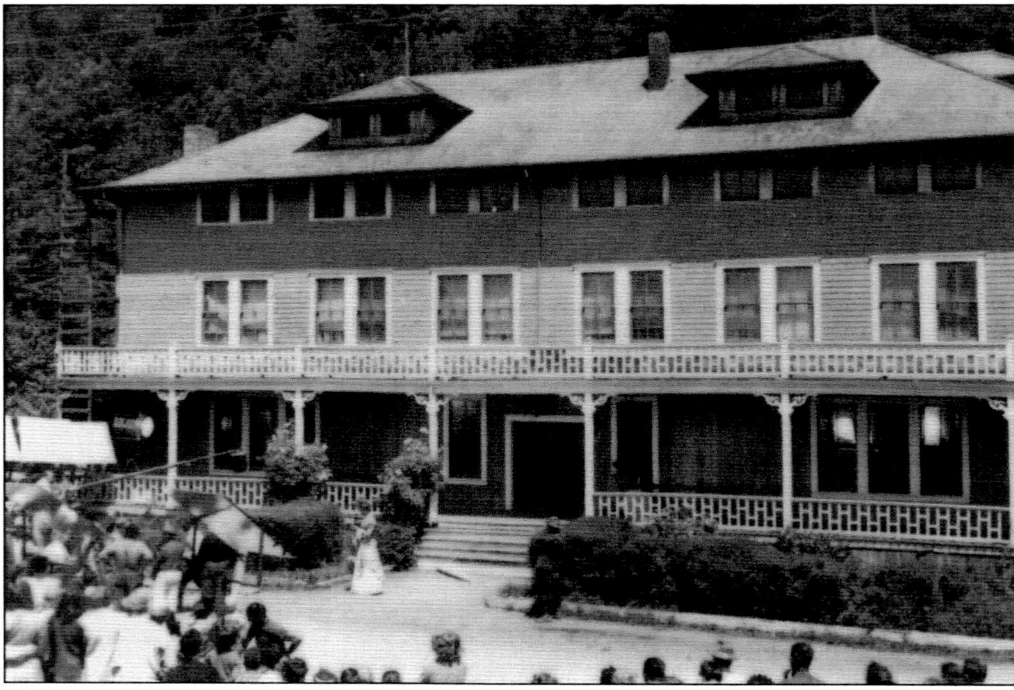

The Big Trees (1952) was one of many redwood-themed films shot in Humboldt County. One location used in the film was the Carlotta Hotel, which was built in 1906 and destroyed by fire in 1995. Carlotta began as a resort town owned by relatives of lumber baron John L. Vance and was named for his youngest great-niece.

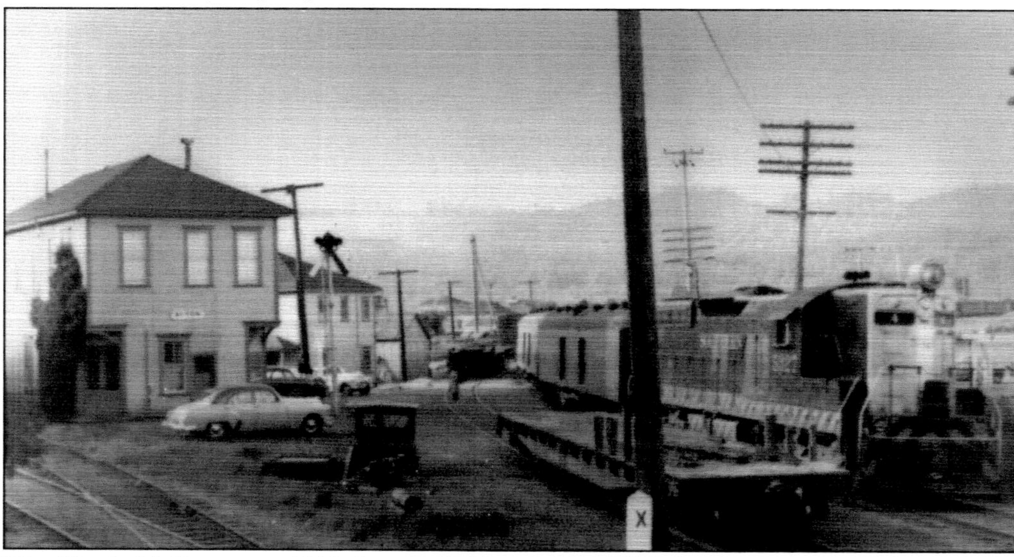

The *Humboldt Beacon* in 1913 described Alton as "a railroad junction, a branch line of the Northwestern Pacific running from the town to Carlotta four miles distant." The main industries of the area were cited as "farming, fruit raising, and dairying." The town's name is attributed to an 1860s settler who named it for his hometown in Illinois, although a rival story claims it was named for local rancher Alta Oliver.

Two

SLIDE, SPRINGVILLE, AND FORTUNA

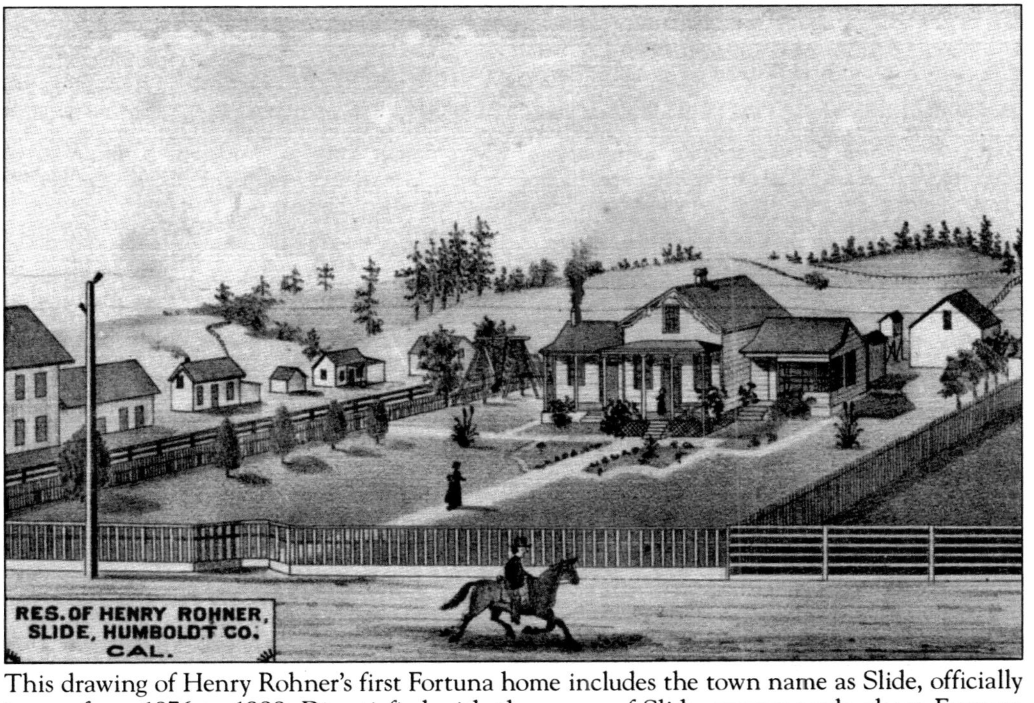

This drawing of Henry Rohner's first Fortuna home includes the town name as Slide, officially in use from 1876 to 1888. Dissatisfied with the name of Slide, townspeople chose Fortuna instead. They may have been inspired by the nearby Cape Fortunas named by 16th-century Spanish explorers.

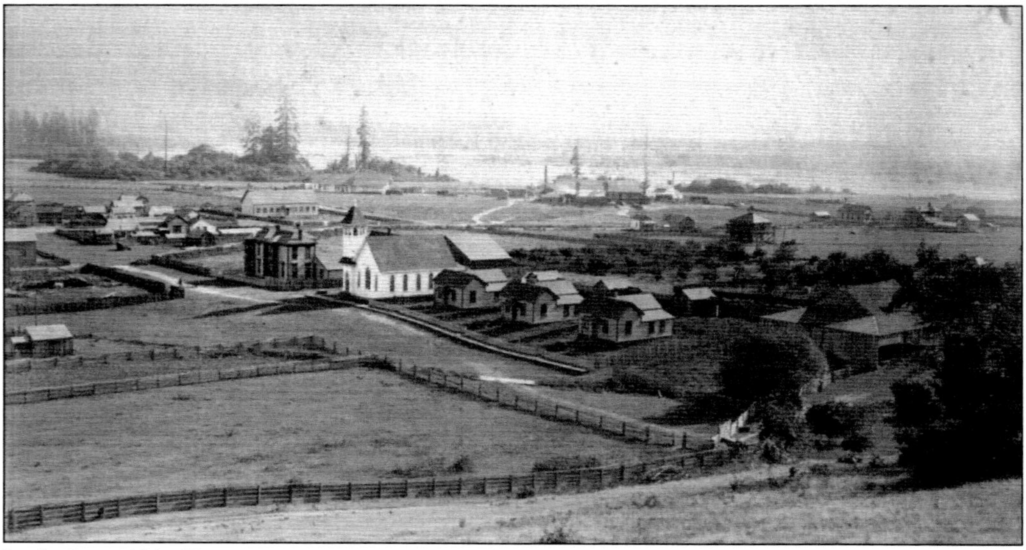

In the late 1880s, Fortuna was a young town with room to expand. Running diagonally through this photograph is Ninth Street. The First Christian Church and the adjacent two-story Gushaw-Mudgett house, both still standing today, are also shown. In the background, the Eel River is visible, with the Fortuna Depot at center and the Springville Mill at right.

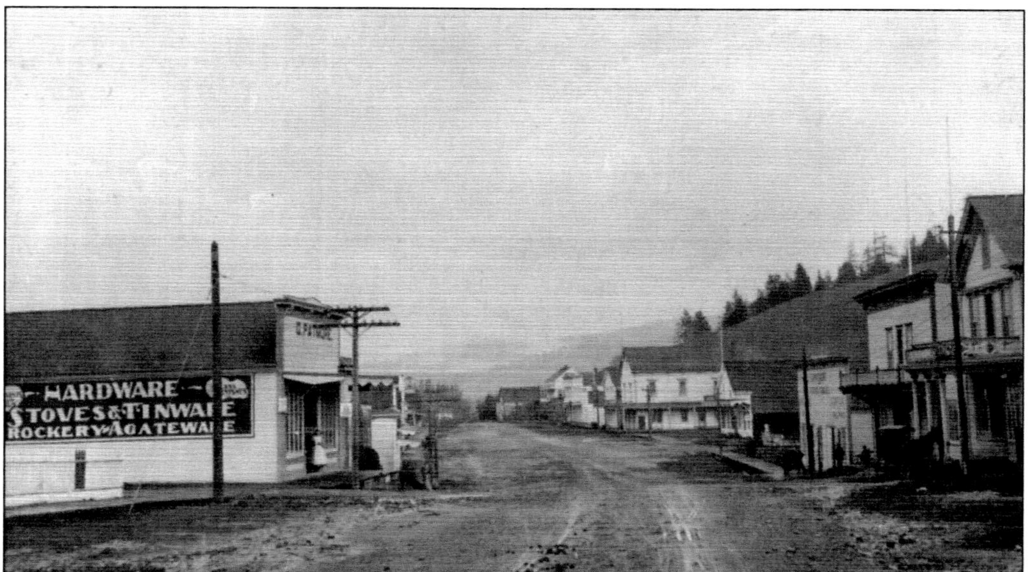

From the 1860s through the late 19th century, Rohnerville was a prosperous community, with the third largest population in Humboldt County in 1870. Named for its founder, Henry Rohner, who built the first store in the area, Rohnerville lost ground to neighboring Fortuna when the Eel River and Eureka Railroad laid its tracks through the younger town. Fortuna finally annexed Rohnerville in 1979.

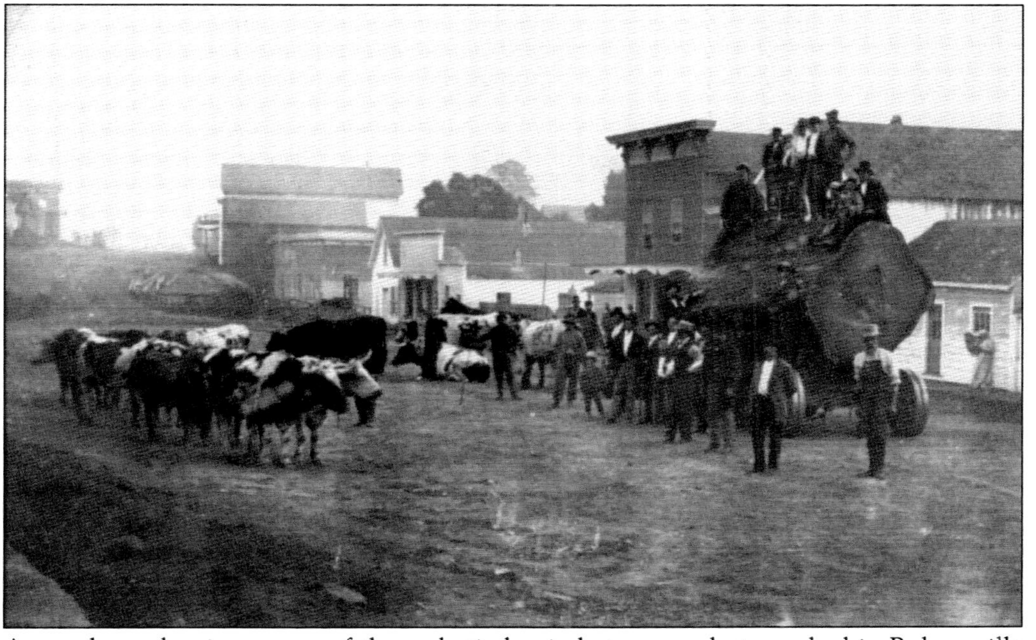

An ox-drawn logging wagon of the early timber industry was photographed in Rohnerville around 1876. In that year, a *West Coast Signal* correspondent wrote that Rohnerville had aspirations to become the Humboldt County seat. The correspondent elaborated, "The location is central and good, and the fogs which are so common nearer the coast do not prevail there. Its proximity to the valuable belt of redwood on one side and fine farming lands on the other assure its permanence."

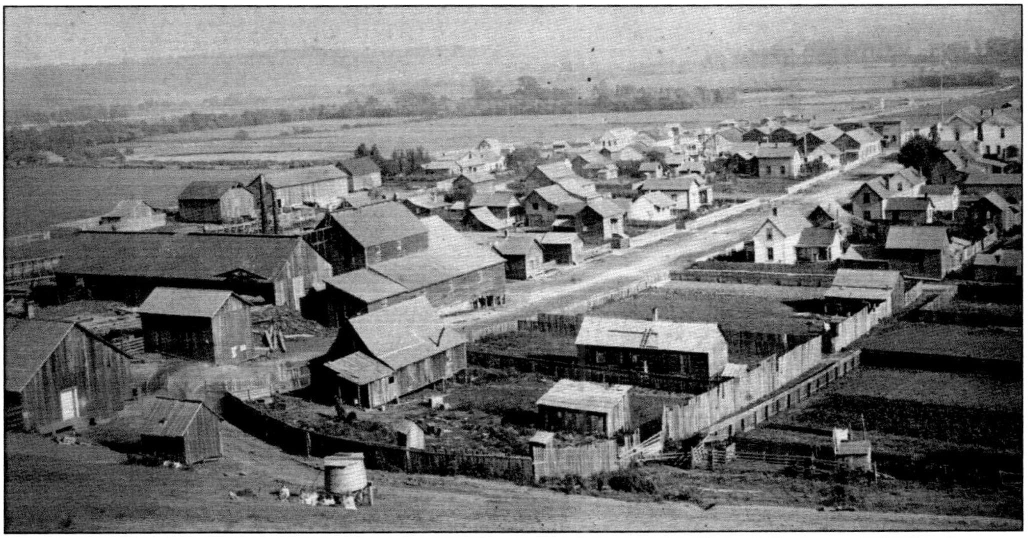

This view of Eleventh Street in the 1880s shows outhouses, backyard farming, clotheslines, a small water tower in the foreground with a group of children sitting in front of it, and a shingle mill at the left. The edge of town is starkly obvious, illustrating the days when open countryside separated Fortuna and Rohnerville.

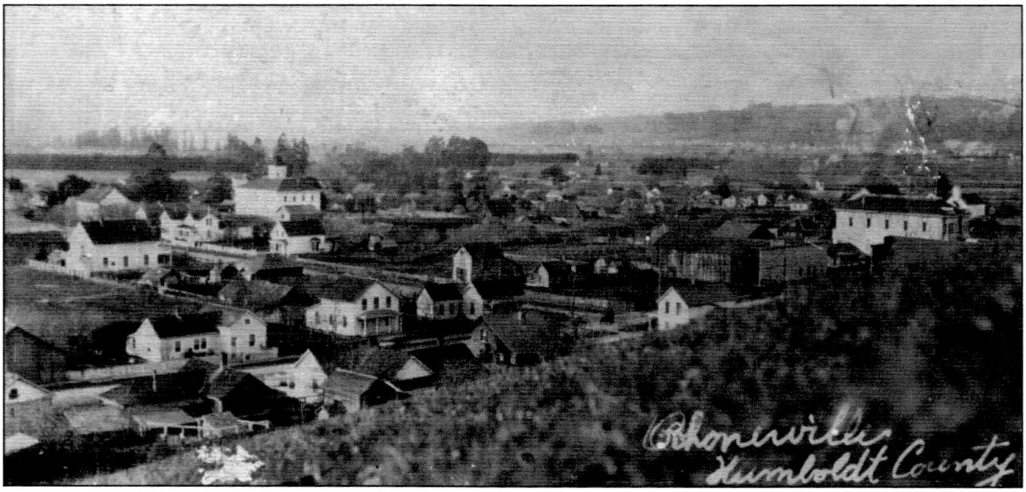

Downtown Rohnerville (misspelled on the original photograph) is nestled beneath the bluff in this late-19th-century view. The towered building with the dark roof is the Rohnerville Grammar School constructed in 1889. The *Humboldt Standard* reported, "We read in the [Rohnerville] *Herald* the new school building soon to be erected in Rohnerville will be an ornament to the town. . . . When ready for use our school grounds and building will be second to none."

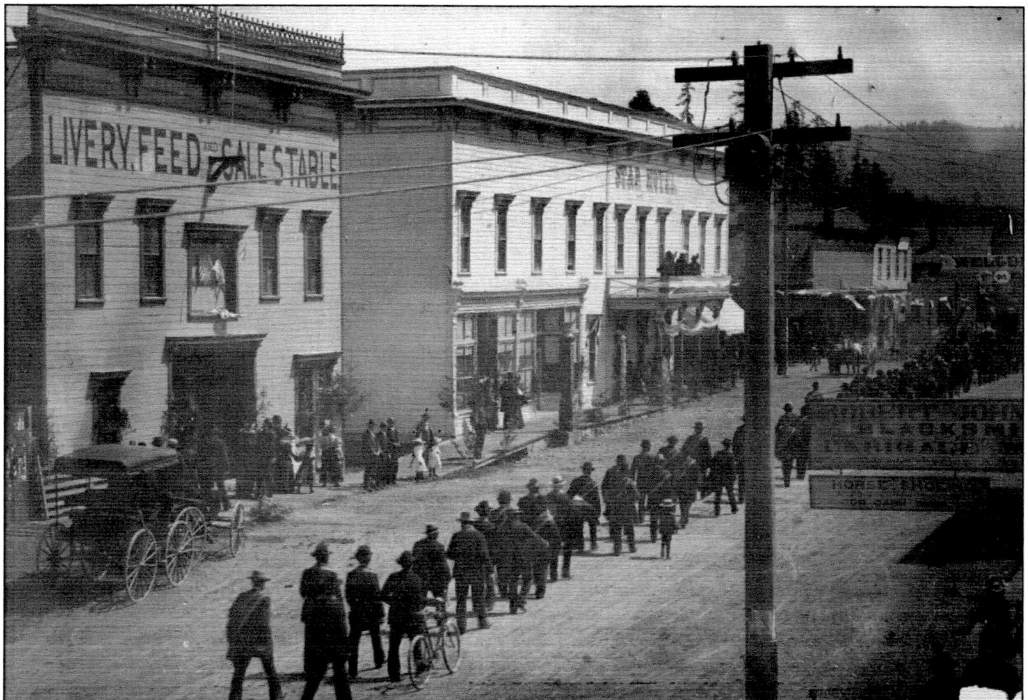

This 1896 parade scene shows early landmarks, including Greig's (later Johnston's) Livery Stable and the Star Hotel. Robert Johnston, who would buy the livery stable, at this point had a blacksmith's shop across the street. Also visible are electric poles installed three years earlier. The man and girls standing between the stable and the hotel are identified on the photograph as George Cooper with daughters Zina and Inez.

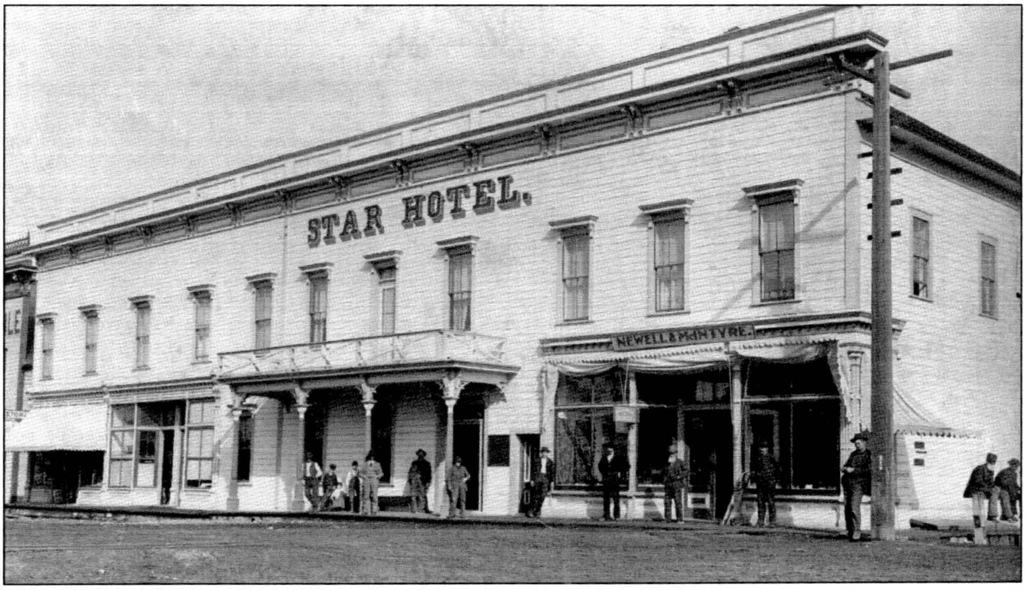

The Star, Fortuna's second and longest-operating hotel, opened in 1876 when the town was still Springville. The central portion with the balcony was originally the entire building. The bench in front was a community gathering point, recalled by Paul Mudgett as the spot where "one could often hear of what was happening in that other world outside of Fortuna, for the Star was a busy and popular hotel."

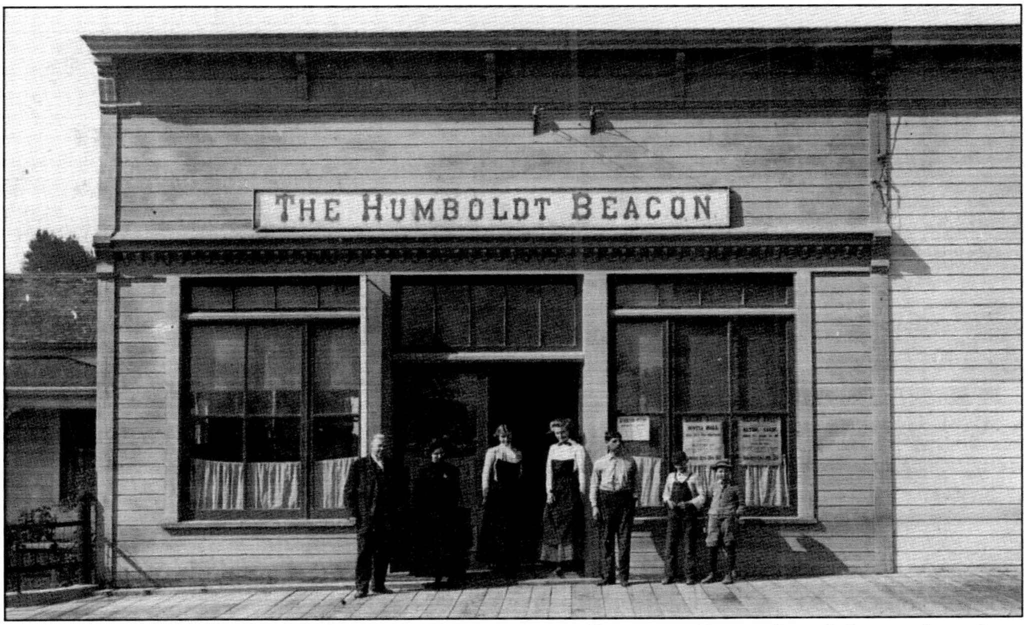

Gathered outside the *Humboldt Beacon*'s Main Street office in 1909 are, from left to right, editor and founder Gustave A. Jasper with staff members Nell Rowley, Ruth Schnoor, Adelaide Mulley, William Bott, Curtis Jasper, and Maurice Bott. Curtis and Maurice were among Fortuna's first Boy Scouts. The Fortuna branch, founded in early 1911 under the leadership of Hazel Swortzel, was the earliest Boy Scout group formed in Humboldt County.

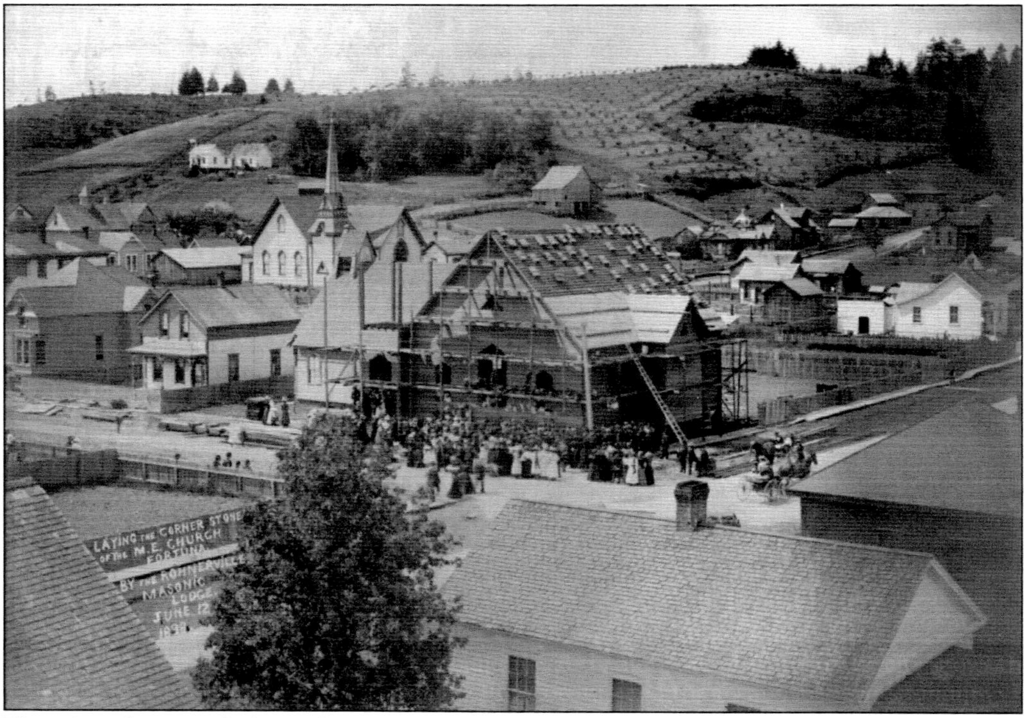

This 1898 photograph shows the construction of an addition to the Methodist Episcopal Church. The earlier building, visible behind the scaffold area, was constructed in 1887. Also founded in 1887 was the First Christian Church, the spired building visible in the background. Both churches still stand over a century later, but the orchards on the hillsides have given way to houses.

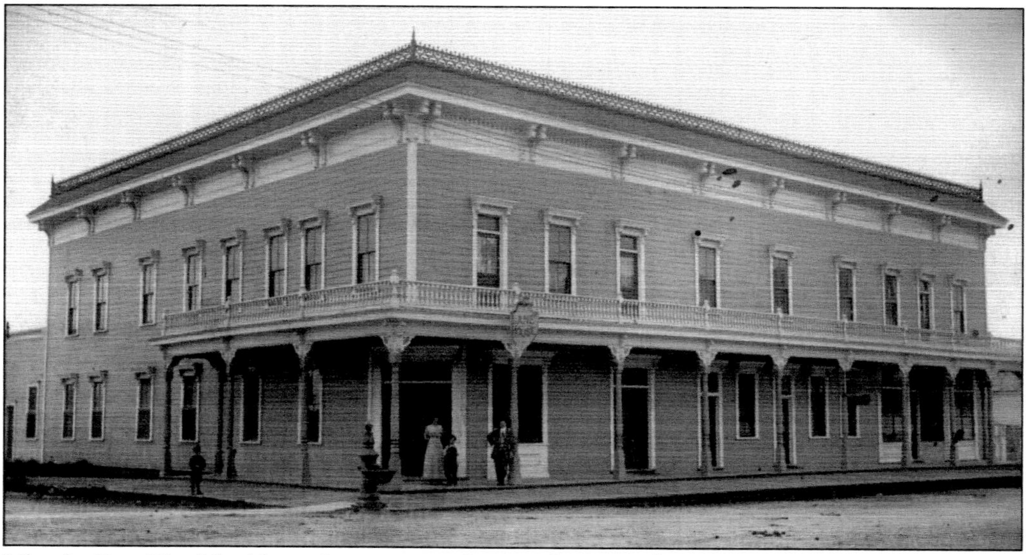

Like the Star Hotel building, the structure that was home to the Lane House boardinghouse still stands along Main Street. The Lane House went through many changes of ownership in the early 20th century, including the father-and-son dental team of Drs. D.L. and W.S. O'Connor, who had offices in the Lane House.

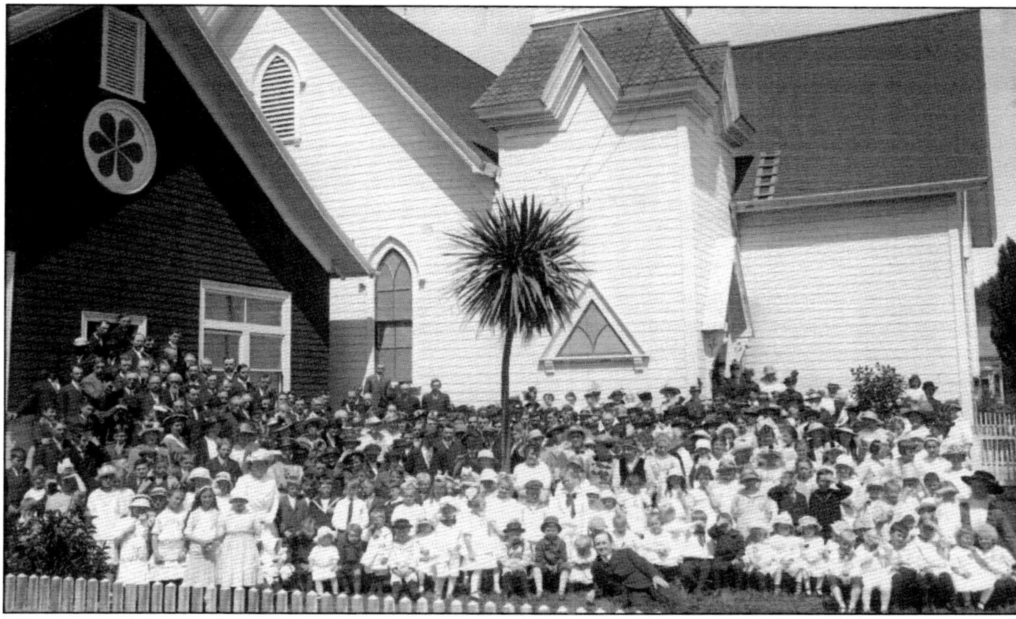

The original First Christian Church building was destroyed by fire. The second, shown in a 1916 photograph, was built in 1889. The first pastor, W.A. Gardner, is one of several men credited with suggesting the town's name. Whether or not this legend is true, Gardner helped to shape early Fortuna. He owned 150 acres, which he sold off in small lots that would become the site of many local homes.

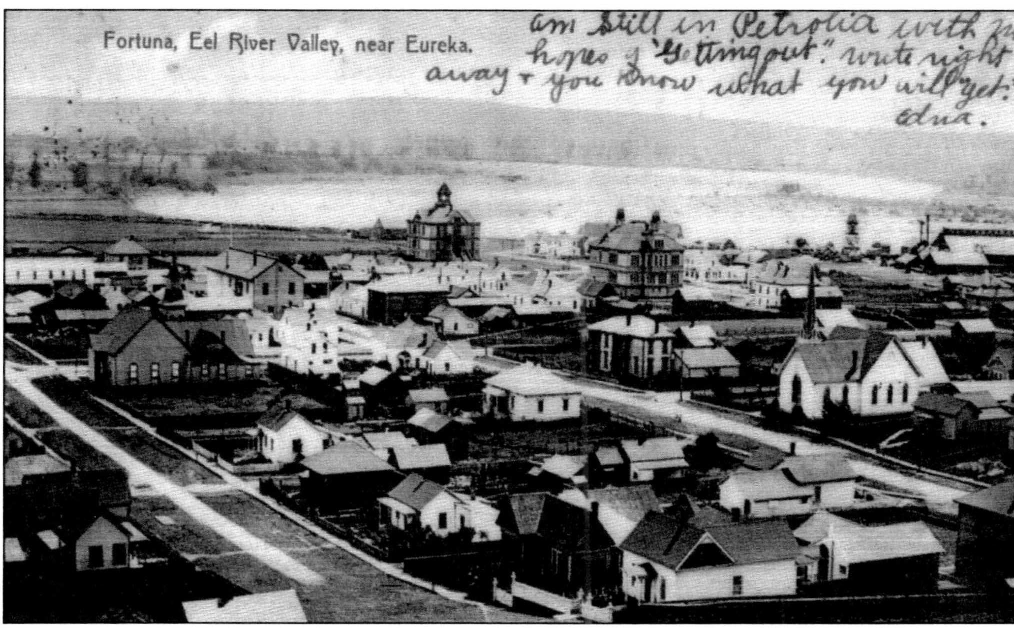

This postcard, sent in 1910, shows the imposing grammar school on Main Street (with two towers near the center of the photograph) and the nearly identical high school in the background. The Springville Mill, around which Fortuna was created, can be seen in the background on the right. The railroad depot is barely visible, peeking out from either side of the grammar school.

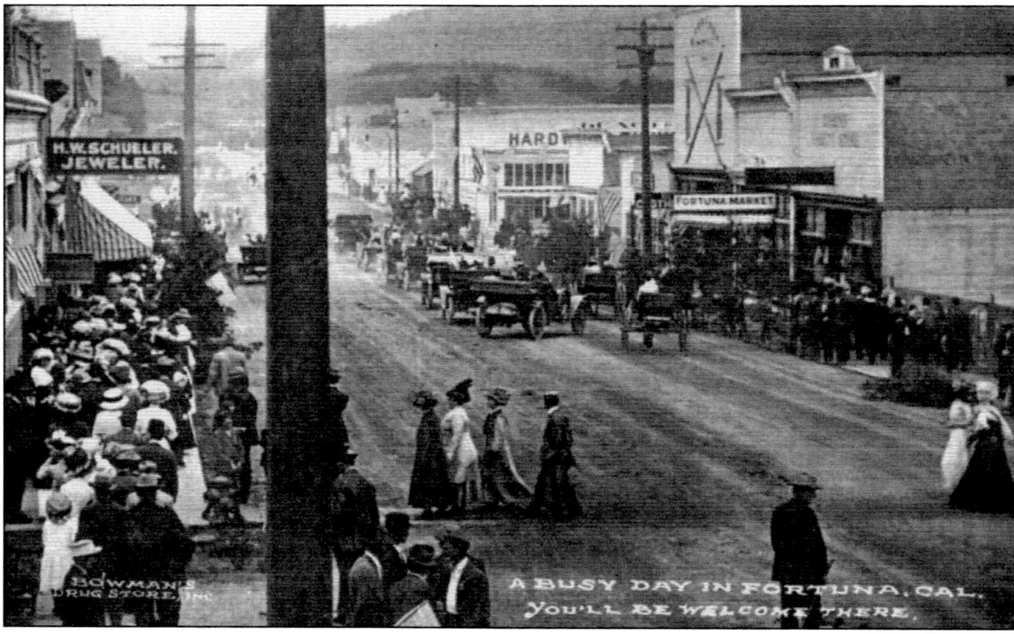

This c. 1910 postcard was printed by Bowman's Drug Store, an integral part of the local business community for generations. Bowman's originally stood across the street from the Star Hotel and on a site earlier occupied by the Fortuna Merchandising Company. The postcard's promise that "you'll be welcome" is echoed decades later in the official adoption of the nickname "the Friendly City."

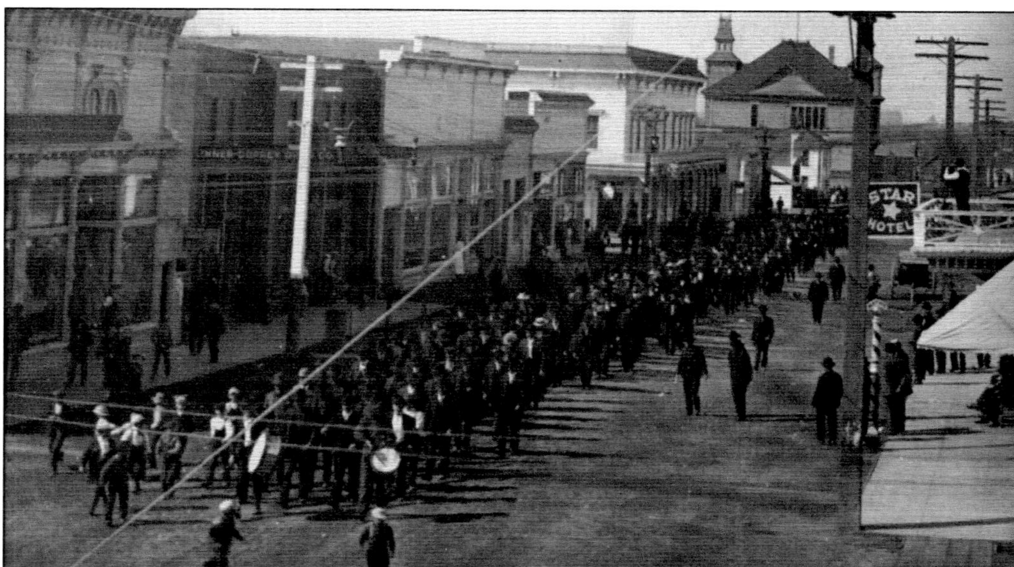

Not everyone could feel welcome in early-20th-century Humboldt County. This 1906 march down Main Street was staged by loggers protesting the introduction of 23 Chinese workers to a salmon cannery in Port Kenyon. The workers were deported from the county, continuing Humboldt's "no Chinese" policy in place since the expulsion of around 320 people from Eureka in 1885. Only in the 1950s did Asians and Asian Americans begin to return to Humboldt.

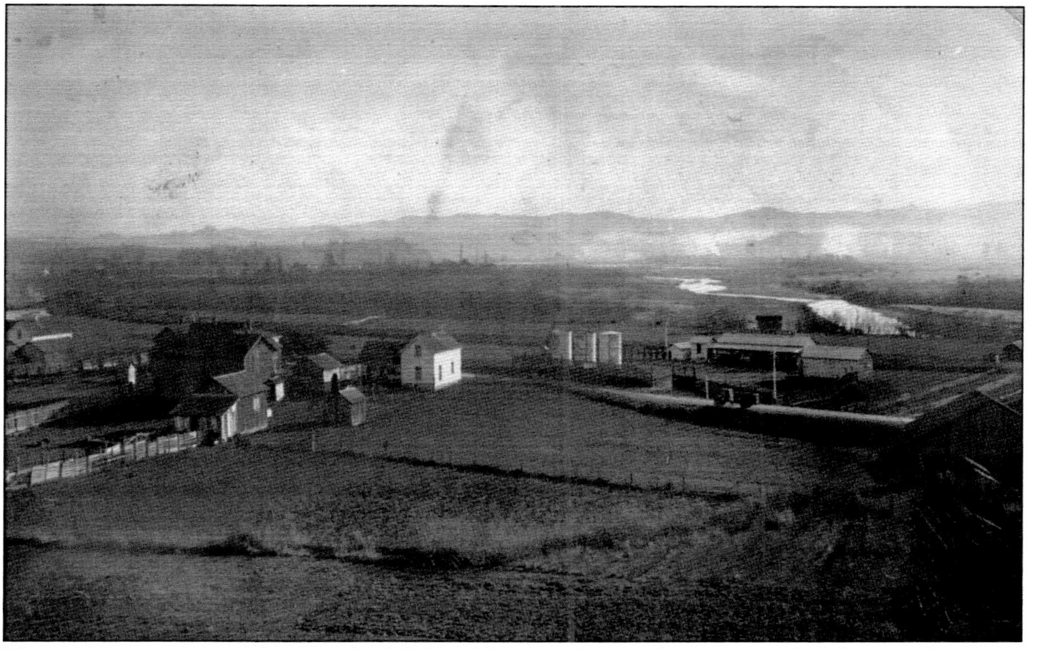

This 1920s snapshot of the Standard Oil buildings at the northwestern end of the city shows the changes in transportation technology affecting Fortuna and the rest of the world. Glimpses of older transportation methods are also seen in this photograph. The railroad track runs behind Standard Oil, and in the background gleam the waters of the Eel River.

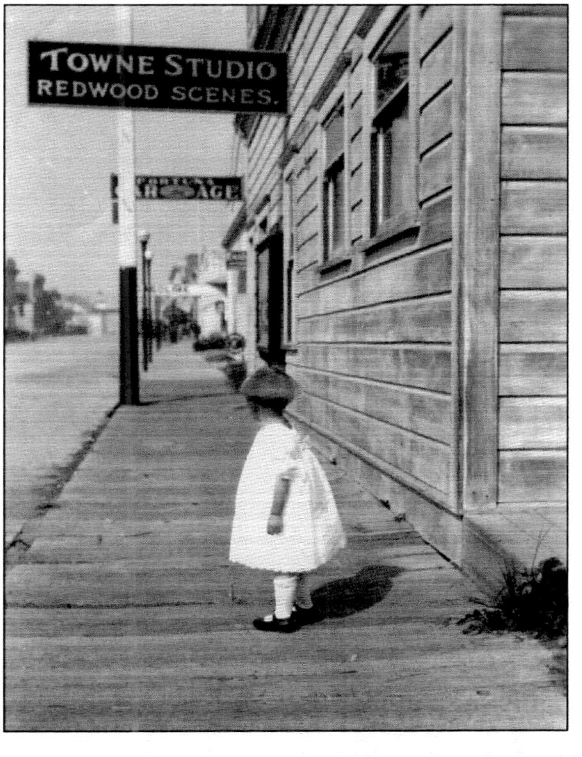

This image of Pauline Towne was captured outside her father's Main Street photography studio around 1922. Paul Towne took a number of the photographs in this book, including several street scenes and redwood forest images. He was also official photographer for the high school's *Megaphone* yearbook for several years.

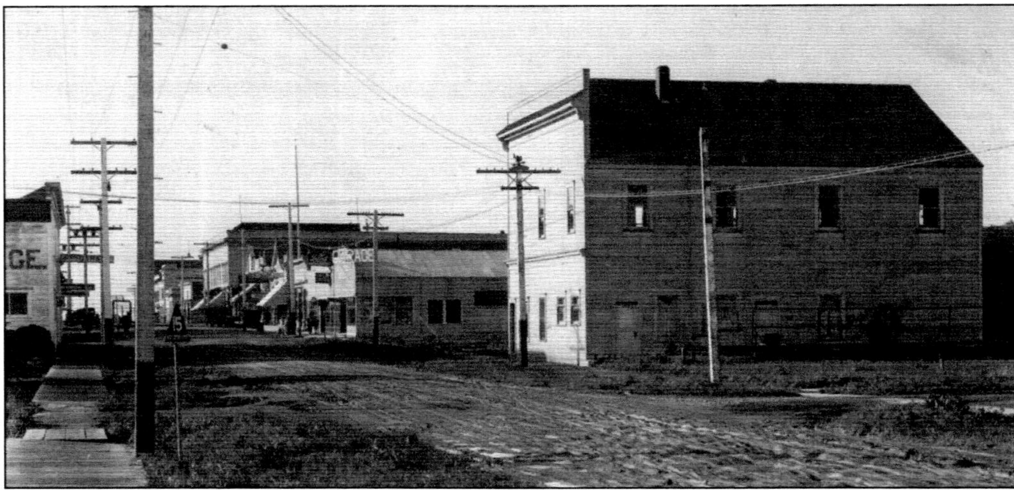

In this photograph from the Towne family collection is the southeastern end of Main Street around 1920. The advent of the automobile age is apparent from the plethora of garages and the 15-miles-per-hour road sign. The Fortuna Garage on the left advertised, "Service Shop, Auto Repairing, Accessories, Samson Tires. Our motto—Fixing not faking." The plank sidewalks and unpaved street evoke earlier days.

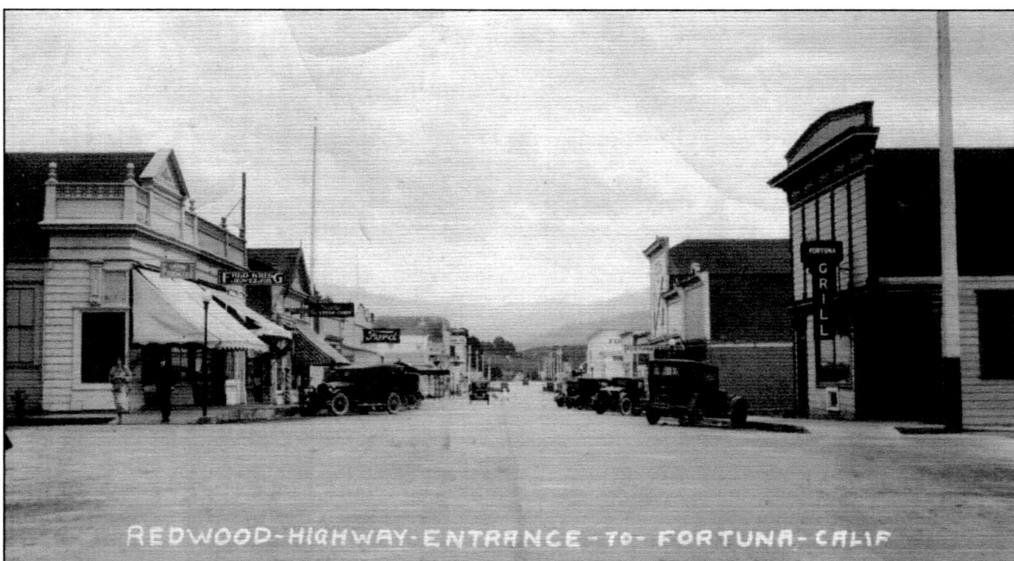

This 1920s view, looking southeast from Eleventh and Main Streets, reflects the era's burgeoning redwood tourism industry. Fortuna now stood on the new Redwood Highway. The 1925 Fortuna High yearbook read, "It has taken many thousands of years to develop the great redwood forest of Humboldt County, and for time to come, people from all parts of the world will come to see these beautiful 'Sentinels of Time.' "

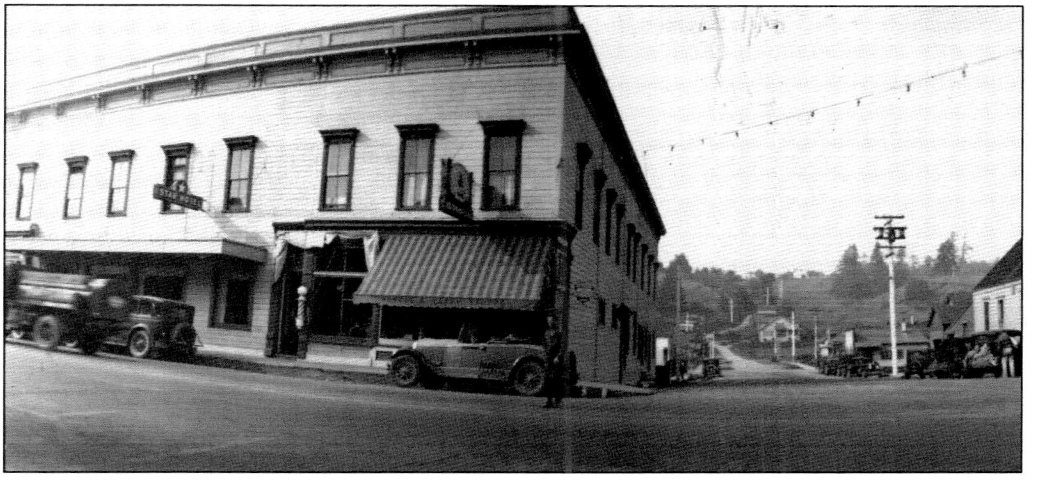

In the 1920s, the space once occupied by Newell and McIntyre's general store housed Newell's Candy Shoppe, but over 40 years after first opening, the Star Hotel was still the Star. Advertisements from the 1920s urged, "When stopping at Fortuna, stay at the Star Hotel for high-class board and lodging" and promoted its "Star-Snappy-Service." The building still stands, but the Star ceased business as a hotel in the mid-20th century.

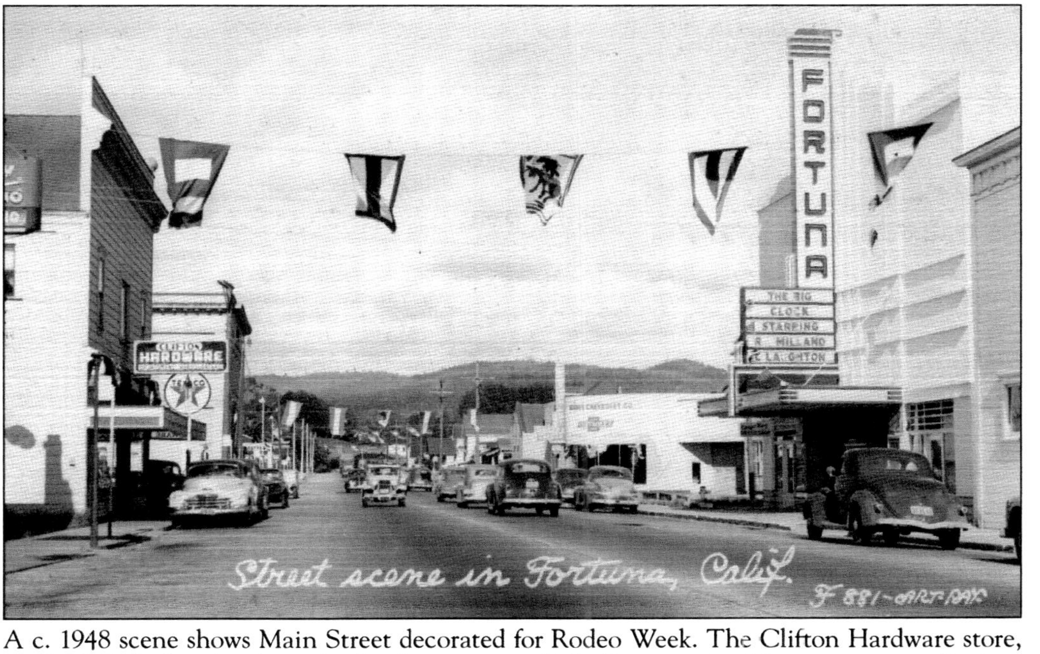

A c. 1948 scene shows Main Street decorated for Rodeo Week. The Clifton Hardware store, on the left, had earlier been the hardware store of L.L. Bryan, a local businessman, politician, and fire department member since the early 1900s. The building still stands and now houses an antique store.

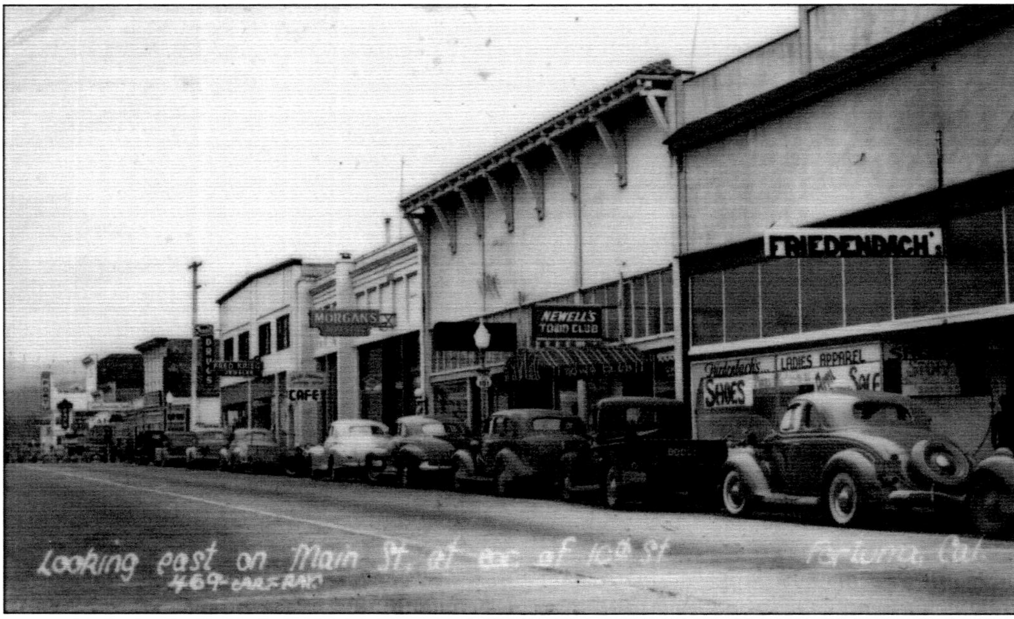

Newell's Town Club downtown bar was a local landmark in the mid-20th century, but from 1912 to 1933, the city was dry. On New Year's Day in 1912, after visiting the saloons, lumberman Stephen Hodgkins stabbed night watchman J.H. Renfroe, who then shot Hodgkins. Renfroe survived, but Hodgkins died, leaving a widow and three children. Shocked by the alcohol-fueled tragedy, Fortuna voted to go dry in a special election in April. The restriction was in place until the repeal of nationwide Prohibition.

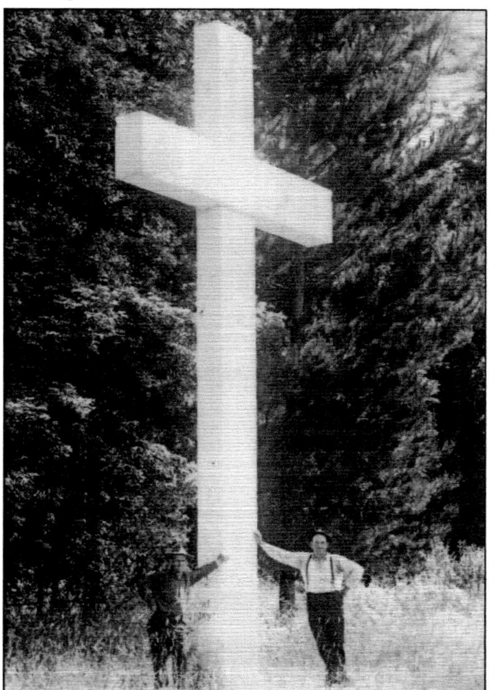

Construction of the 24-foot cross on what was then known as Campfire Ridge in Rohner Park was proposed to the Fortuna City Council in 1941 by Rev. F.C. Zimmerman, who represented a group of Fortuna churches. The cross was first used in Easter services in 1942. Standing with the cross in 1947 are Charlie Conant (right), a lifelong member of the First Christian Church, and J. Boynton of Petaluma.

Three

THE REDWOODS

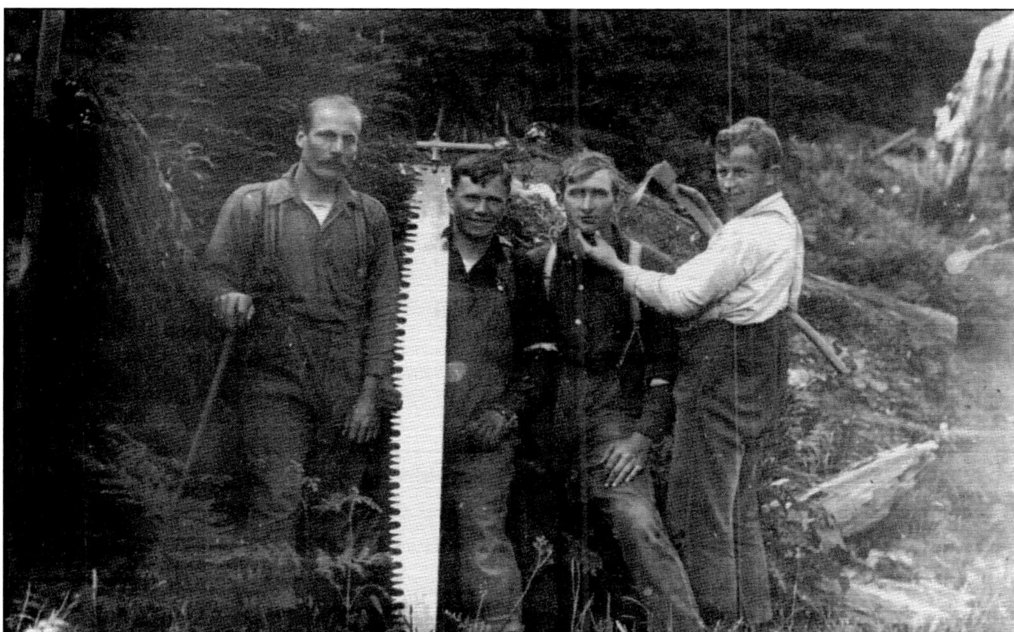

The redwood trees around Humboldt Bay were first harvested in the early 1850s. Specialized tools and equipment were invented to fell them. By the 1870s, the first mill and woods operations were located in the Fortuna area. In 1874, the Springville Mill Company began logging the redwoods in the region. Men who worked in the woods prized their tools. These included, as pictured, the ax, crosscut saw, and adze.

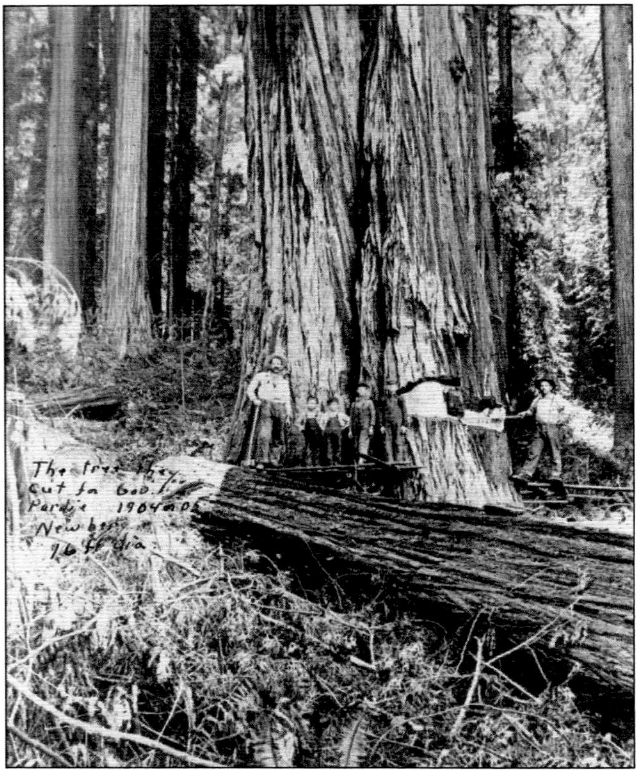

Loggers in the late 1800s began cutting a redwood by chopping notches to set springboards above the butt swell of the tree. They used the boards to stand on while making the undercut, which took several days of chopping. These choppers are shown in the Newburg woods cutting a 16-foot-diameter tree for the visit of California governor Pardee to the Fortuna area in 1904.

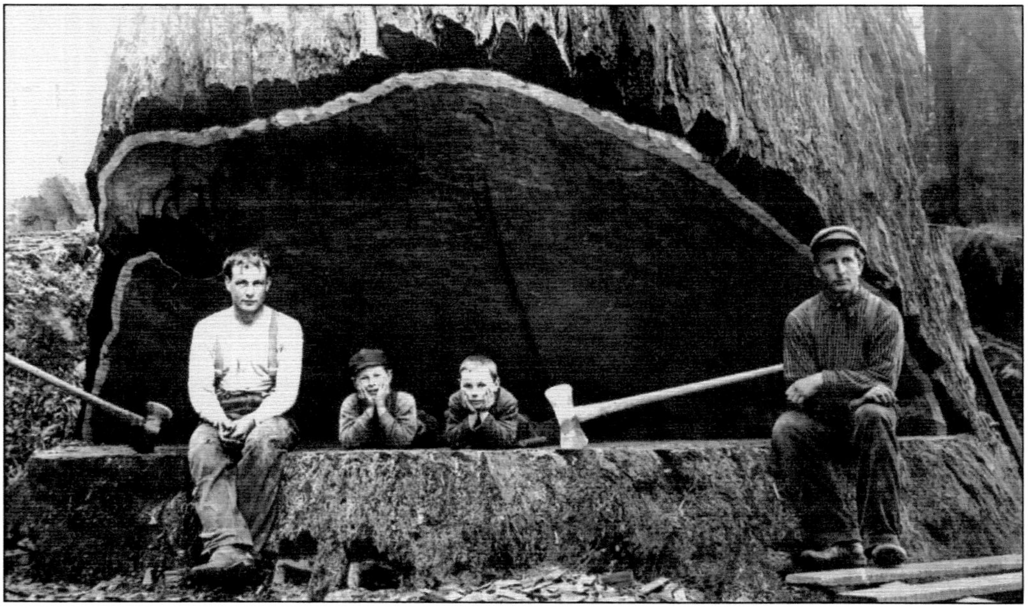

The loggers made undercuts to guide the tree's fall. Undercuts could be very large and often were used photographically to demonstrate the size of the trees. This picture features chopper Guy Larison (far right) with, from left to right, younger brother Jim and sons Mervin and Leonard. The picture was taken above Rio Dell at Monument Flat.

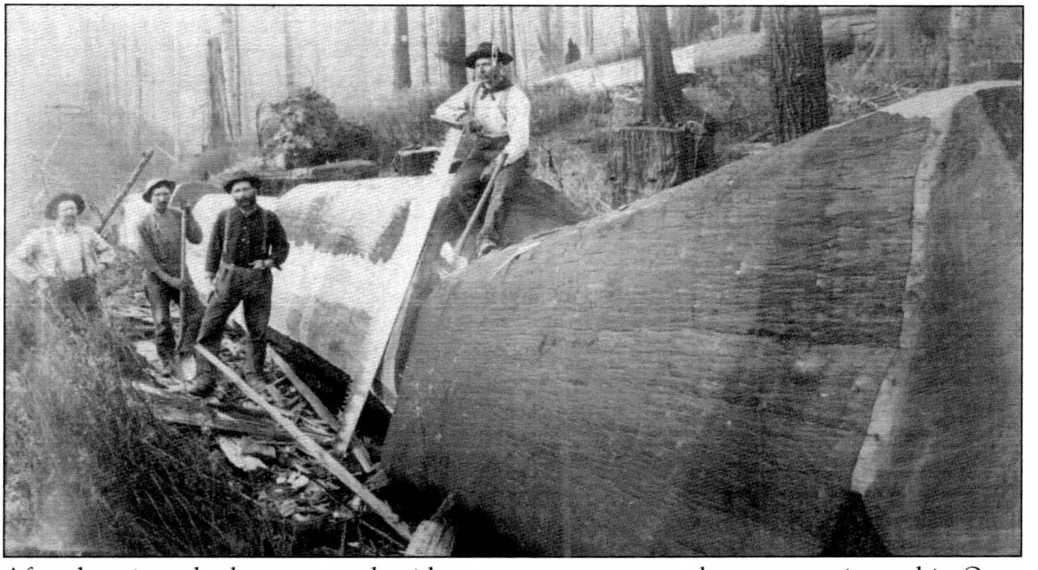

After chopping, a back cut was made with a two-man crosscut saw known as a misery whip. Once the tree was felled, it was sawed into manageable lengths (referred to as bucking the log). Logs were debarked with long peeler bars. The six-inch bark was discarded, allowing the log to be pulled more easily by oxen or mule teams. The Newburg woods operation is seen in this image.

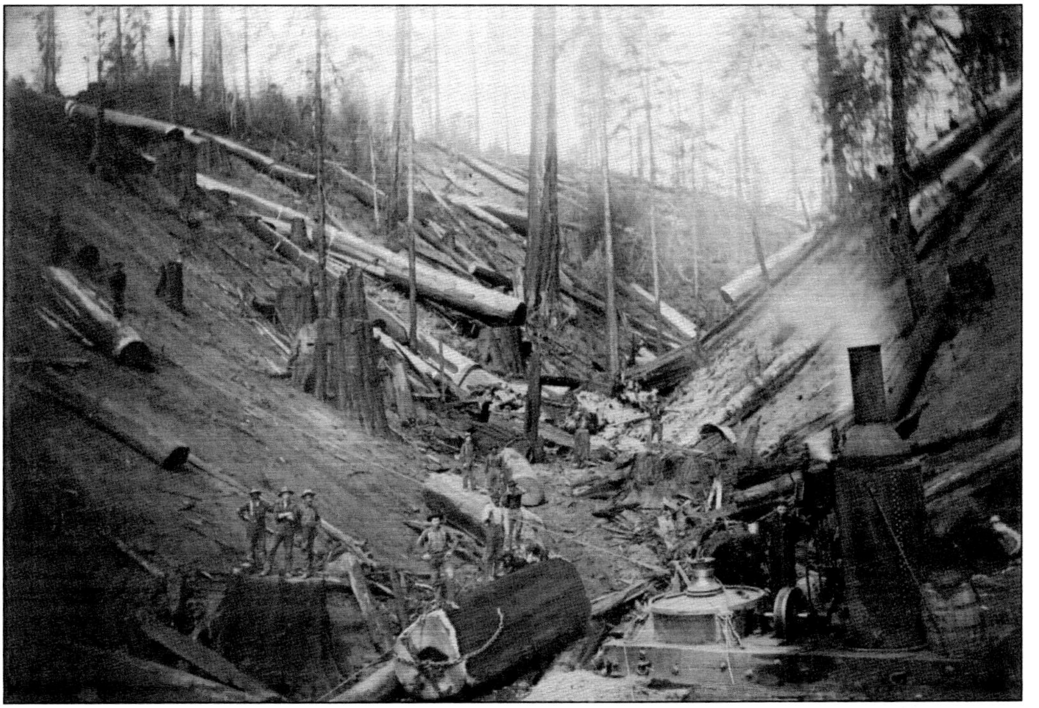

In 1882, John Dolbeer of Eureka invented an upright steam engine that revolutionized logging on the Pacific coast. Called a steam donkey, it provided a mechanical means of harvesting redwoods. A log was felled in a remote woods operation and yarded down to a landing where it was pulled to the mill by mule or oxen teams or loaded on the emerging railroad systems.

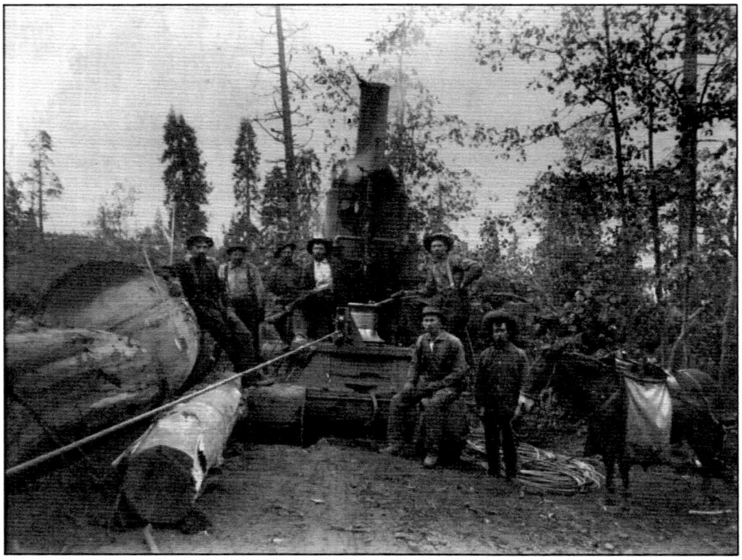

Mounted on wooden sleds for mobility, steam donkeys were anchored to a stump during operation. The donkey engineer, or skinner, and crew fed wood and water into the boiler for power. The main line pulled logs, but a mule was used to pull the line back to the next log, as the early machine had a single one-way drum. The bag on the mule was used to carry the choker that attached the log to the main line.

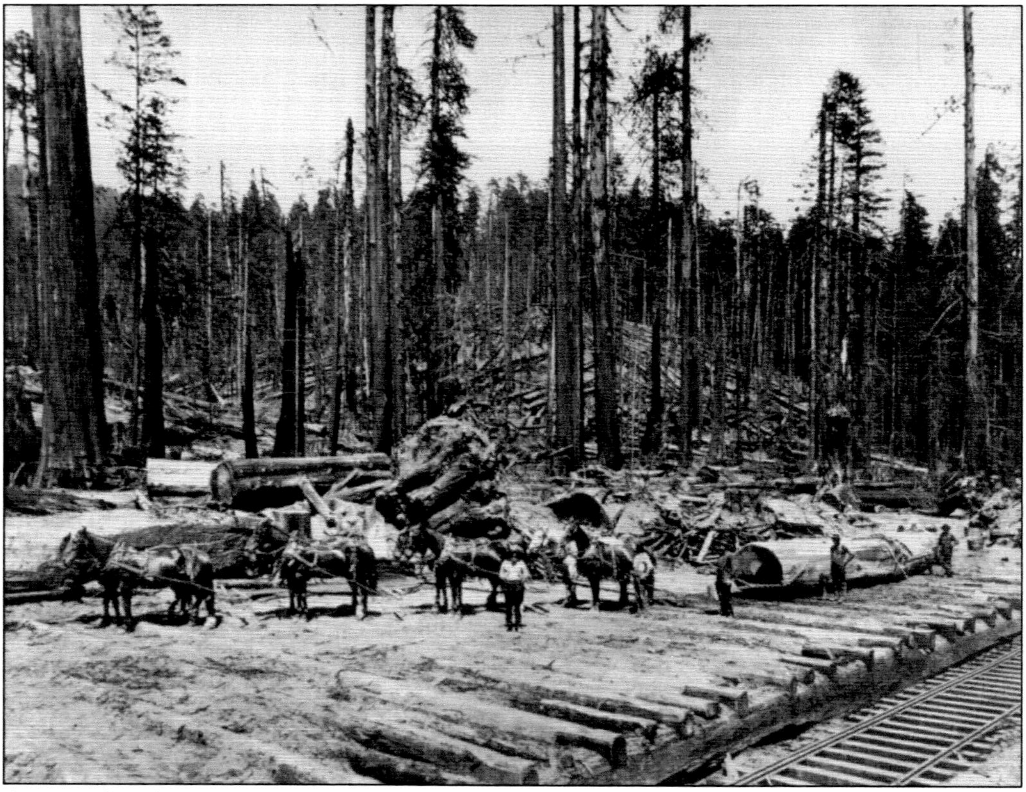

Oxen and mule teams were used to drag logs either to the mill or to a railhead. They pulled or skidded the timber over corduroy roads that were made of logs laid crossways on the roadbed. This picture features Dan Newell's mule team near Scotia in 1895. Newell is in the center of the photograph. There were opposing opinions over whether mules or oxen were better for pulling logs, but both were used in the region.

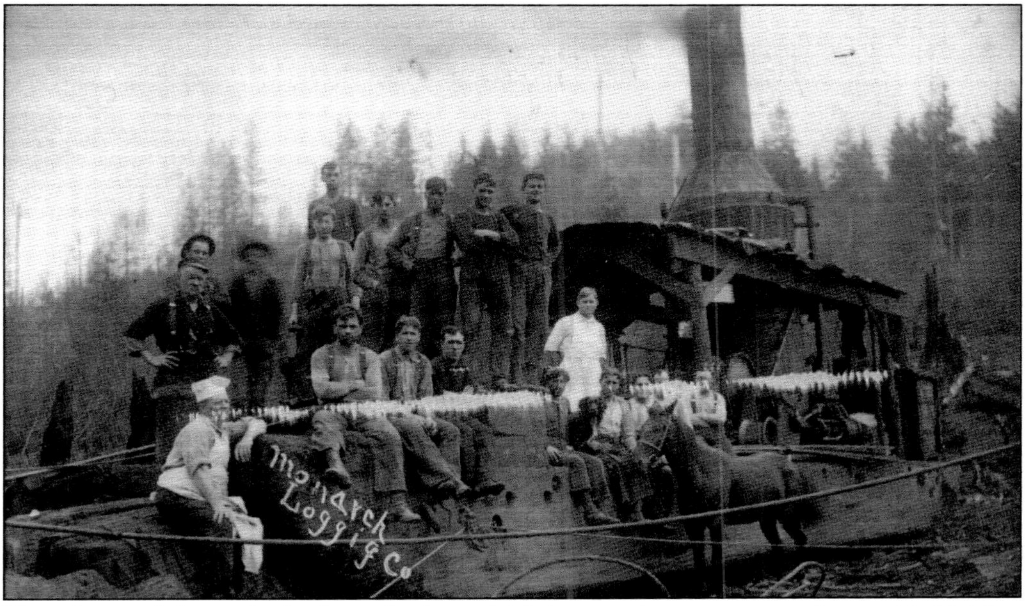

The advent of the multiple-drum donkey, which became known as a yarder, enabled higher production. The machine could pull out its own lines, as well as pull logs. This 1912 Monarch Logging Company photograph shows the entire woods crew. The cook was an important crew member. A good cook ensured that the lumber company kept a quality crew. Standing fourth from the left is Charles Hellard, age 22.

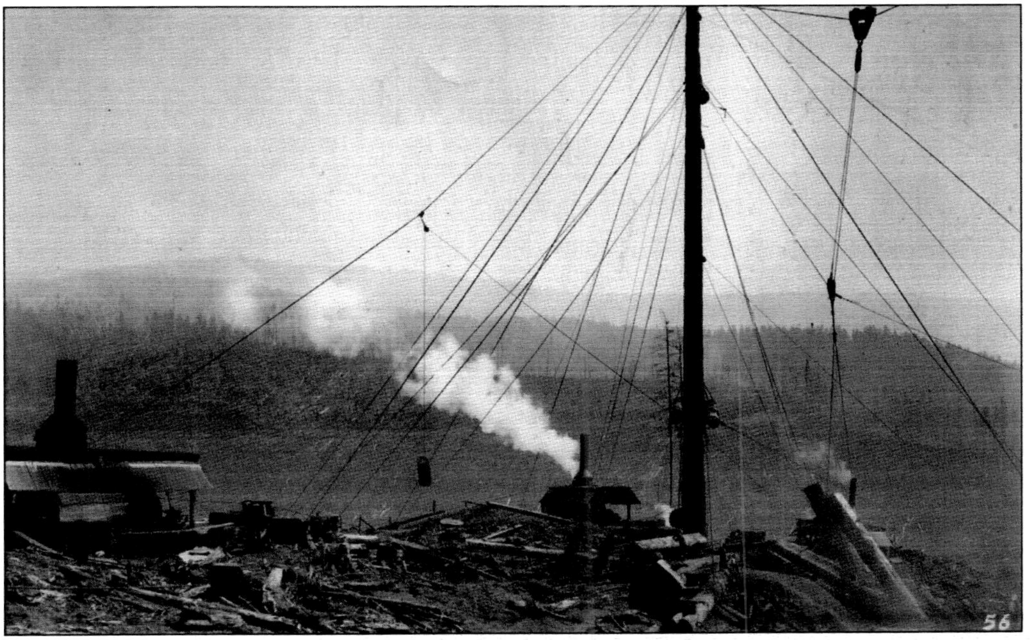

With the advent of the yarder, the spar tree became an important part of woods operations. A spar tree enabled logs to be lifted above stumps and other debris. It was also used to load logs onto railroad cars. The spar tree was rigged with blocks and guy wires to support it. They were created when a climber topped a tree and rigged it.

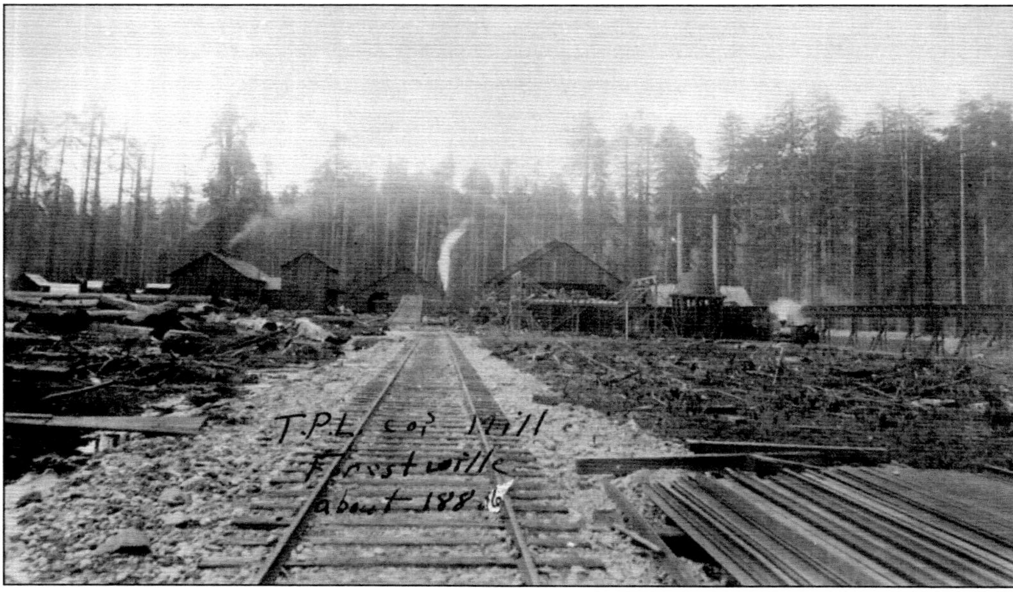

The Pacific Lumber Company (T.P.L. Co.) began at Scotia in 1869. However, no logging or milling operations took place until 1886, when a mill was built, employing 150 men. First given the name of Forestville, the town was renamed Scotia in 1888. The company ran its own woods crews, railroad, and shipping fleet and operated until 2008 when it was sold to Mendocino Redwoods.

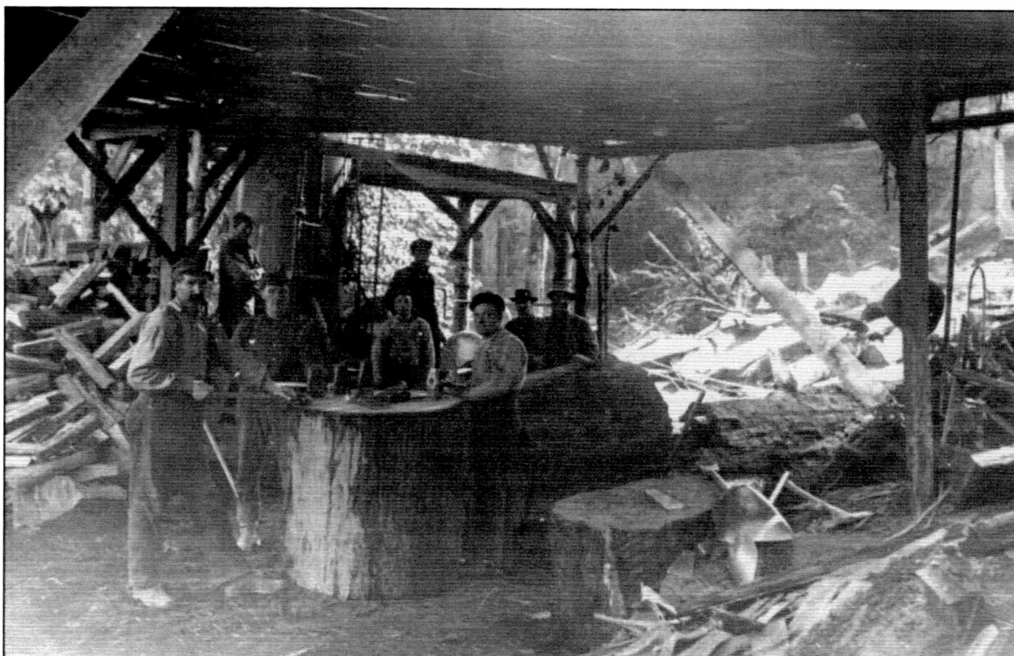

The blacksmith shop was an important workplace for the lumber industry. In the woods, the blacksmith's work included making saws, adzes, splitting awls, and axes, as well as shoes for the mules and oxen. Blacksmiths were known for their skill, and loggers would often be hired at a new location based on the maker of their tools.

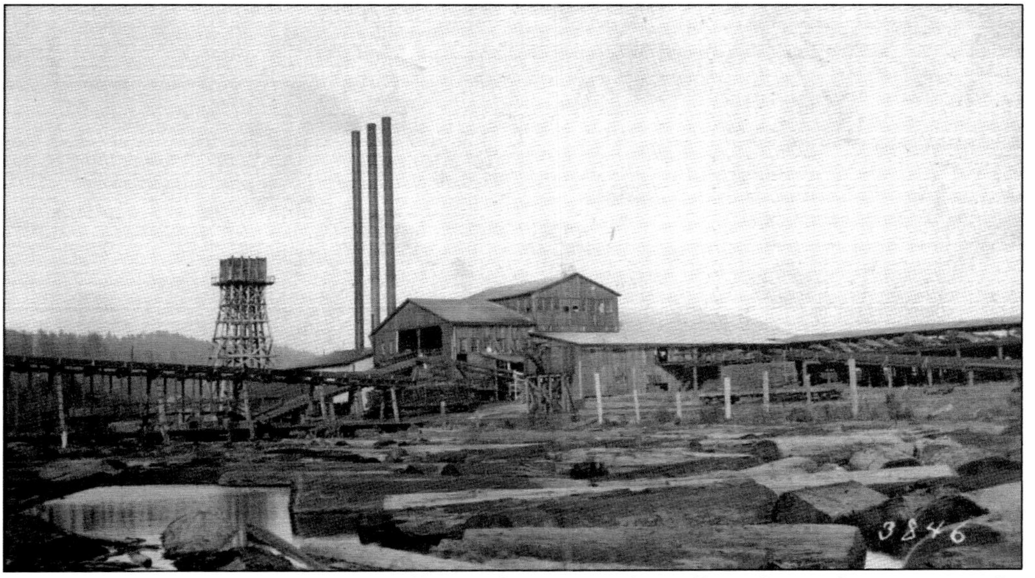

Mills were located throughout the valley. Built in 1904, the mill at Metropolitan supported a town of 25 houses, a store, and a hotel. One resident, Grace Wilber, wrote in 1917 that it was "not as nice as the mill at Caspar [California]. All mills look the same to me." Mills of the era were uniform, including ponds to hold logs before they were milled and boilers to power the mill.

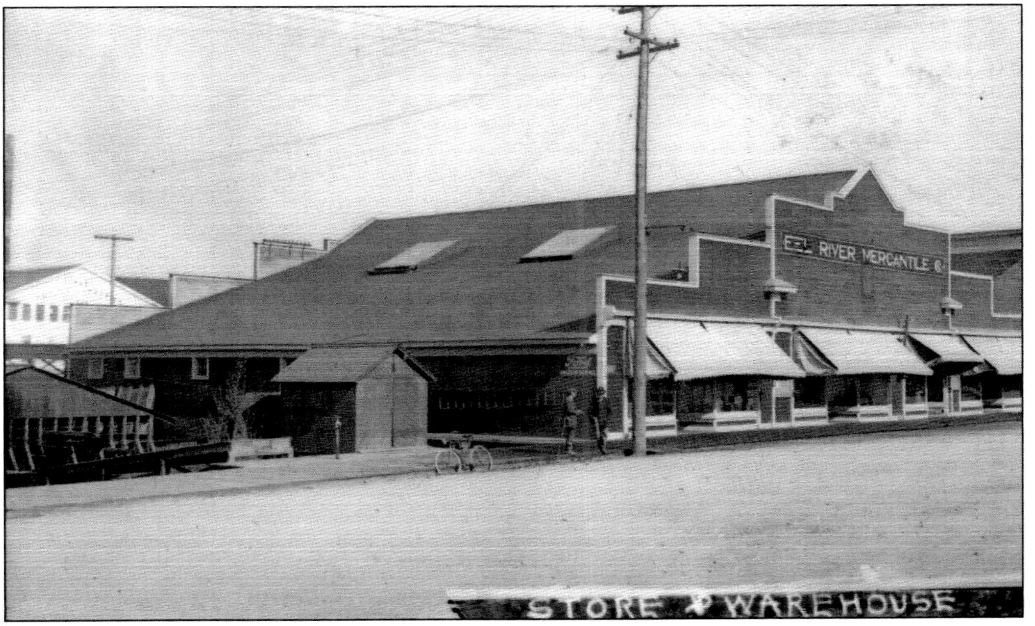

Larger mills, such as the one at Scotia, created their own communities. Scotia was a company town. The Pacific Lumber Company owned all of the houses, which were rented to its employees. They also operated their own shops where workers could buy necessities. The company store, Eel River Mercantile, was an important place for the employees and their families.

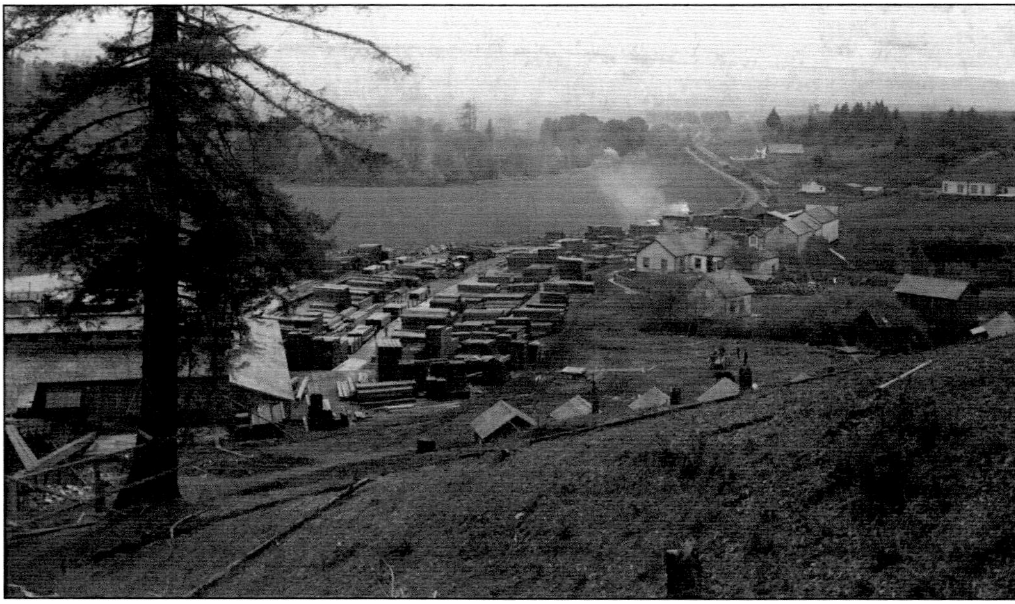

Fortuna began with the Springville Mill Company, but others followed. In 1884, the Eel River Valley Lumber Company's mill was built near the redwoods along Strong's Creek. Becoming one of the largest mills in the region, the town site was named Newburg, after founder E.J. Dodge's hometown in New York. In 1914, Dodge became sole owner and changed the mill's name to the E.J. Dodge Lumber Company.

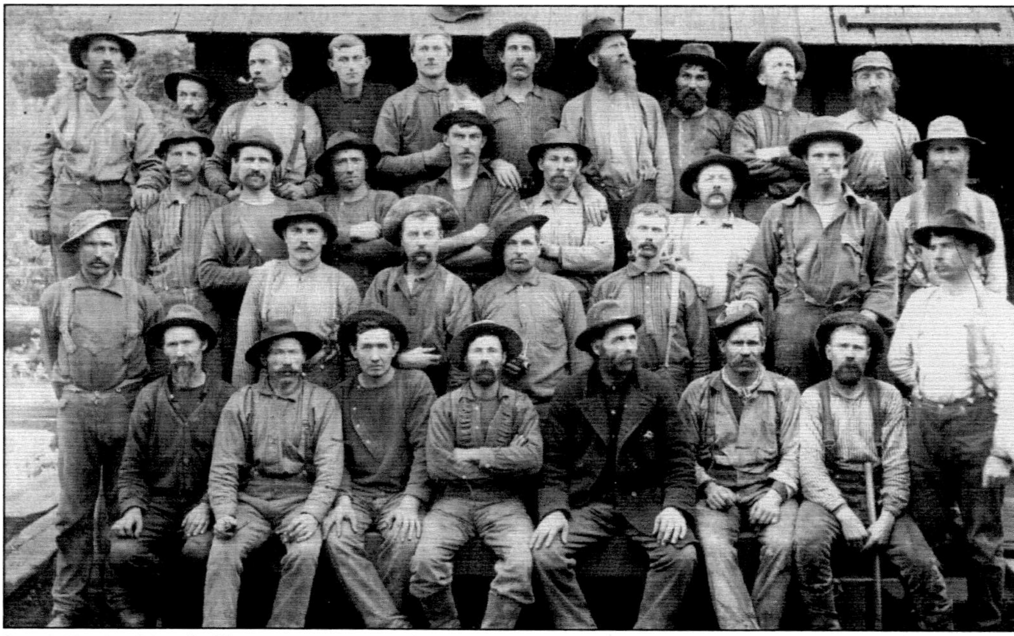

In 1912, the *Humboldt Beacon* reported that the Eel River Valley Lumber Company at Newburg, two miles east of Fortuna, was "up to date in all of its appearances. Employment is given to some 200 men in the milling and logging industry, all of whom are furnished with board in the two boarding houses of the company." The Newburg mill crew is shown in an undated photograph.

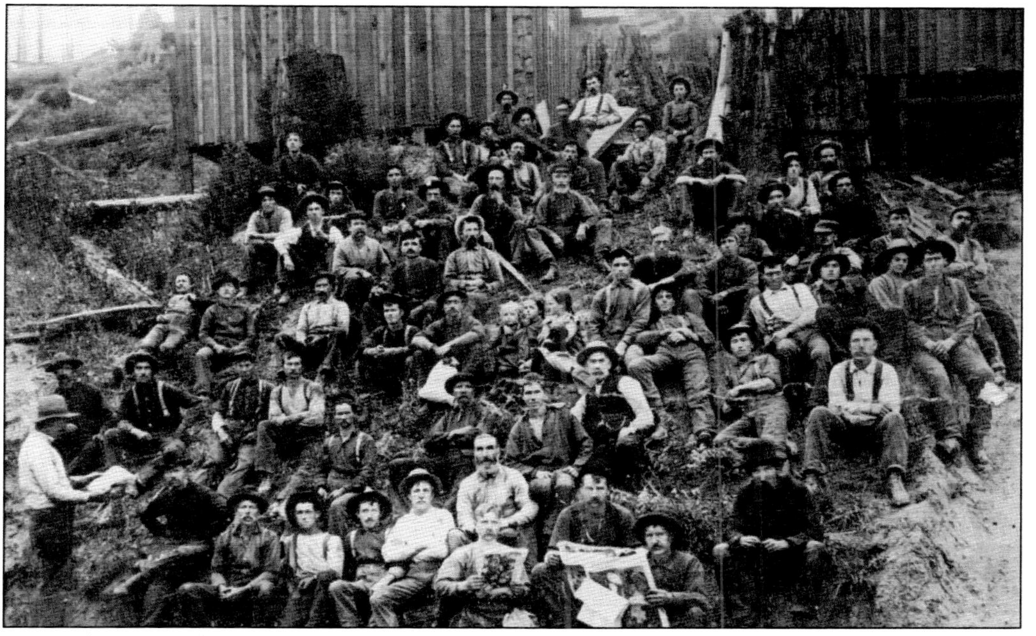

Pictured in 1902, the Eel River Valley Lumber Company's woods crew consisted of men of many nationalities. Tim Fielder started work at the Dodge woods camp at the age of 14. He recalled that he "worked with a crew of rough Irishmen. [I] saw a logger throw a double-bitted axe at the boss, and the boss caught it and threw it back. Then, they went on working."

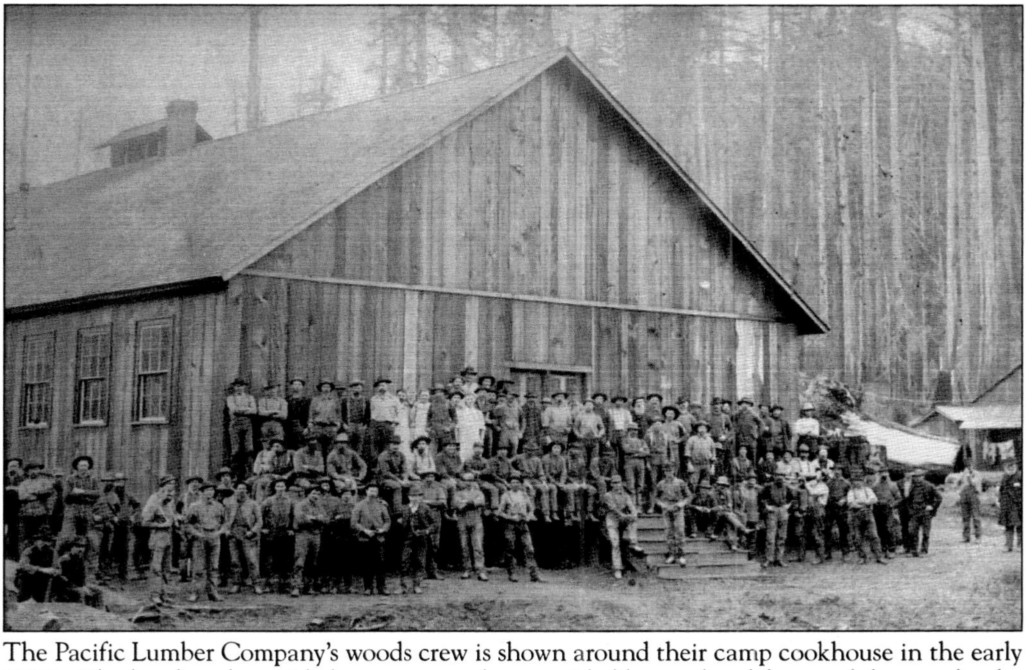

The Pacific Lumber Company's woods crew is shown around their camp cookhouse in the early 1900s. The head cook presided over a crew that provided hearty breakfasts and dinners for the lumbermen. Lunch was taken from the spike table to be eaten in the woods by the crew. Mills also had cookhouses for their crews.

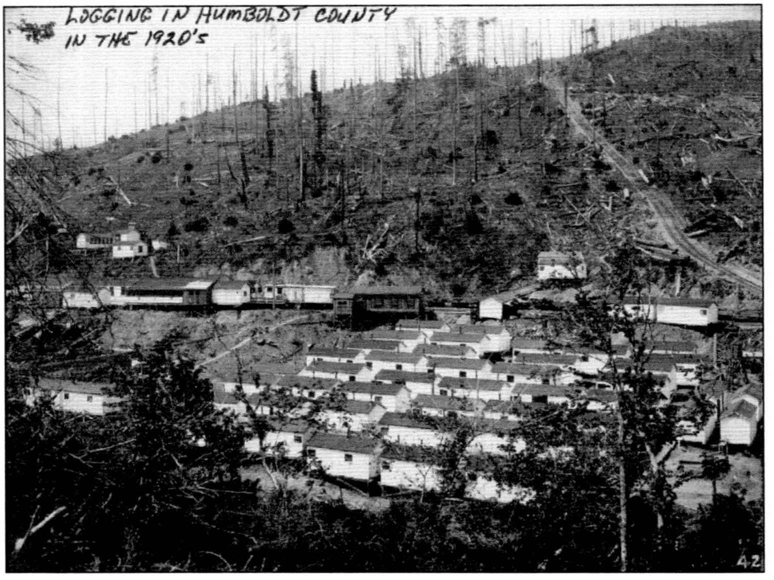

By the 1920s, logging camps had become mobile. The loggers' cabins and other buildings of the camp were on skids so they could be dragged to new locations. The "bull of the woods" was the boss of operations, who had an office and quarters. Bull was used to describe the head or the largest of anything in the woods. (Courtesy of Bob Lutz.)

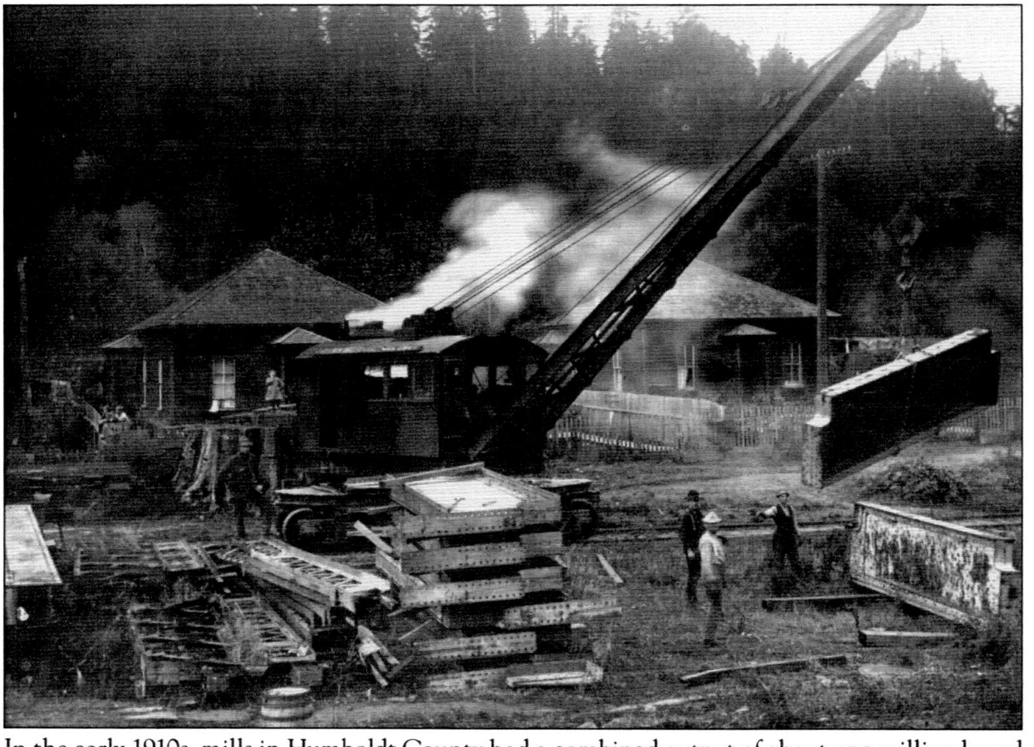

In the early 1910s, mills in Humboldt County had a combined output of about one million board feet of lumber a day. Trees closest to most mills had been harvested, and lumber companies extended operations farther away from their mill sites. For example, in 1906, the Holmes Eureka Lumber Company constructed a railroad with a steel trestle from Shively across the Eel River to its timber holdings. Shown are the construction crew and building materials at Shively.

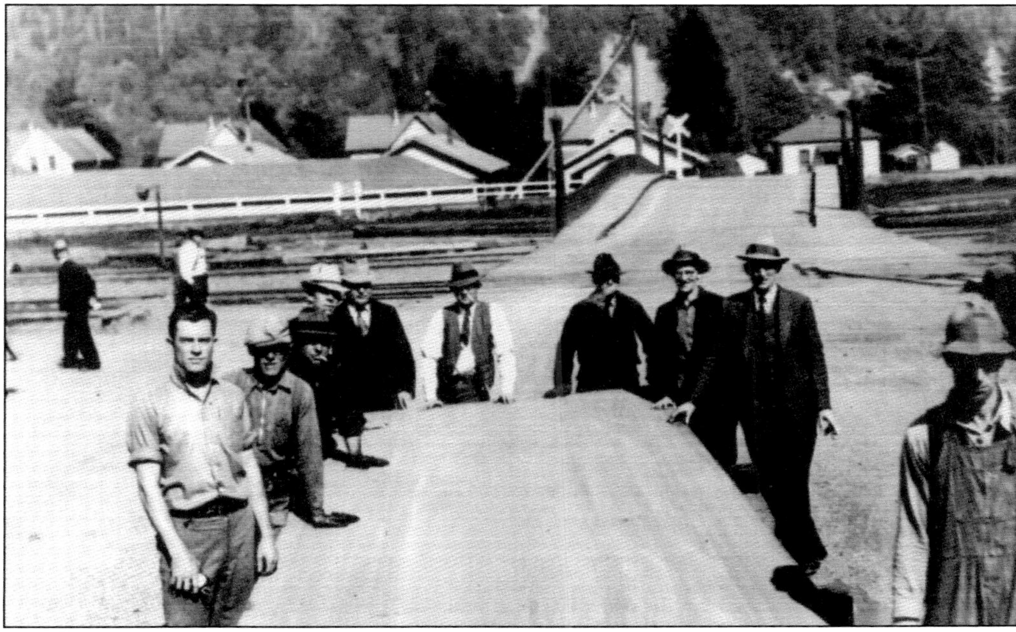

Celebrating and advertising the advantages of using redwood began when the trees were first harvested. In the late 1930s, for the world's fair in San Francisco, this impressive board was cut from one redwood at the mill in Scotia. The men shown here are listed on the back of the photograph as being Hollis Rollins, James Strobridge, Jess France, Preston Cook, Adolph Kanke, Roy Latman, Jonny Laresen, Lonal Arman, Terry McGowen, John Silva, Dan Coakley, and Harry Kesser.

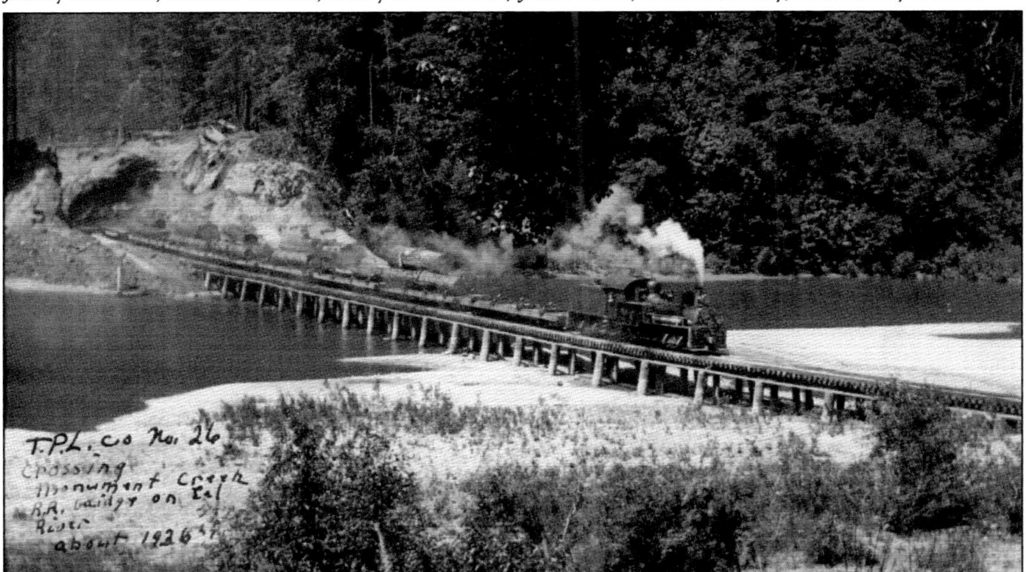

To maximize its operations, T.P.L. Co. had its own railroad line. The company owned 22 different locomotives. No. 26 was a Shay locomotive purchased by the company in 1906 and scrapped in 1950. The engine is shown making its way over the Eel River across from Scotia on Monument Creek in 1926. Many lumber companies had diverse railroad lines that accessed redwoods along various watersheds.

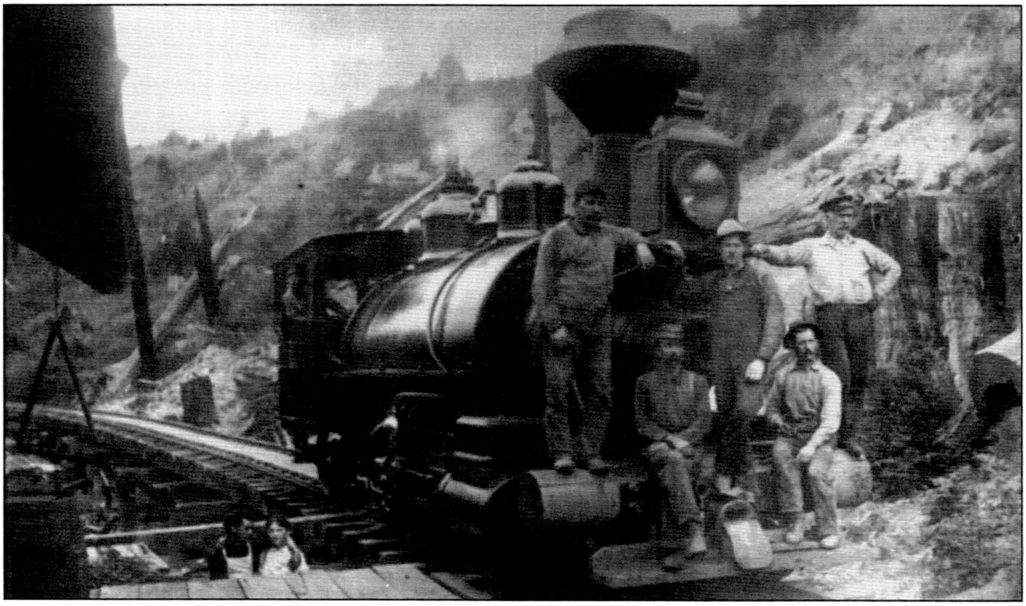

The Eel River Valley Lumber Company, later the E.J. Dodge Company, owned four locomotives. The company purchased their No. 3 engine in 1916. Built in 1895, the locomotive hauled logs from woods operations to the mill and retail yards in Fortuna. These operations expanded from Strong's Creek to Wolverton Creek and Alton. From there, the company built a trestle over the Eel River and rail lines along Howe Creek.

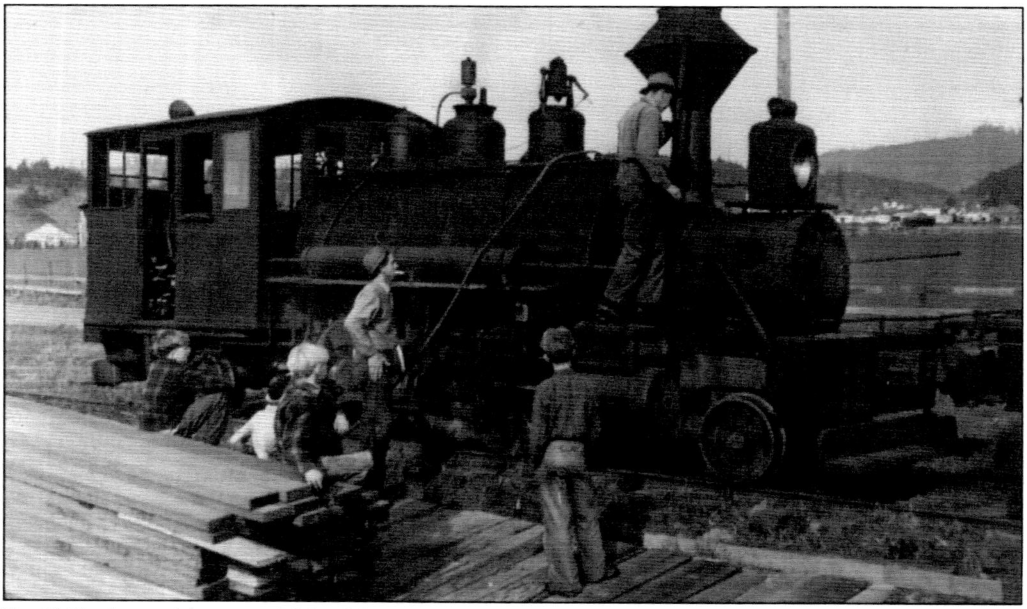

By 1943, the rail lines and No. 3 locomotive were becoming obsolete. Shown at the retail yard at the junction of Newburg Road and Twelfth Street, No. 3 made its last trip that year. The mill ceased operations during the Depression and was dismantled, along with the rail lines, in 1943. The company continued to operate the retail yard for five more years. Its closure brought an end to the E.J. Dodge Company.

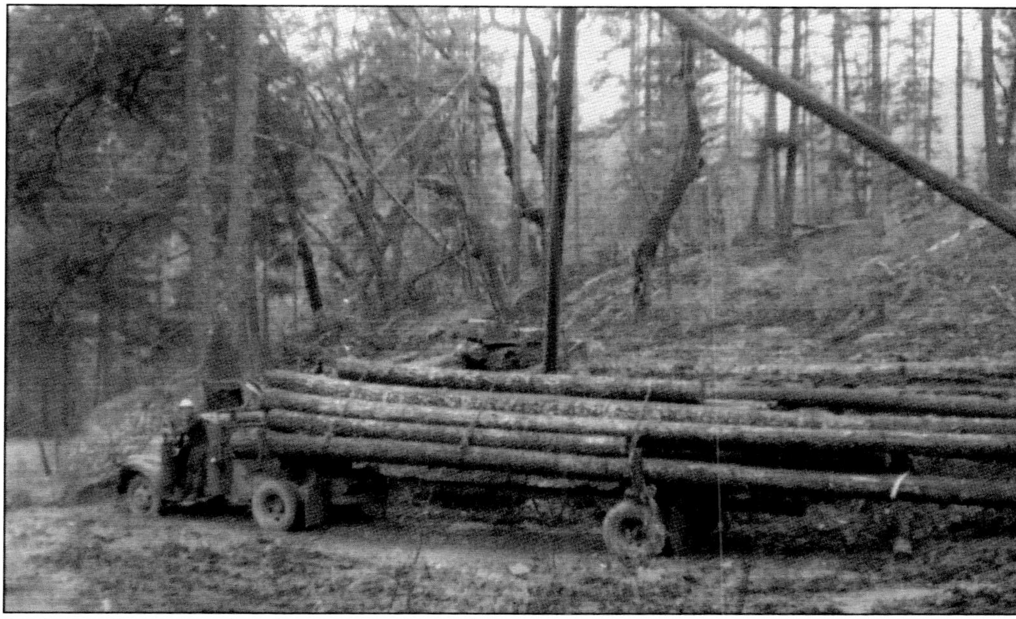

In the mid-1940s, railroads began to be replaced by trucks. The log truck gave the lumberman more mobility, operated at a lower cost to the company, and accessed more remote logging operations. Some companies maintained their own fleet of trucks, while others contracted the job out to truckers. This logging truck, operated by Bob Umland, shows the large load the trucks could haul.

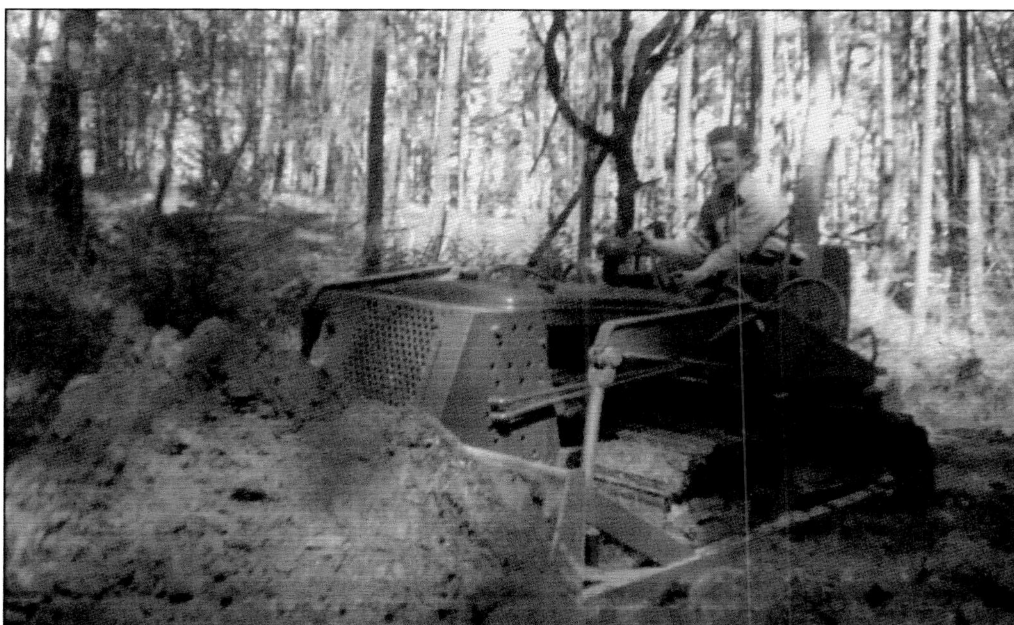

By the late 1920s, the steam donkey was replaced by the tractor crawler. Known as a bulldozer to woods crews, it could pull logs to landings and make roads. The bulldozer not only increased harvesting capabilities, it also changed the landscapes of the woods by making skid roads.

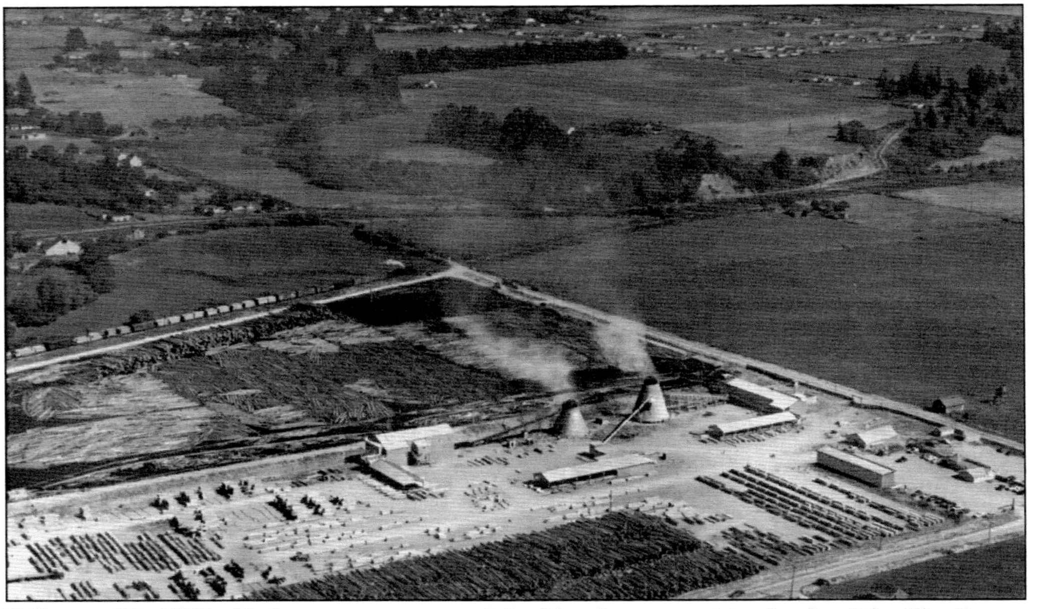

Following World War II, there was a nationwide building boom requiring lumber. The Clay Brown Redwood Lumber Mill was one of 30 sawmills, plywood mills, veneer mills, and tie mills found in the Fortuna vicinity in 1956. These mills had a combined output of over a million board feet of lumber a day and employed over 695 workers, according to a 1956 publication of the Eureka and Humboldt County Chambers of Commerce. (Courtesy of Doug and Marilyn Strehl.)

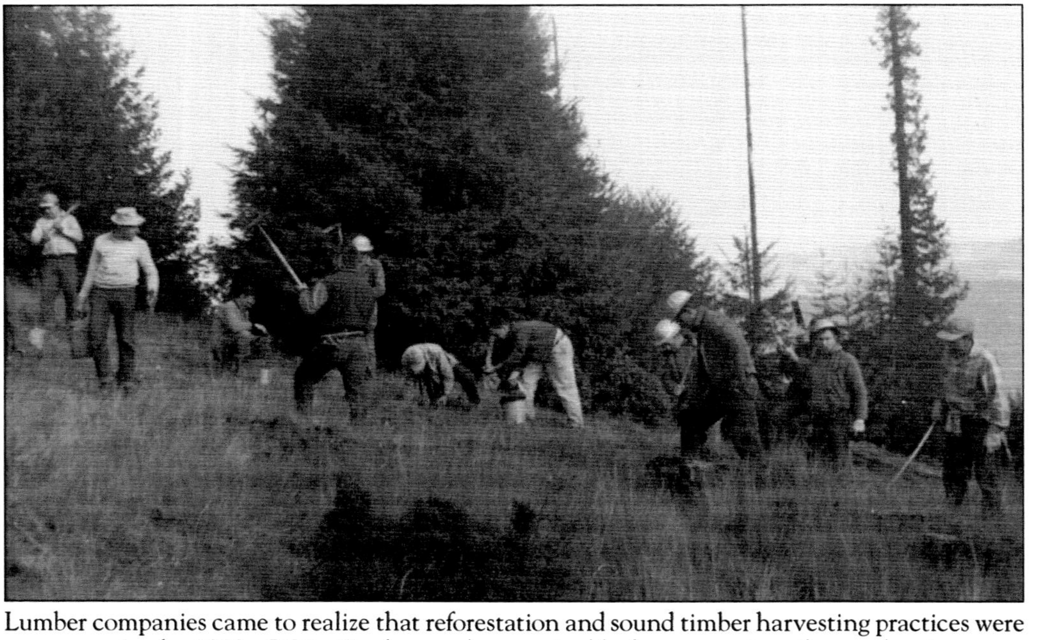

Lumber companies came to realize that reforestation and sound timber harvesting practices were necessary. In the 1920s, T.P.L. Co. began the sustainable forest practice of never logging more than could be replanted. This tree planting at Jordan Creek in 1962 reflects that practice. The lumber companies started their own greenhouses to raise trees and often paid people to collect redwood cones and seeds.

Technological changes that advanced logging and milling of redwoods also allowed visitors to travel to see the magnificent trees. Touring in 1917, San Francisco professors and scientists John C. Merriam, Henry Fairfield Osborn, and Madison Grant were dismayed by logging damage. Forming the Save the Redwoods League in 1918, they preserved the first grove in Humboldt County near Myers Flat, dedicating it in 1921 to Colonel Bolling, the first high-ranking US officer killed in World War I.

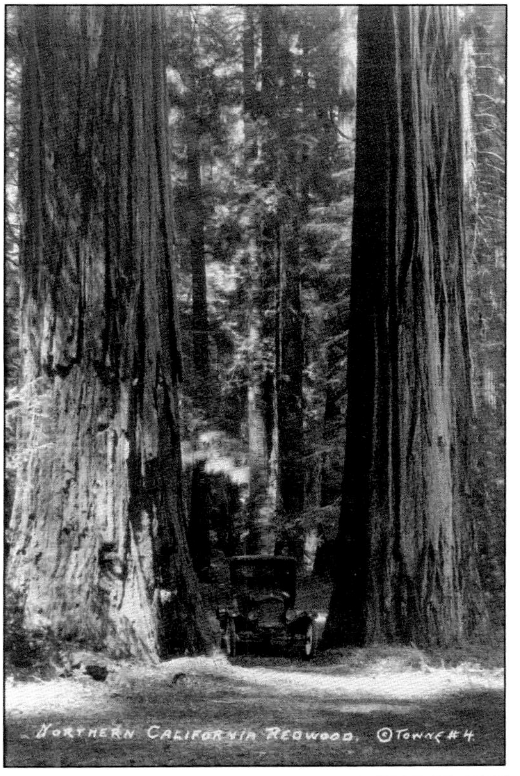

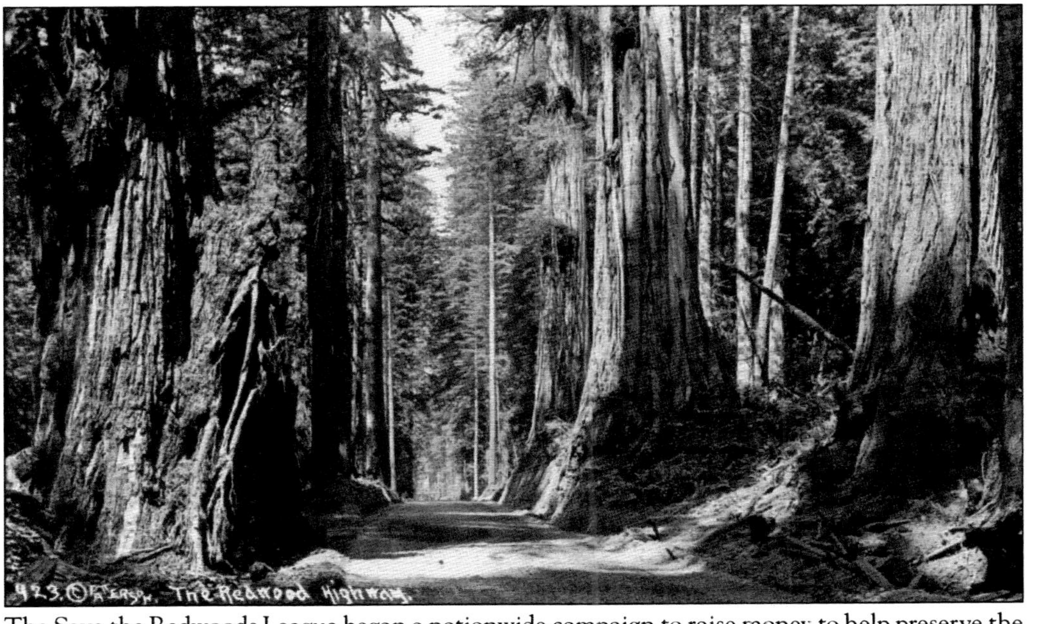

The Save the Redwoods League began a nationwide campaign to raise money to help preserve the redwoods in Humboldt County. They also sparked local interest in preserving the majestic trees. A Humboldt Save the Redwoods League was formed, as well as a Women's Save the Redwoods League. There had been a movement to create a local Redwood National Park as early as 1910.

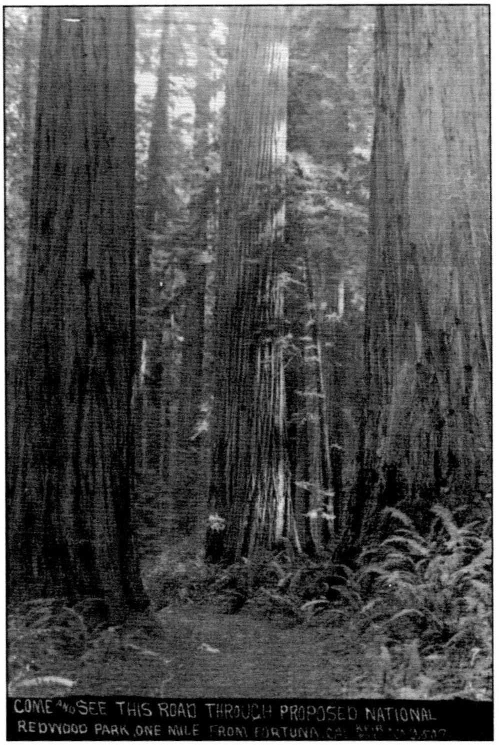

Thomas A. Greig, son of Fortuna's early livery stable owner, was actively engaged in preserving redwoods, joining the Save the Redwoods League soon after it was founded. He served as a leader in the acquisition program of the league, working to obtain the stands of redwoods along the Avenue of the Giants from T.P.L. Co. He was recognized with a grove dedication near Pepperwood.

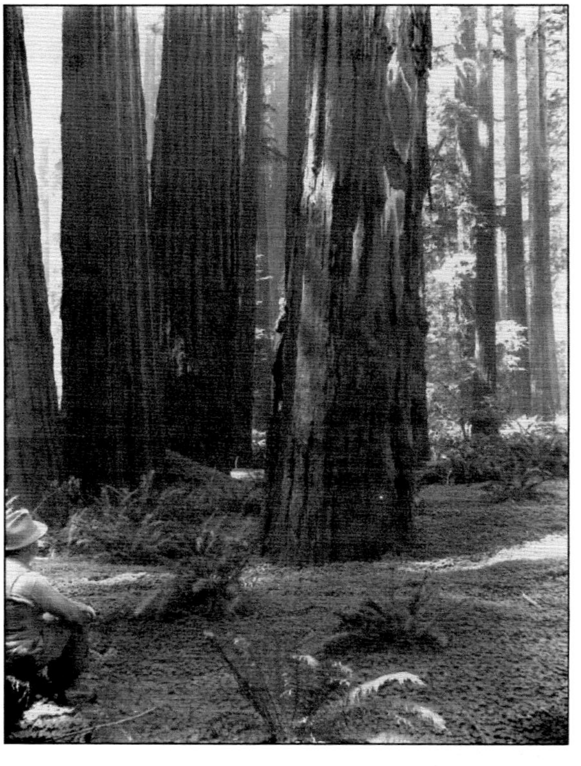

Redwood groves throughout Humboldt County were preserved through the efforts of Save the Redwoods League and other local groups. Both the logging and the preserving of the redwoods are intimately tied to the growth and development of the Eel River Valley. An unidentified man gazes at the giant trees in a 1920s photograph, symbolic of those who continue to enjoy the protected redwood forests.

Four

Ways to Make a Living

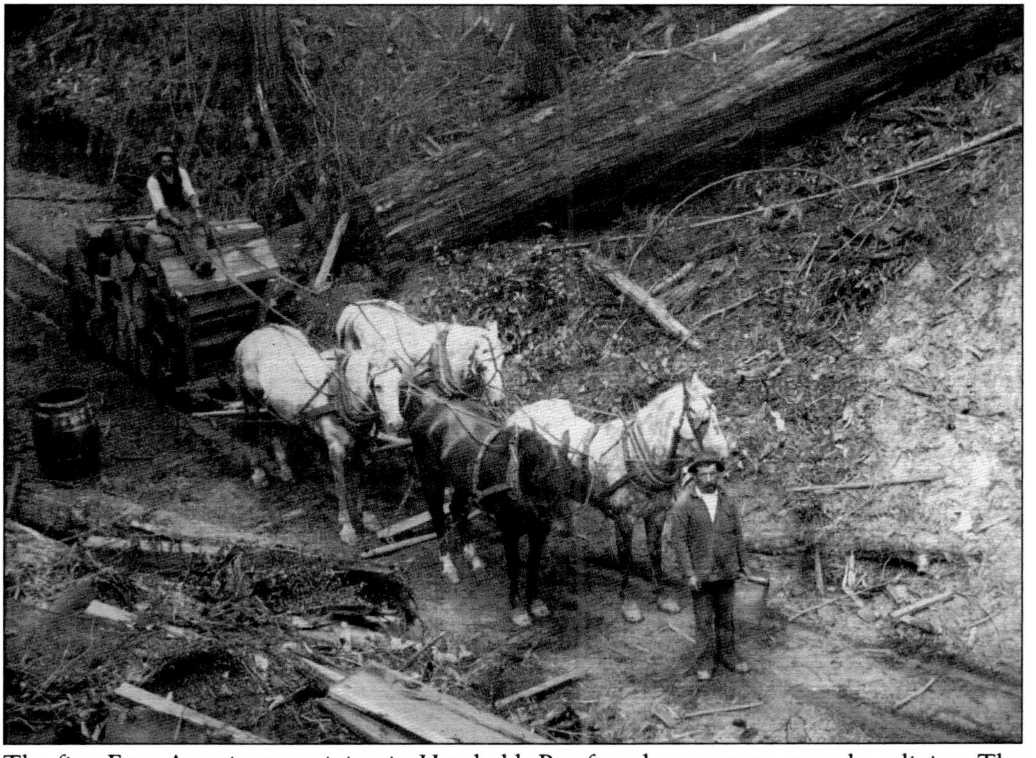

The first Euro-Americans arriving in Humboldt Bay found many ways to make a living. The primary industry in the region was logging and milling redwood trees. Additionally, there was an industry based on the splitting characteristics of redwood. Called the split-products industry, this smaller offshoot of the timber industry provided income for many individuals, including Sam Guthrie and Enos Jackson, pictured here near Newburg in 1895.

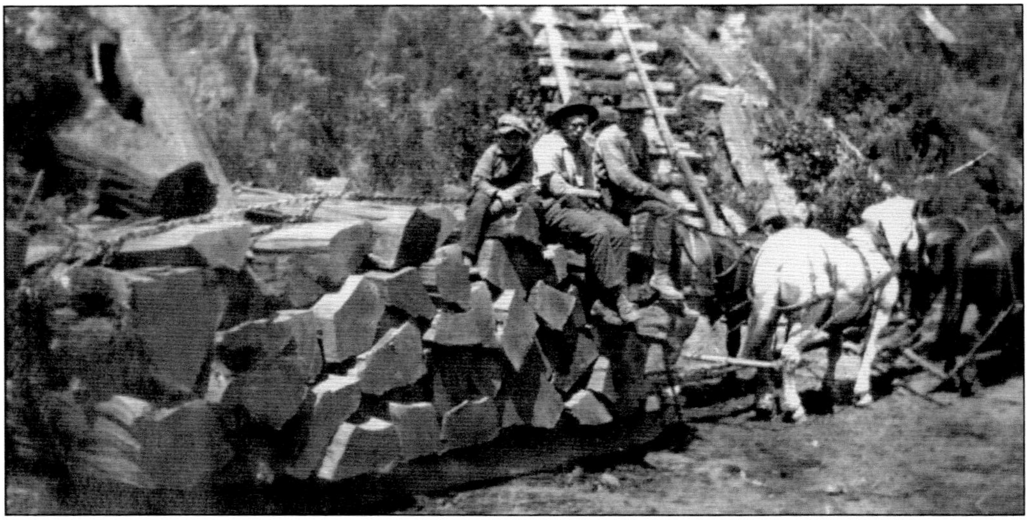

Redwood logs were cut into shingle bolts or split into grape stakes, railroad ties, or fence posts. Redwood shingle bolts were large chunks of wood that would later be split into shingles for covering roofs and, with the rise of the craftsman bungalow style, the sides of buildings. Al Daggett (middle) is sitting atop this load. (Courtesy of Bob Lutz.)

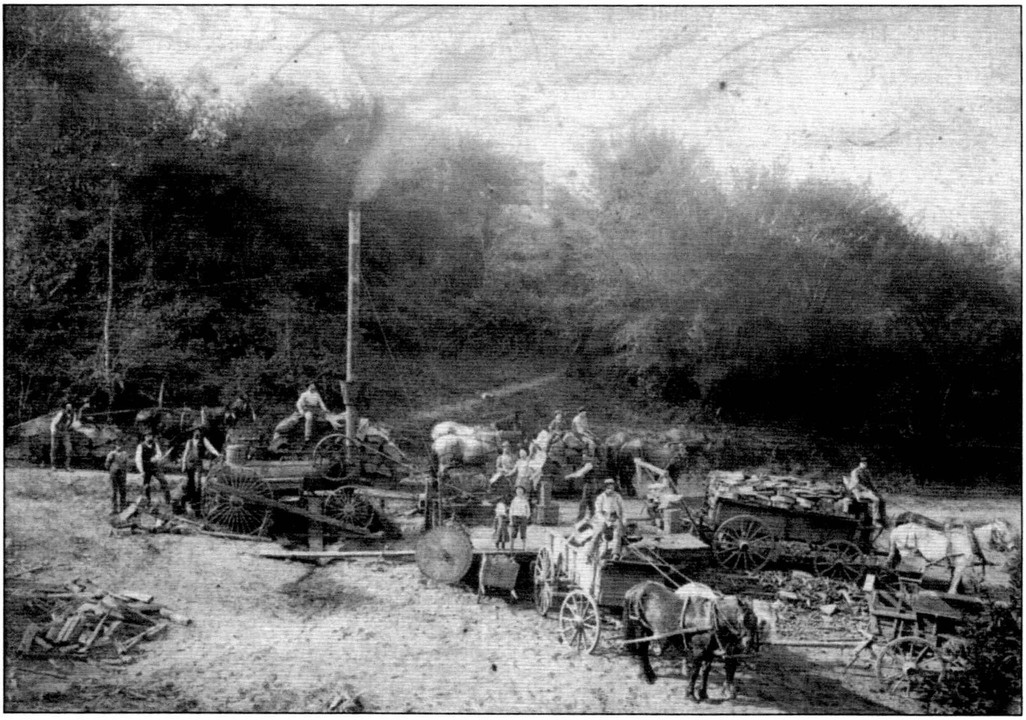

The advantage of cutting logs into shingle bolts or other split products was that they could be more easily hauled from the woods. Bolts and other products were often cut from the tree where it had fallen. Shingle bolts were hauled by wagon to shingle mills, and grape stakes and railroad ties could be taken directly to market. Therefore, tie camps were found farther from railheads.

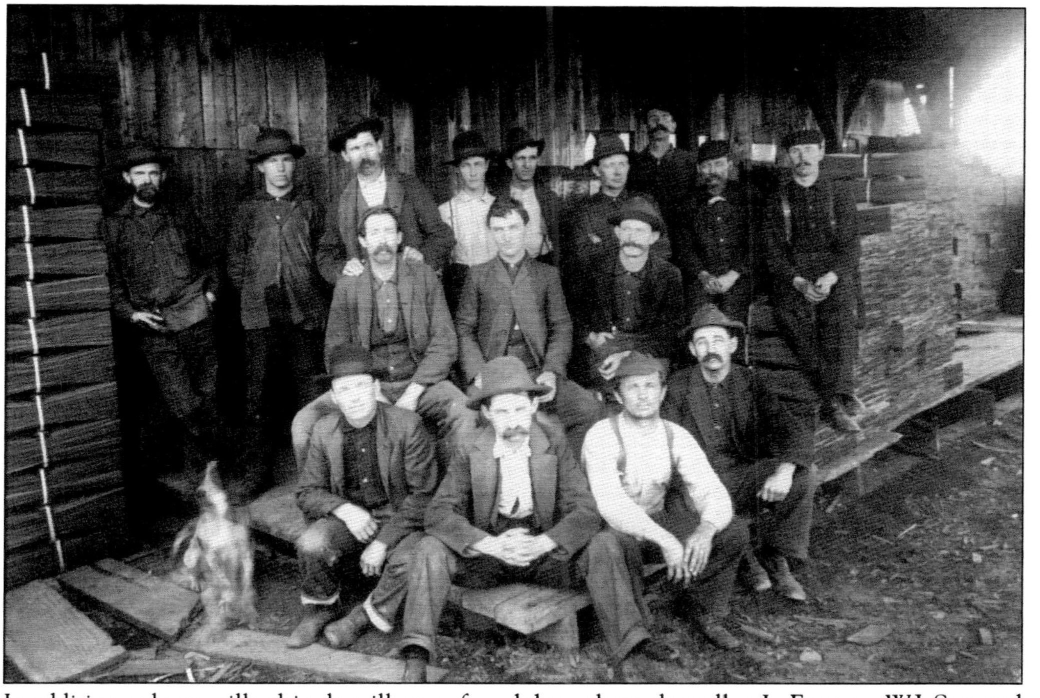

In addition to large mills, shingle mills were found throughout the valley. In Fortuna, W.J. Swortzel was part owner of the Humboldt Milling Company, which made moldings, doors, windows, shakes, and shingles. In 1895, the value of the shingles the mill produced was $25,C00. The shingles made in Fortuna were shipped throughout California, and the mill employed over 60 men.

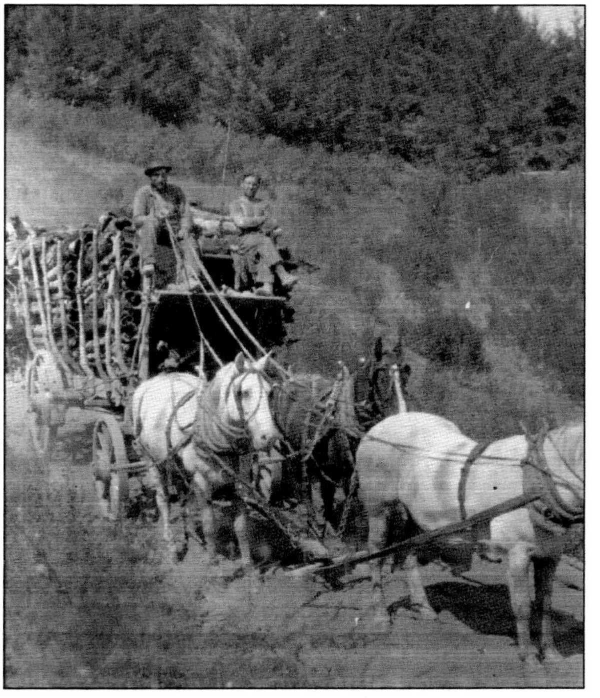

Another woods product–based business, the tanbark industry, depended on the acidic nature of the bark of the tan oak. Trees were ringed, and the bark peeled from the tree. After it dried, the bark was ground and used to tan hides. Some tanbark was shipped to tanneries in the San Francisco Bay area, and some was used in local tanneries, including one in the Rohnerville area.

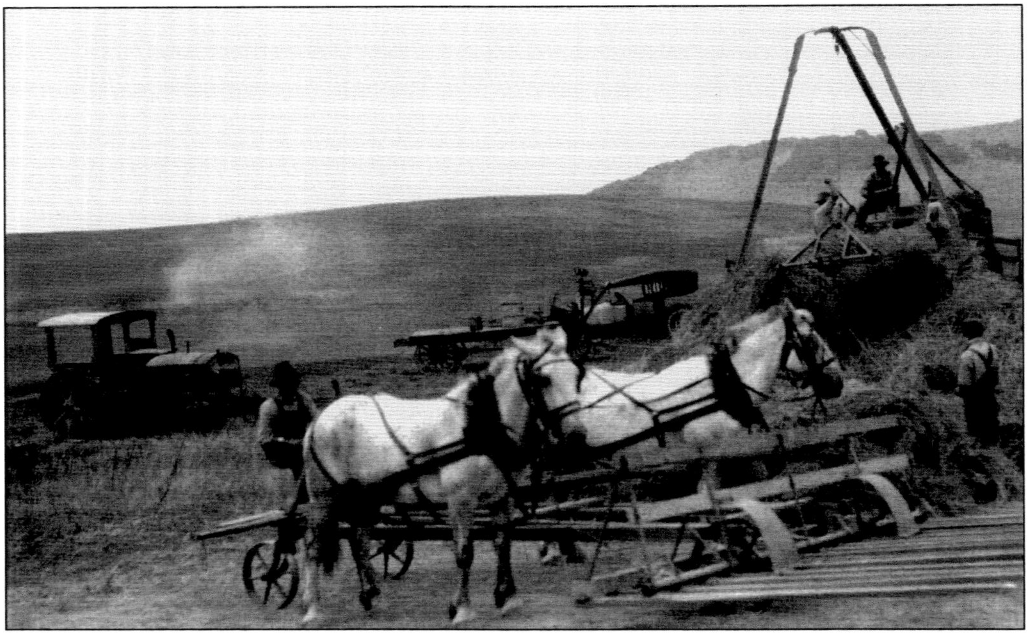

Another important agricultural product in the Eel River Valley in the 1890s was oat hay. During that time, Humboldt County produced nearly one-third of the oats grown in California. In 1893, an oat field on William Dinsmore's farm near Alton yielded 98.5 bushels of oats per acre. The oats grown in the Eel River Valley were considered exceptionally plump and were sought for milling purposes.

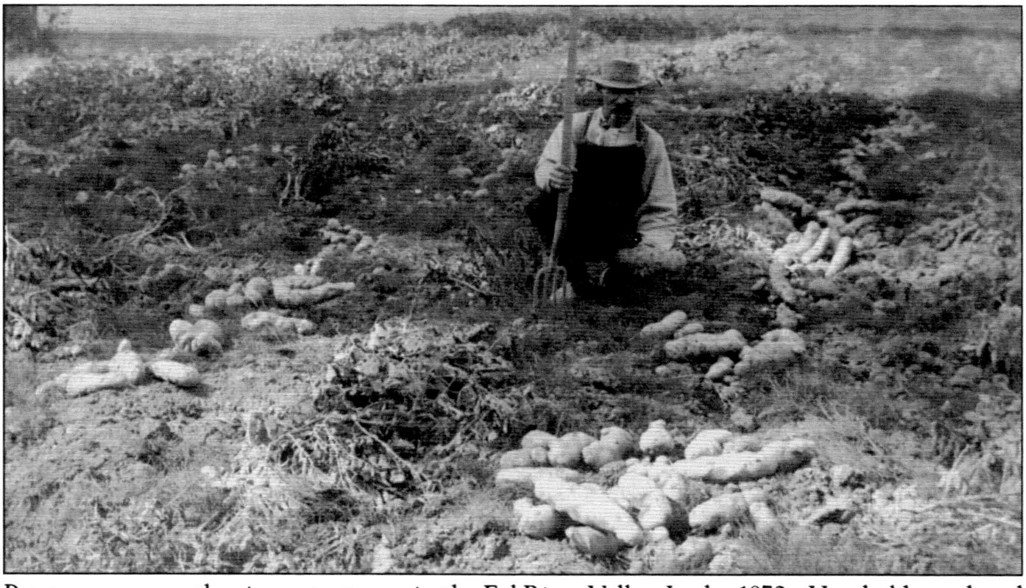

Potatoes were another important crop in the Eel River Valley. In the 1870s, Humboldt produced one-third of the potatoes grown in California. The yield, size, and quality of the potatoes first established Humboldt's agricultural reputation. Although a blight damaged the crops in the 1880s, potatoes remained an important crop for many years. In 1893, the potato crop in Humboldt County averaged a value of $60,000.

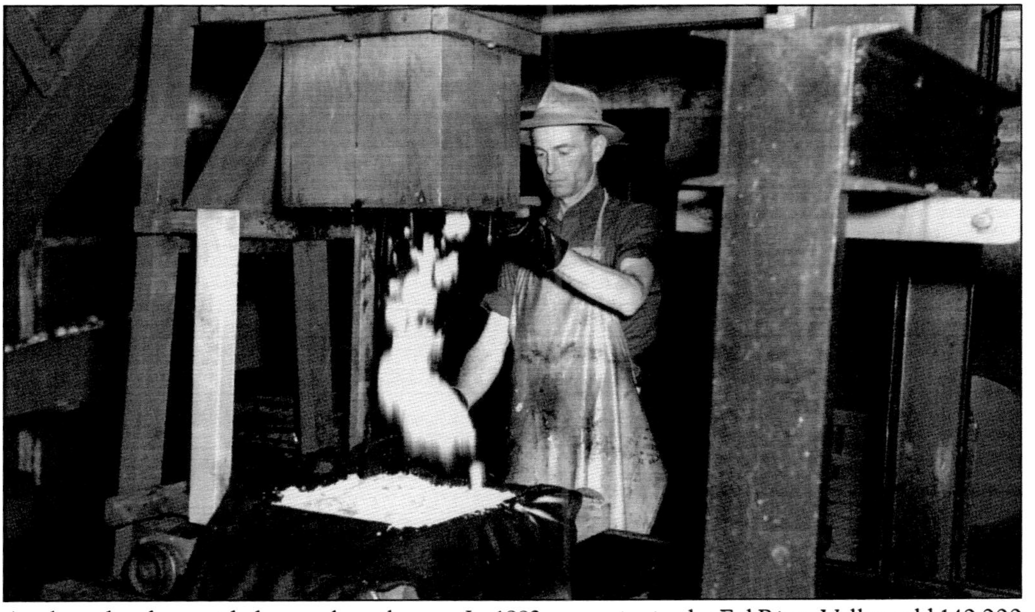

Apple orchards provided an early cash crop. In 1893, nurseries in the Eel River Valley sold 140,000 apple trees. Apples continued to be an important crop in the 20th century, as illustrated by this 1949 photograph of Andrew Clendenen using his 1916 Mount Gilead No. 4-C Cider and Fruit Press. The Clendenen Cider and Vinegar Works began operating in 1909. The same cider press is still in use today. (Courtesy of Clendenen's Cider Works.)

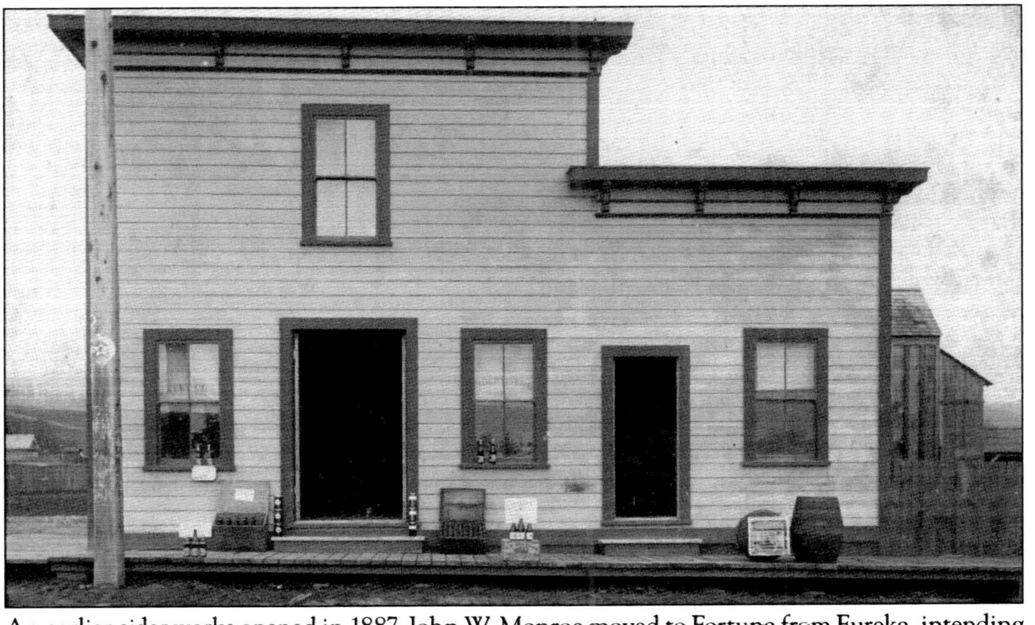

An earlier cider works opened in 1887. John W. Monroe moved to Fortuna from Eureka, intending to open a new business. His bottling works manufactured carbonated temperance (nonalcoholic) beverages. Monroe's sparkling Champagne Cider was much in demand as a temperance drink at weddings and other celebrations and was advertised as being "equal to champagne." In addition to cider, apple vinegar was produced, as it was important in food preservation.

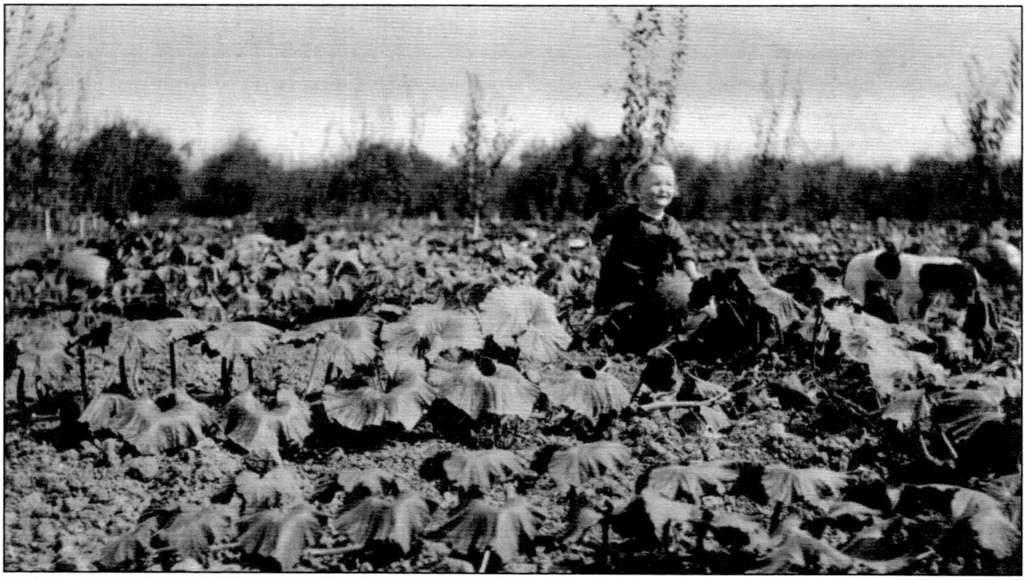

Other crops that were grown in the valley included peas, oats, barley, and pumpkins. Then, as now, a farmer's entire family was involved in planting, weeding, and harvesting the crops. Here, an Umland child was photographed in the family pumpkin field near Rohnerville in the 1920s.

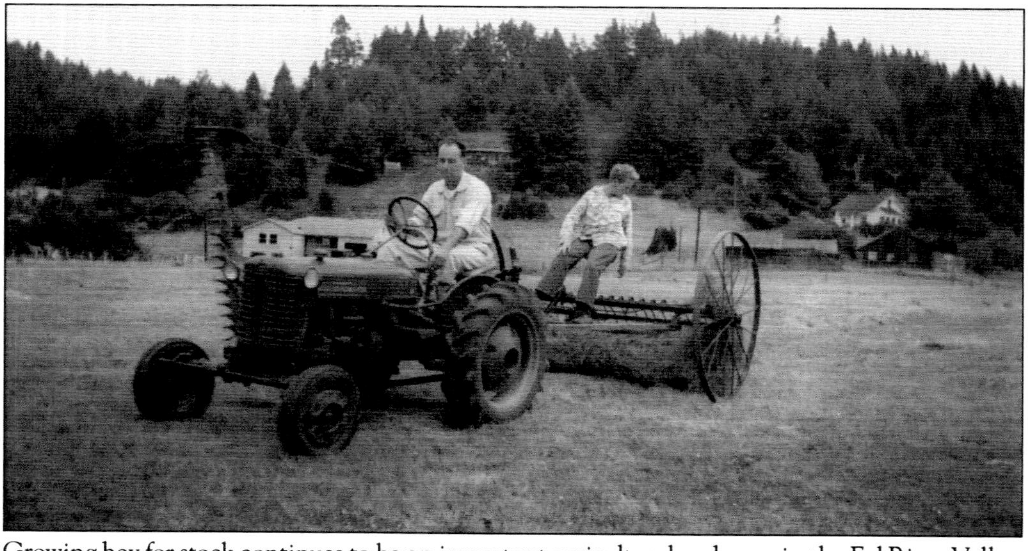

Growing hay for stock continues to be an important agricultural endeavor in the Eel River Valley. This photograph from the 1940s shows the Umland family using their Farmall Model A tractor with a mounted mower. It is pulling a dump rake to make rows out of the hay so that it could be gathered.

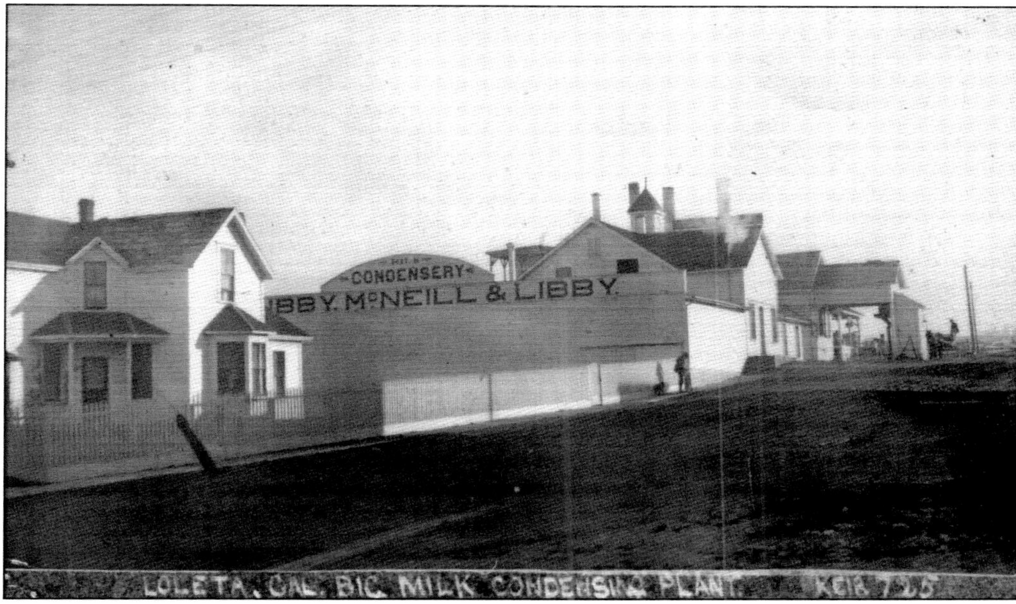

The hay most often found its way to the dairy industry of the Eel River Valley. The Libby, McNeill, and Libby Creamery in Loleta opened in 1893 and was originally called the Diamond Springs Creamery. According to the *Humboldt Beacon* in 1913, the Libby firm bought the creamery "following an extensive investigation by eastern experts as to the quality of the milk produced in the valley."

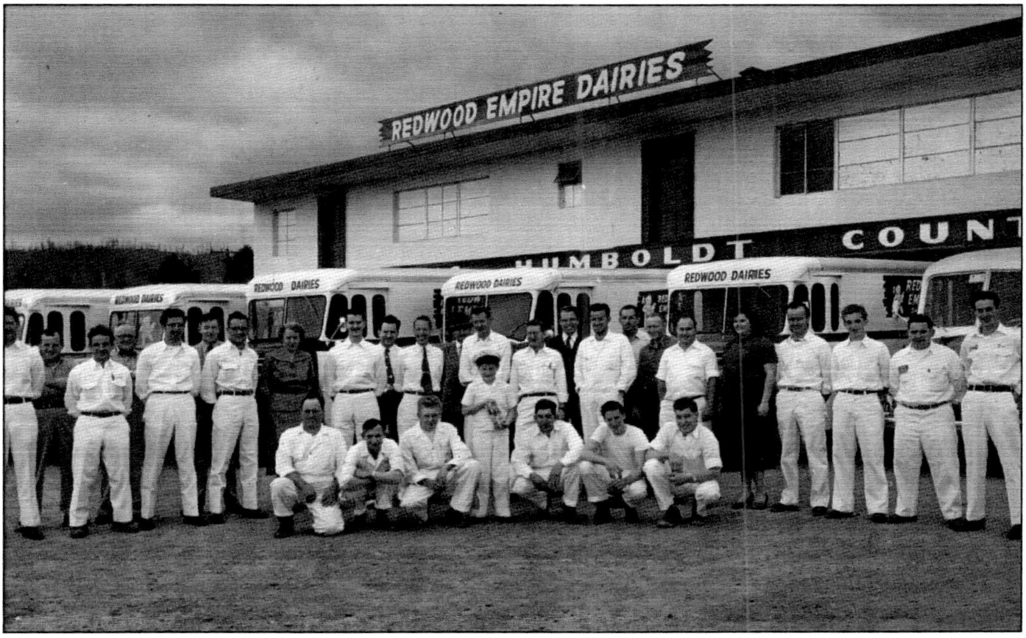

The Humboldt Creamery, also known as Redwood Empire Dairies—a consortium of local dairymen—was formed in 1929. This 1950s-era photograph shows the staff in front of their delivery trucks. The creamery's largest export was powdered milk. (Courtesy of Clarke Historical Museum.)

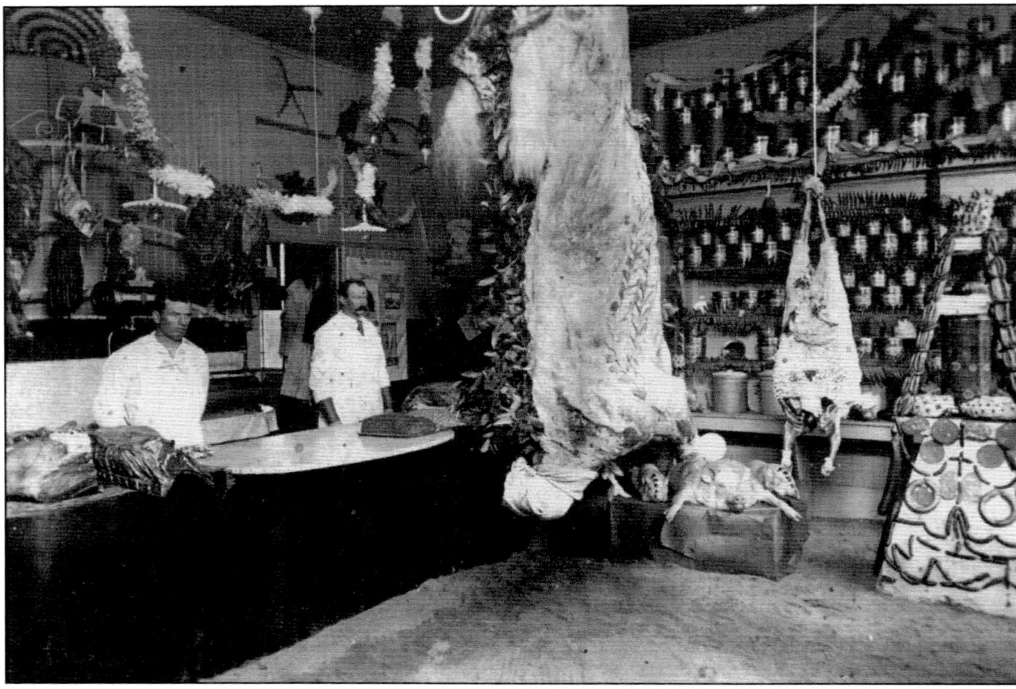

In the towns of the valley, businesses soon sprang up to meet the needs of loggers and farmers. In 1913, the Fortuna Meat Market advertised in the *Humboldt Beacon* that owner F.C. Thompson's market was the "only meat market south of Eureka that handles county inspected meats." His business also carried "meats of all kinds." (Courtesy of Clarke Historical Museum.)

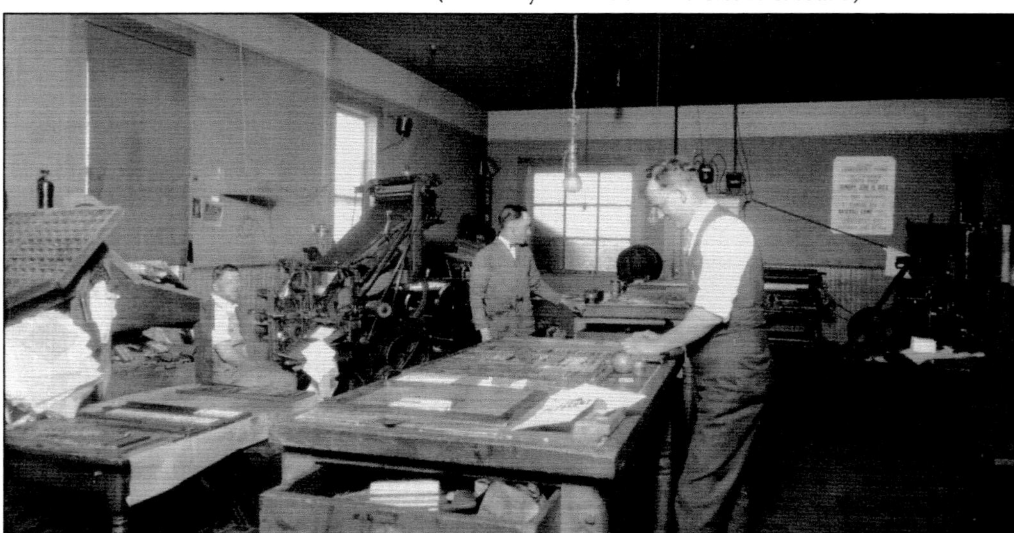

Newspapers were the main source of information for valley residents. Fortuna's first newspaper, the weekly *Eel River Valley Advance*, began publishing in 1888. In March 1902, the *Humboldt Beacon*, another weekly, was formed by the Reverend Gustave A. Jasper. Beginning operations in Loleta, he moved his paper to Fortuna in June. In this photograph are Paul Jasper (foreground), Gustave's son and second editor of the paper; Fred Scribner (seated at left); and an unidentified man.

Fortuna native H.I. Gushaw owned Humboldt Pharmacy, one of two drugstores in Fortuna in 1896. Located on Main Street, the *Eel River Valley Advance* described it as "a cozy and attractive dispensatory of antidotes for the ills which come in childhood, youth, manhood, and old age." Gushaw carried a "stock of drugs and medicines commensurate with the demands of this community . . . as well as fine cigars and choice confections."

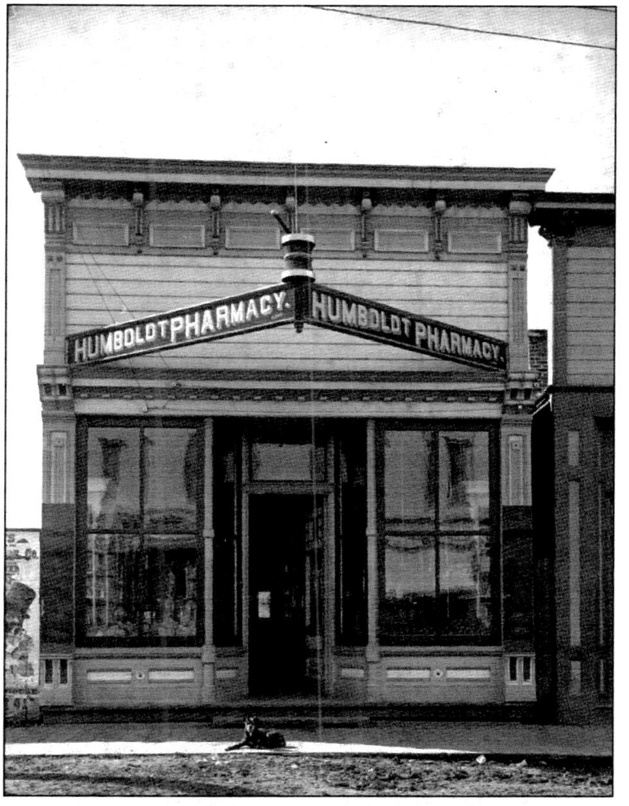

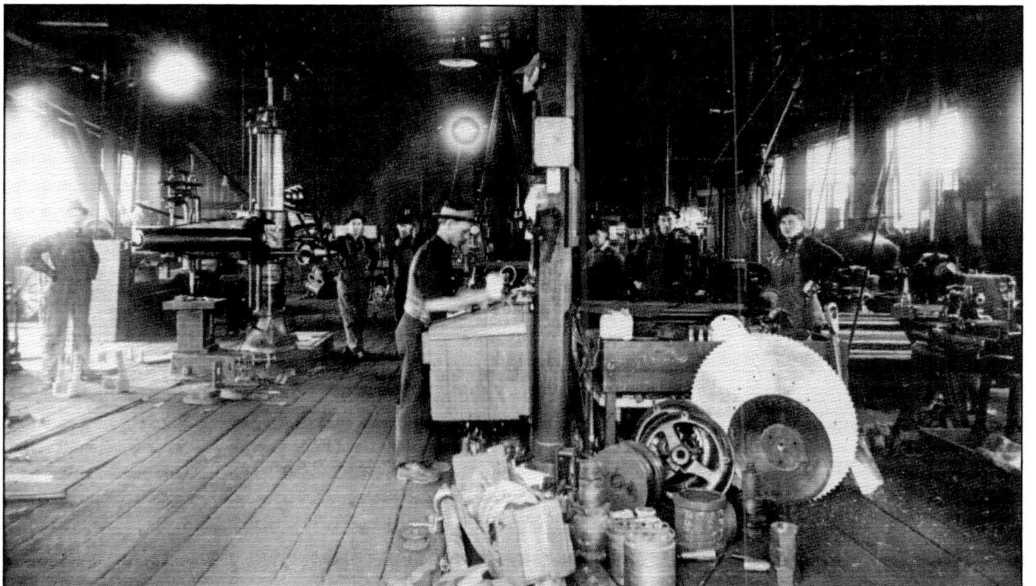

A specialist, the machinist manufactured and repaired all the parts of the mill, including the saws, for the millwrights. The size of the redwoods required special saws, many of which were made on-site. Les Perrott is seen standing at the workbench in the Scotia machine shop.

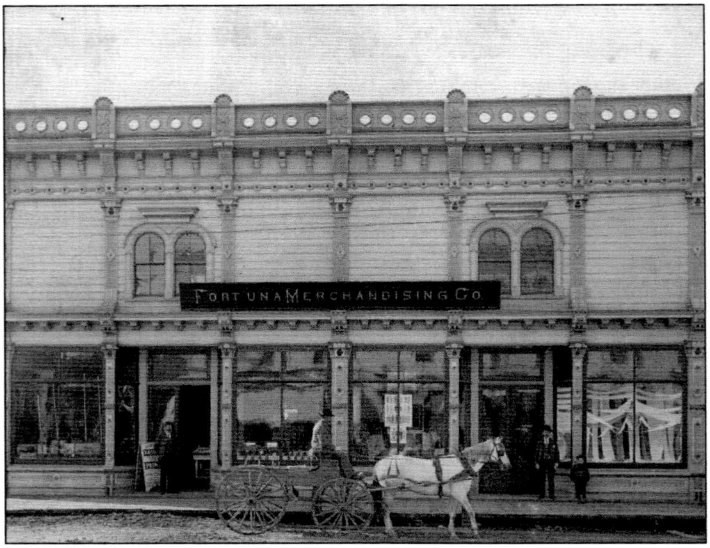

Formed in 1880 by W.J. Swortzel and originally called Swortzel and Williams, the Fortuna Merchandising Company was located on Main Street and renamed in 1895. The *Eel River Valley Advance* noted in 1896 that "more than likely at the present time, although more than one mercantile store is in the Eel River Valley between the ocean shore and Scotia, none sells a greater quantity of general merchandise annually than the Fortuna Merchandising Company."

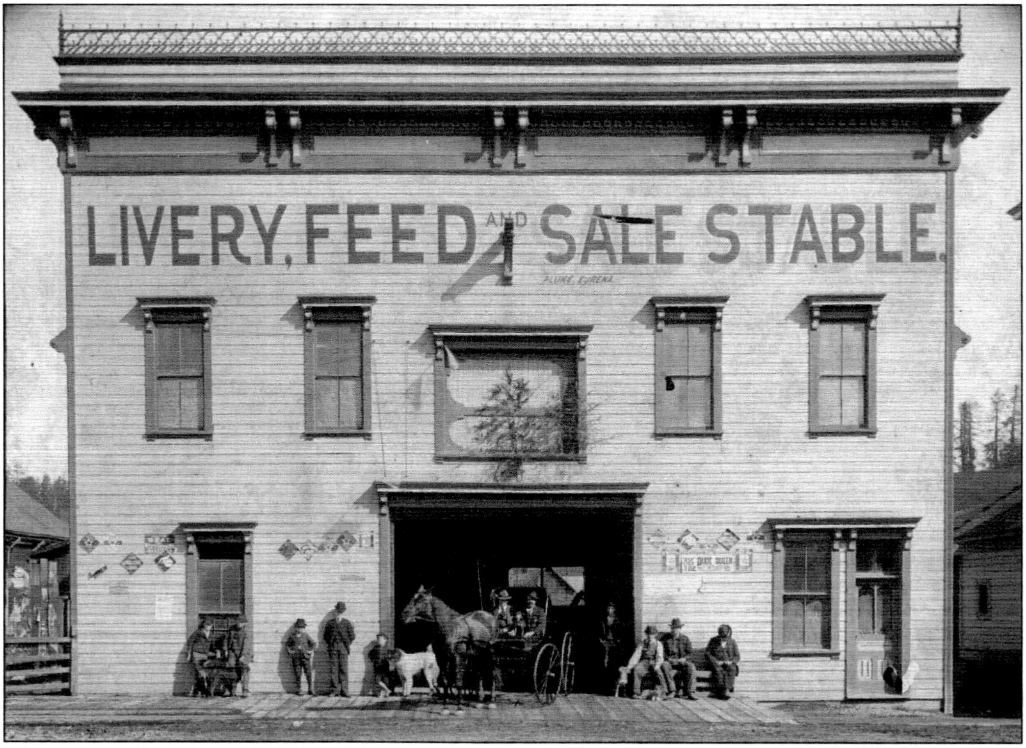

Thomas G. Greig's livery stable was near the corner of Main and Redwood (now Tenth) Streets. The livery opened in 1876, and Greig was known, according to the *Eel River Valley Advance*, for never renting a vehicle that "would excite the slightest suspicion of unsafety [*sic*]."

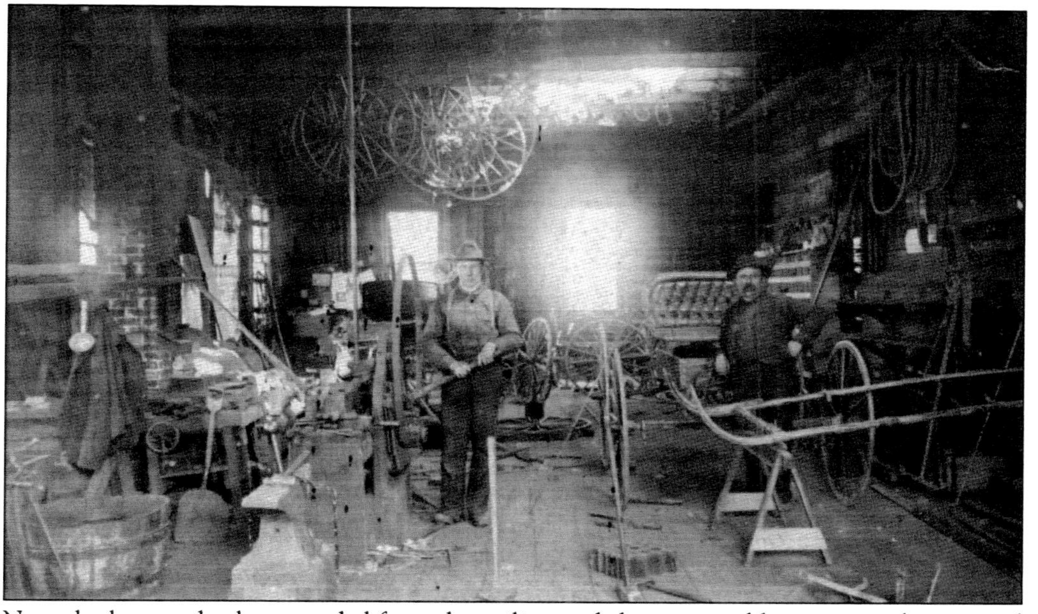

Note the buggy wheels suspended from the ceiling and the seats and harnesses to be repaired in this interior photograph of an unidentified Fortuna blacksmith shop. In 1896, James Hamner advertised that he would give a buggy whip away to whoever bought one dollar's worth of goods from his harness shop on Main Street. He also noted that he had purchased a bicycle-enameling oven and was prepared to do all kinds of repair work.

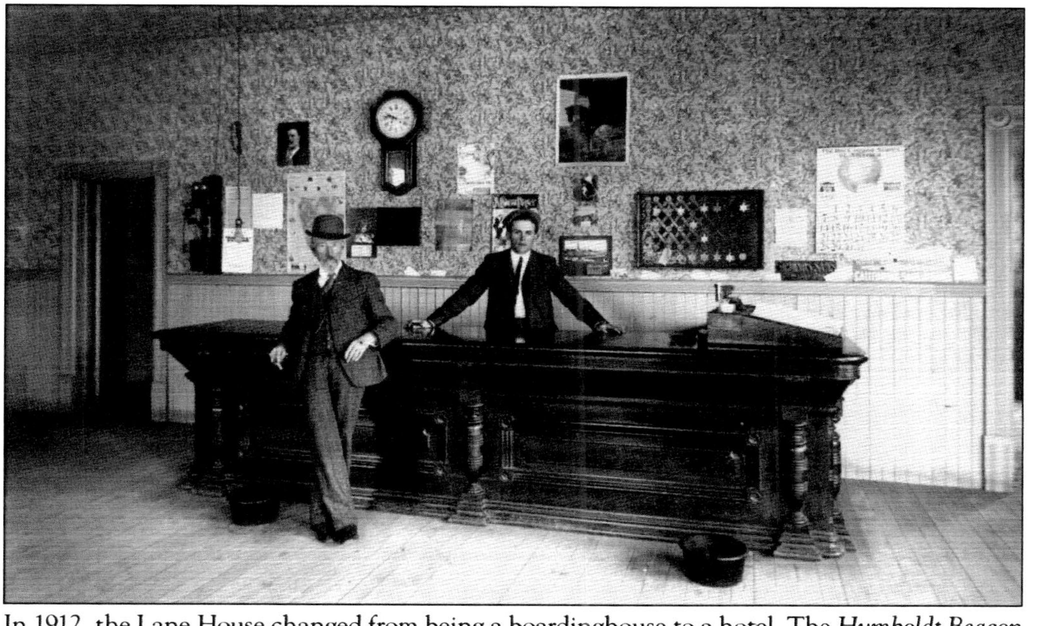

In 1912, the Lane House changed from being a boardinghouse to a hotel. The *Humboldt Beacon* observed that the Lane, by "changing its nature from being one for lodgers only to a first-class hotel provide[d] something Fortuna had needed for months." Standing behind the desk is W.S. "Wid" O'Connor, who, with his father, had a dentist's office in the Lane House building and owned the hotel for some time. (Courtesy of Clarke Historical Museum.)

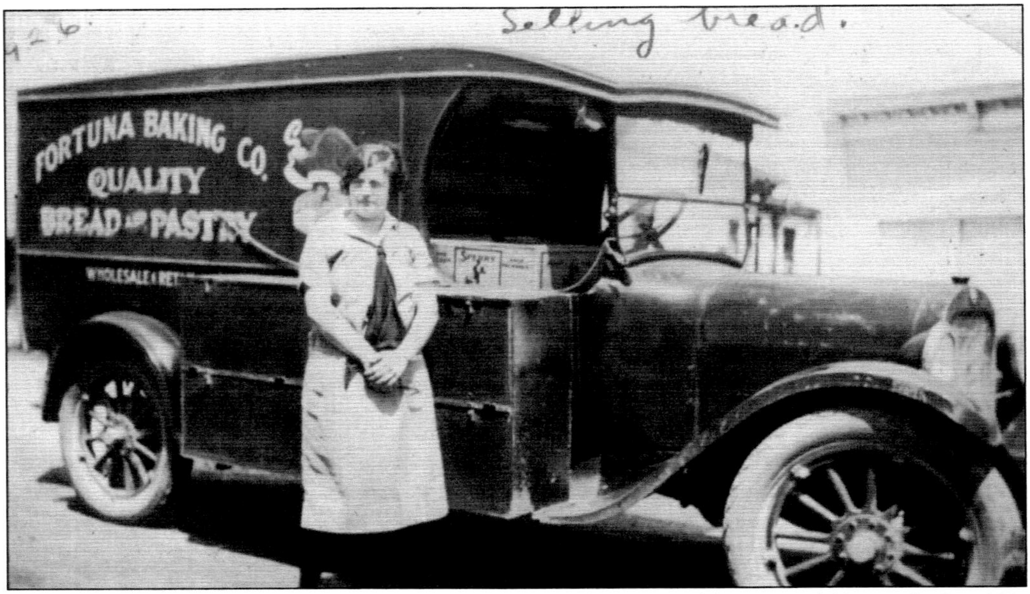

By the early 1920s, Fortuna was established as a place where a good living could be made. In 1922, at the age of 16, Faye Patton moved to Fortuna from Alderpoint to find work to support herself. Her first job was delivering bread for the Fortuna Baking Company. She used the money she made to attend the Eureka Business College. She would serve as city clerk for Fortuna. (Courtesy of Marguerita Nichols.)

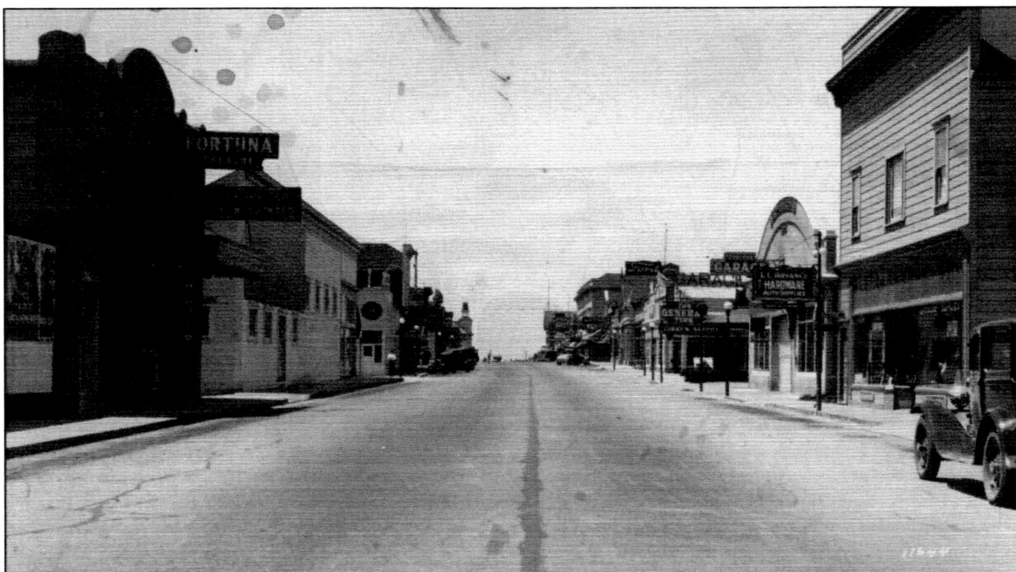

In the early 20th century, new technologies resulted in even more varieties of businesses and ways to make a living. One such business was the Fortuna Theater, opening near Thirteenth and Main Streets in 1920. It replaced the town's first cinema, the Theater Trilma, at Tenth and Main Streets, which opened as early as 1909.

Another new technological advance, the telephone reached Fortuna by 1895. The switchboard is shown here in the early 1900s. The operator is believed to be Maude Hedley, who retired in 1944 after more than 30 years as a Fortuna operator. Her 1964 obituary read, "She will be remembered by many county residents for her cheerful, efficient service during those years long before dial phones were even heard of." (Courtesy of Clarke Historical Museum.)

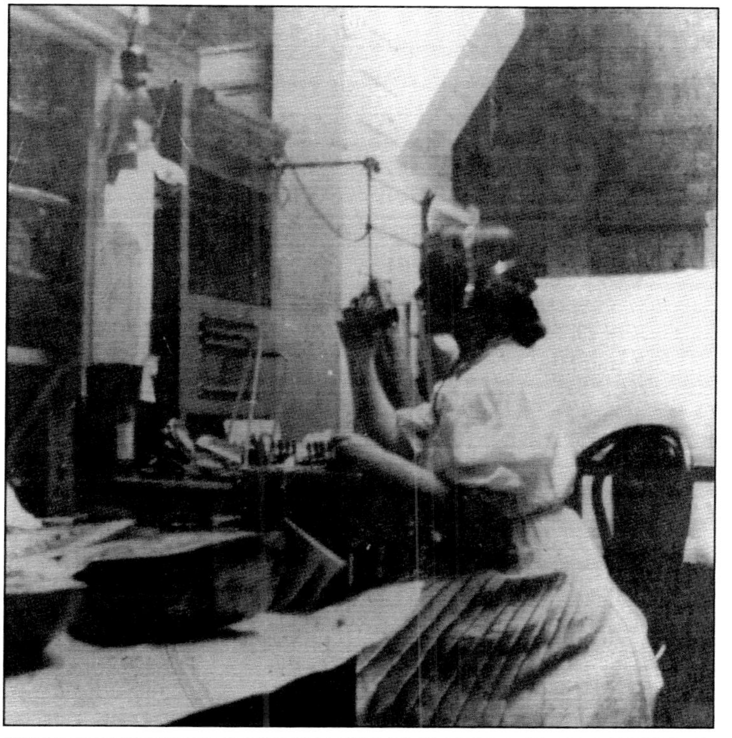

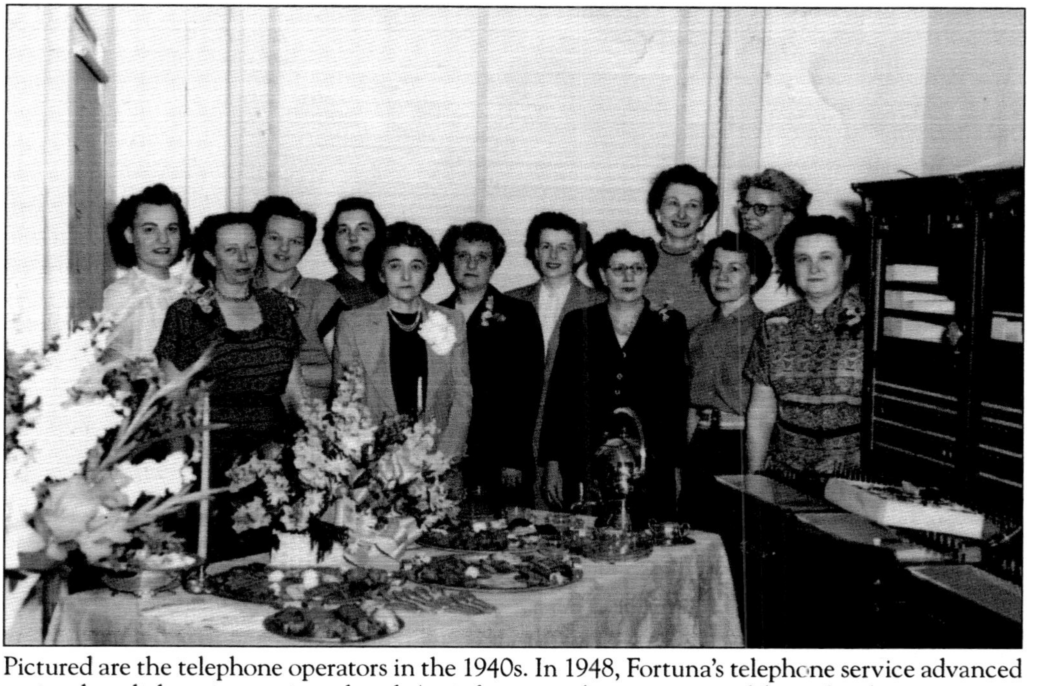

Pictured are the telephone operators in the 1940s. In 1948, Fortuna's telephone service advanced again when dial service was introduced. An informative demonstration of the unfamiliar new system was given at the *Humboldt Beacon*'s offices. Residents were assured that there would be no reduction in services and that they could pay their bills at Marjorie's Dress Shop on Main Street.

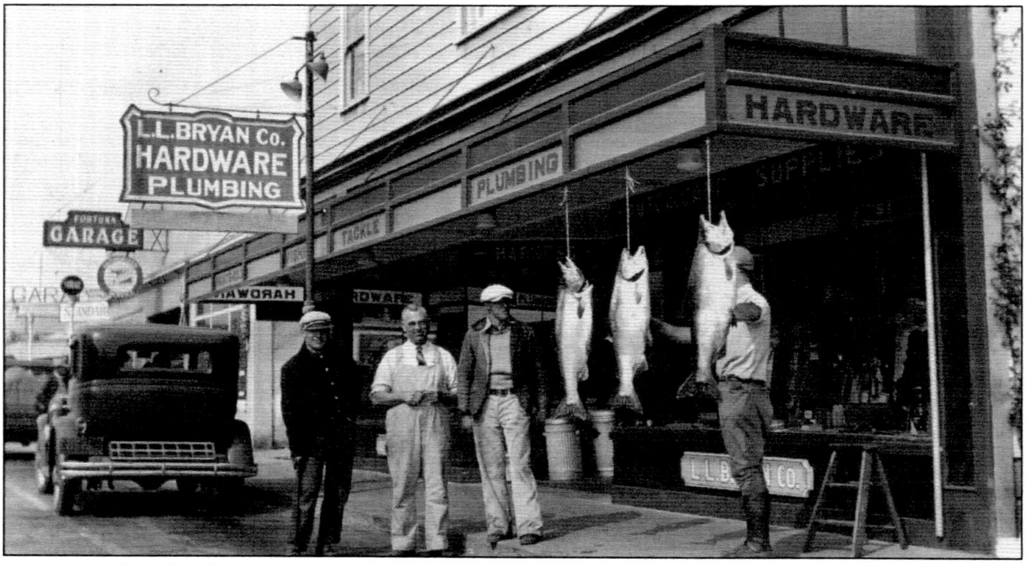

L.L. Bryan Co. Hardware and Plumbing served the public for many years on Main Street. Hardware stores were important places for supplies, as many did their own repairs. L.L. Bryan also sold fishing tackle. Bryan was an involved citizen for decades, serving on the fire department and in the town band in the early 1900s. (Courtesy of Marguerita Nichols.)

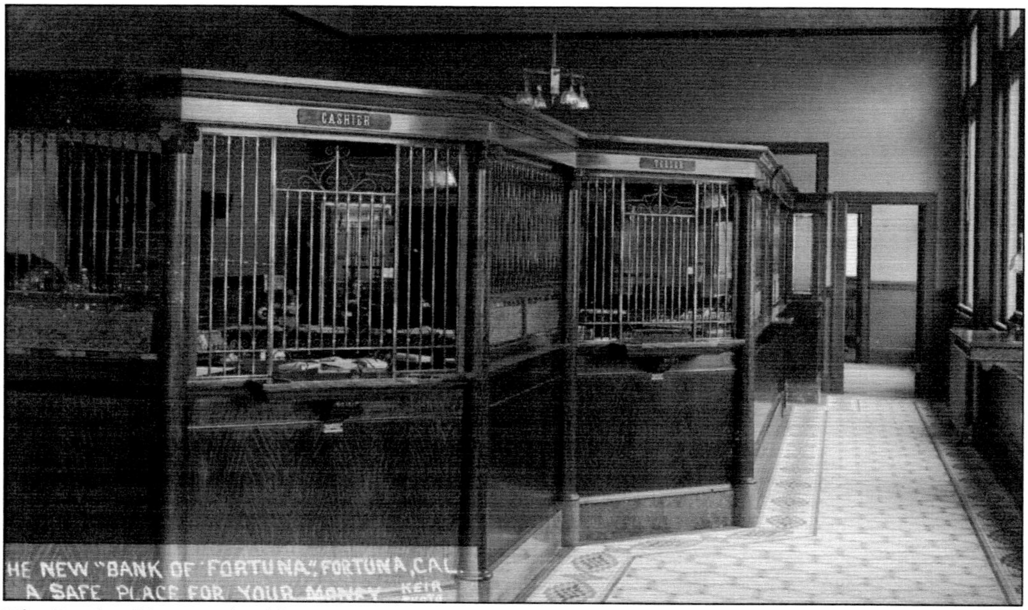

The Bank of Fortuna building can still be seen on the corner of Tenth and Main Streets. Opening for business on March 5, 1905, the concrete building was constructed in 1912. The vault was considered to be burglar and fireproof. E.W. Haight was president, I.H. Van Duzer was vice president, and Fred P. Newell was cashier. In 1913, the *Humboldt Beacon* noted bank management made a "specialty of accommodating the agricultural interests."

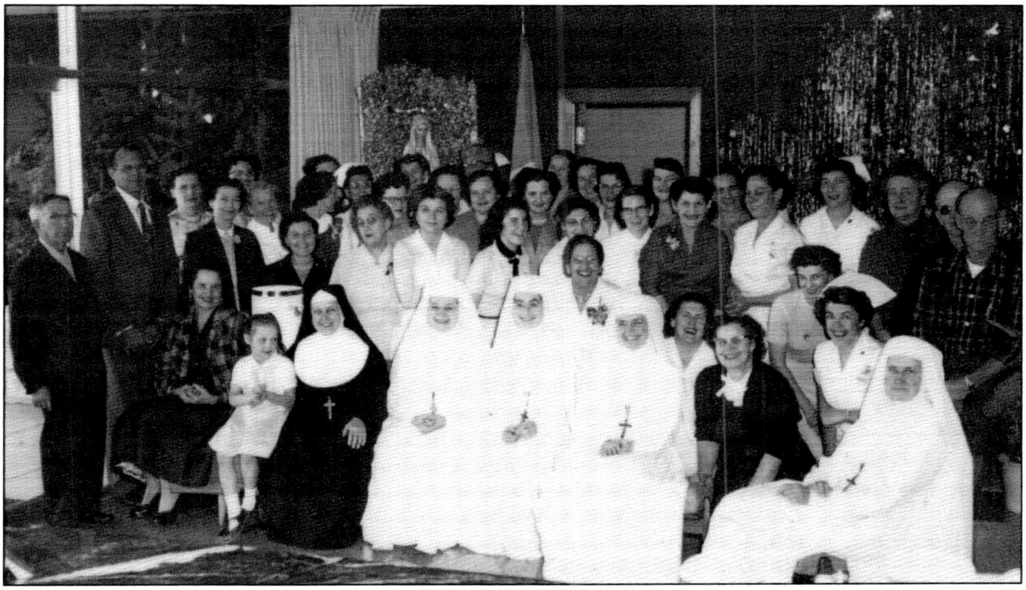

In 1957, through the fundraising efforts of the local community, Redwood Memorial Hospital opened. Replacing the hospital in Scotia and the nursing home operated by Dr. Comfort, the hospital opened through a partnership with the Sisters of St. Joseph of Orange. The sisters had operated St. Joseph's Hospital in Eureka since the 1920s, and they earned a positive reputation in the region with their efforts during the 1918 flu epidemic.

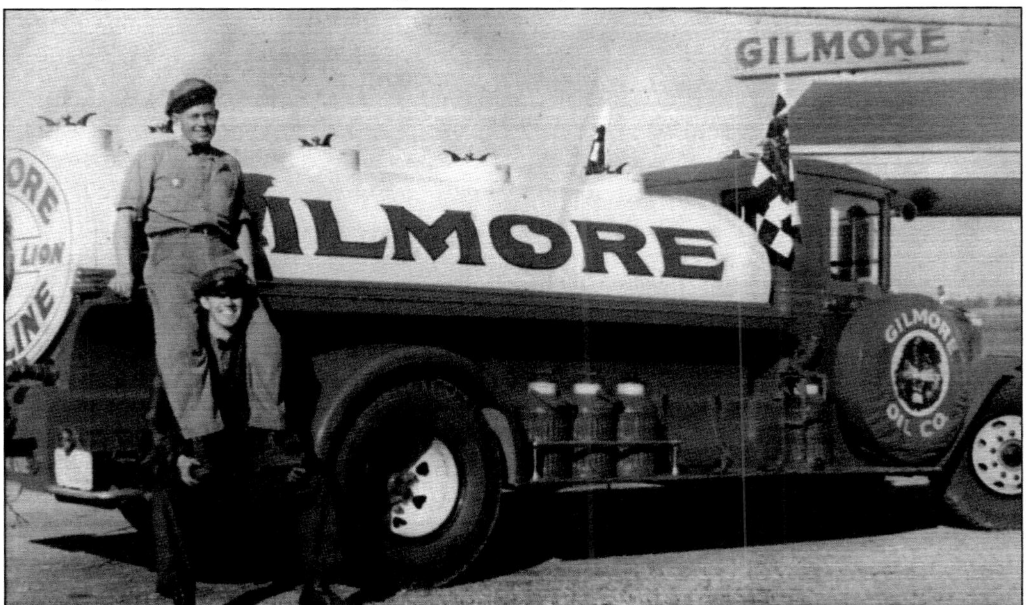

The increased availability of automobiles led to business opportunities in the valley. In 1911, the first car dealership opened in Fortuna, and the Leach and Smith Hardware store began to also sell cars. Not far behind was demand for gasoline stations. Al Daggett is shown sitting on the shoulders of an unidentified man by a Gilmore Gasoline delivery truck at his service station in Loleta in the 1940s. Gilmore was a popular gasoline company from Los Angeles.

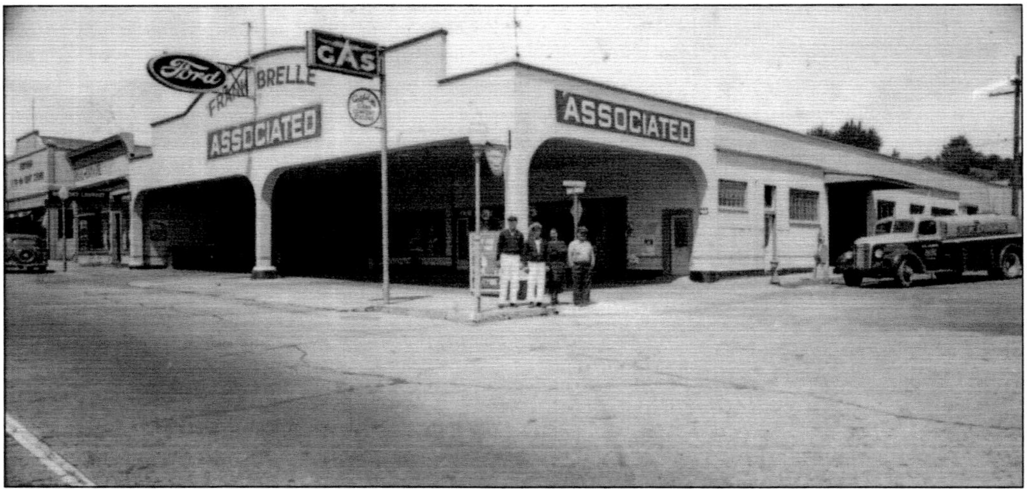

In 1915, Frank Brelle established his Ford dealership in Fortuna. His was one of the earliest car dealerships in the region and one of the first that was not part of another business. Brelle's business stood at the corner of Twelfth and Main Streets. The showroom was in the main building, and the car lot was across the street.

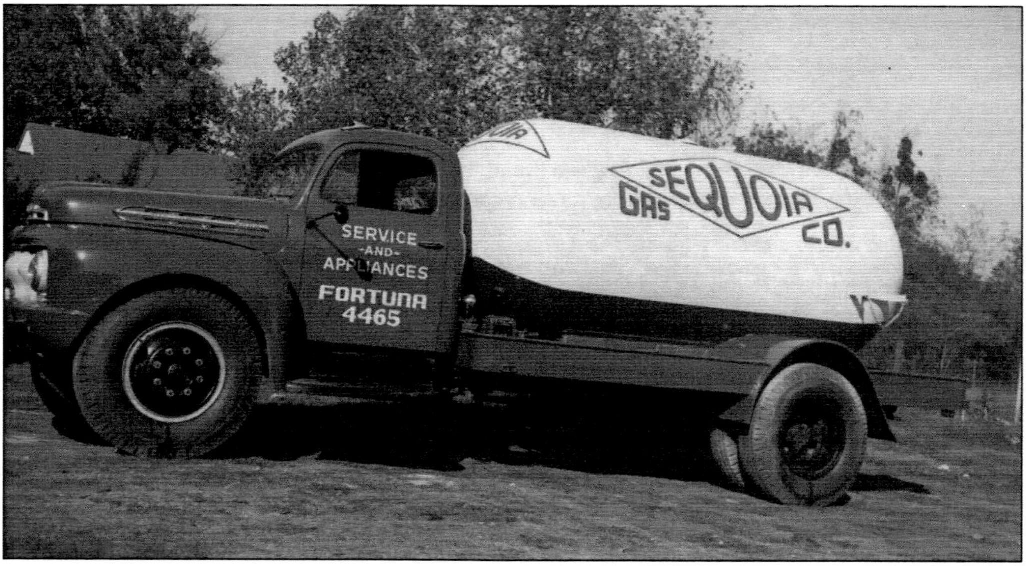

Gene Youngreen started Sequoia Gas in 1943. Propane had been discovered as a heating fuel in 1913 and was a popular source for cooking and heating. In 1954, Sequoia Gas was purchased by Ben McWhorter, who became a partner in 1948. The company has always used trucks to deliver its product to customers. The tank on this 1948 truck is still in use as a bulk storage container. (Courtesy of Shannon McWhorter.)

Five

TRANSPORTATION

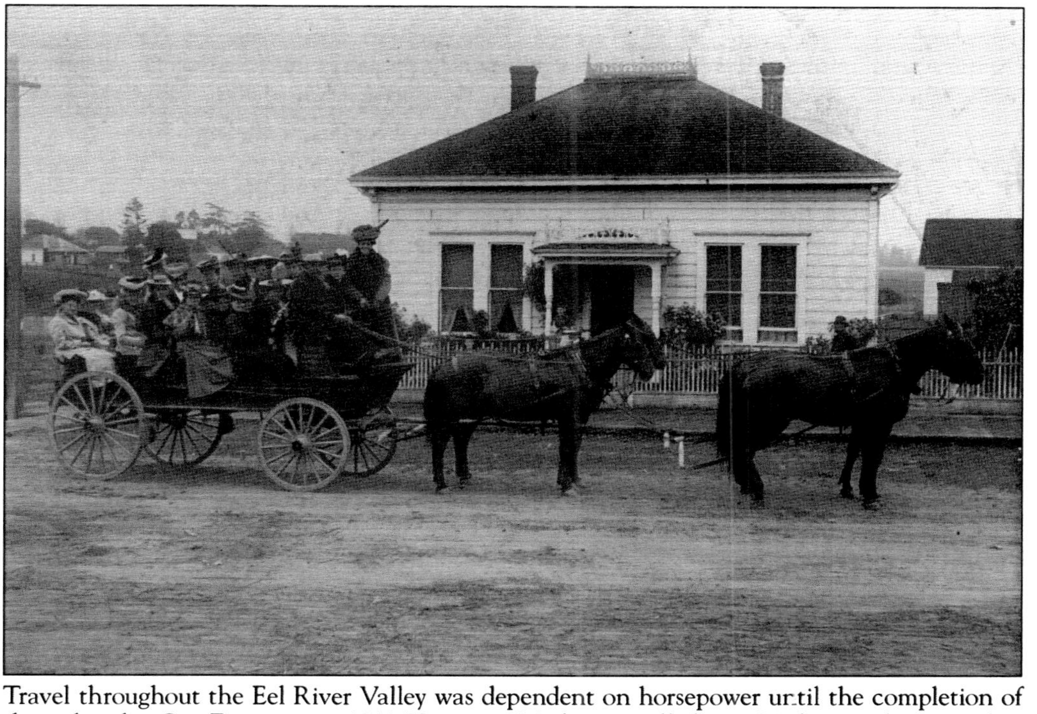

Travel throughout the Eel River Valley was dependent on horsepower until the completion of the railroad to San Francisco in 1914. Henrietta Mudgett recalled in 1978 that, in the 1910s, her future husband would come to visit her in Rohnerville from Fortuna. It cost him $1.50 to rent a horse and buggy to travel four miles. Pictured in Rohnerville, this open stage was rented at Johnston's livery stable in Fortuna.

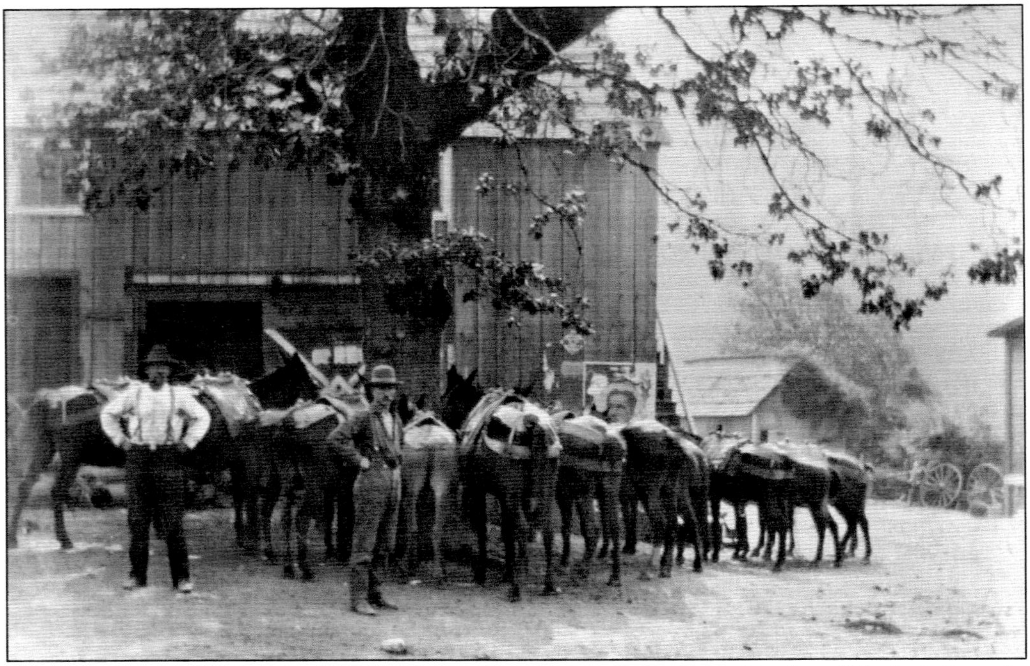

The earliest land routes out of Humboldt County were trails. In 1866, Absalom Schultz followed a mule trail with his wagon, pioneering the route as he went. Pack-mule trains, like this one shown in Hydesville in the late 1800s, carried supplies to homesteads and ranches in the back country, as well as to the Trinity County mines.

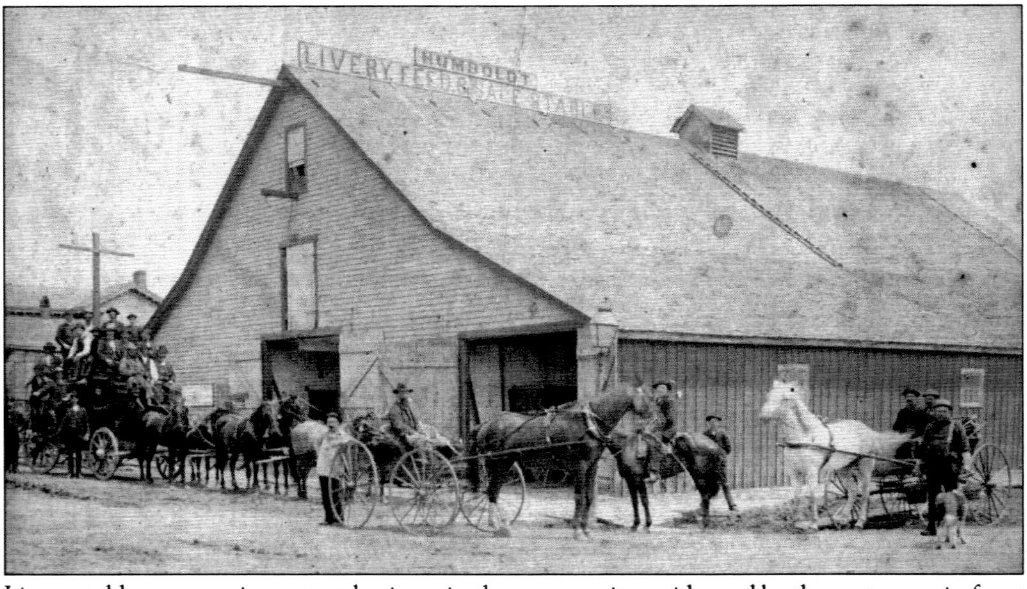

Livery stables were an important business in the community, evidenced by the customers in front of this Rohnerville stable. Not only were horses, buggies, and wagons available for rent, the stable also was a place for animals to be cared for and kept. In 1896, at his livery stable in Fortuna, T.G. Greig advertised, "Horses well cared for, buggies and carriages for hire at very reasonable rates." (Courtesy of Clarke Historical Museum.)

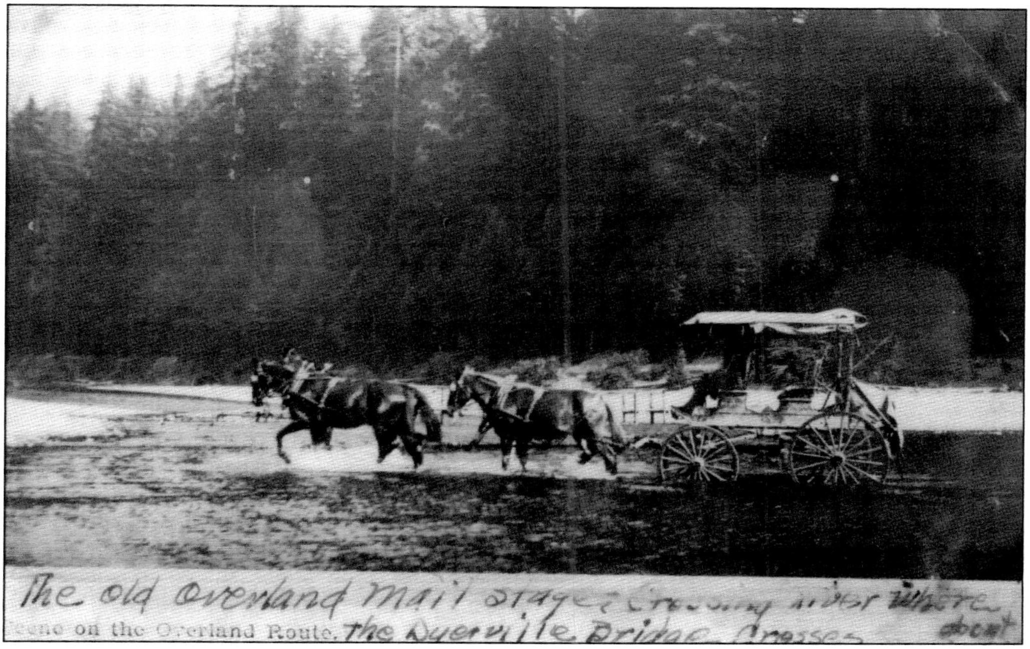

Until the railroad's completion, people who traveled overland rode stagecoaches that linked the rail's ends at Scotia and Willits. In 1896, the stage left Scotia at 6:00 a.m. In this image, the overland mail stage crosses the South Fork of the Eel River at Dyerville. Jim Boots, a stage driver in the 1890s, recalled that travel was challenging, and "mud was axle deep in places, and there was lots of snow."

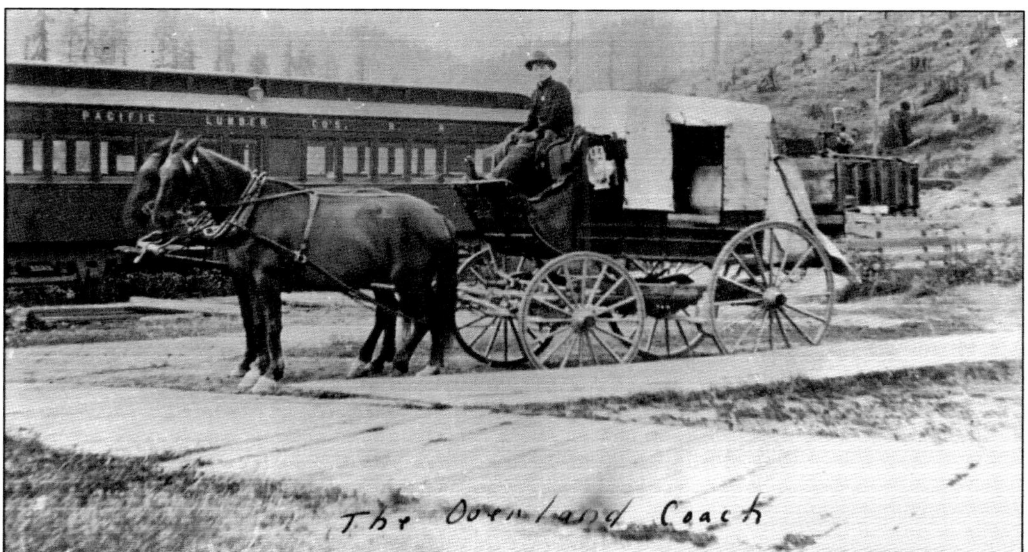

The overland stage was patronized by those who did not want to travel by boat, the only other way to reach southern destinations. A two-horse team went to Garberville, while a four-horse team traveled over the mountains to Willits. The train's terminus, pictured here at Scotia, was the departure point for the overland stage.

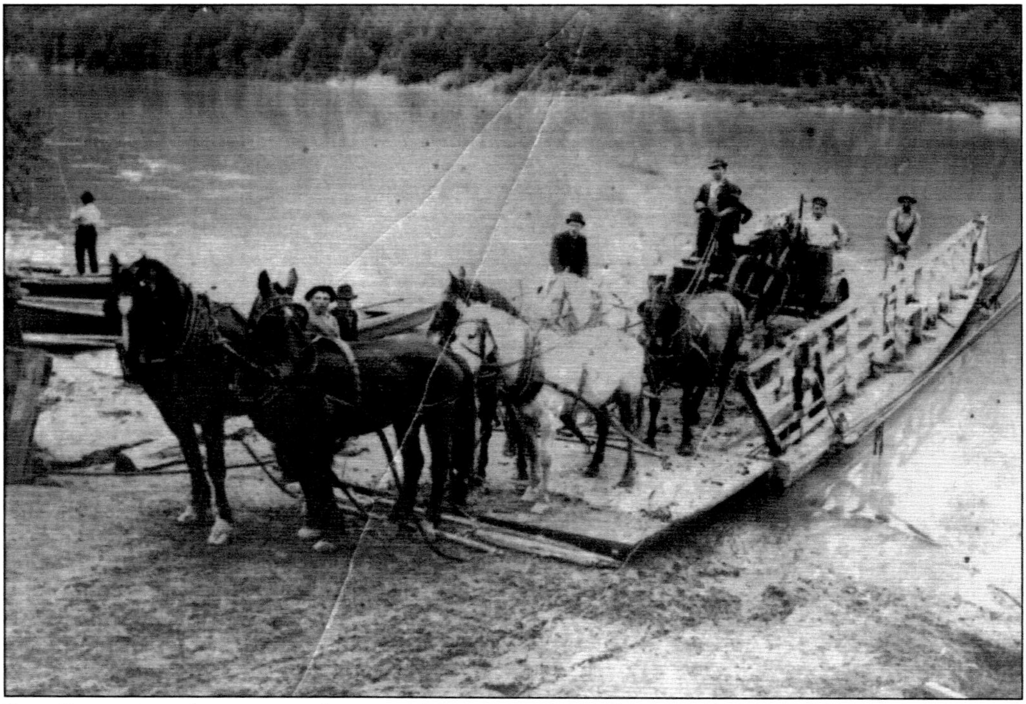

For all travelers, ferries served a critical function along the meandering Eel River. Ferries were found along the river at Singley (near where Fernbridge now crosses the Eel) and near Alton. Rio Dell had two ferries, one connecting to Metropolitan and the other crossing to Scotia. Different rates were charged for different modes of transportation, even for herd animals.

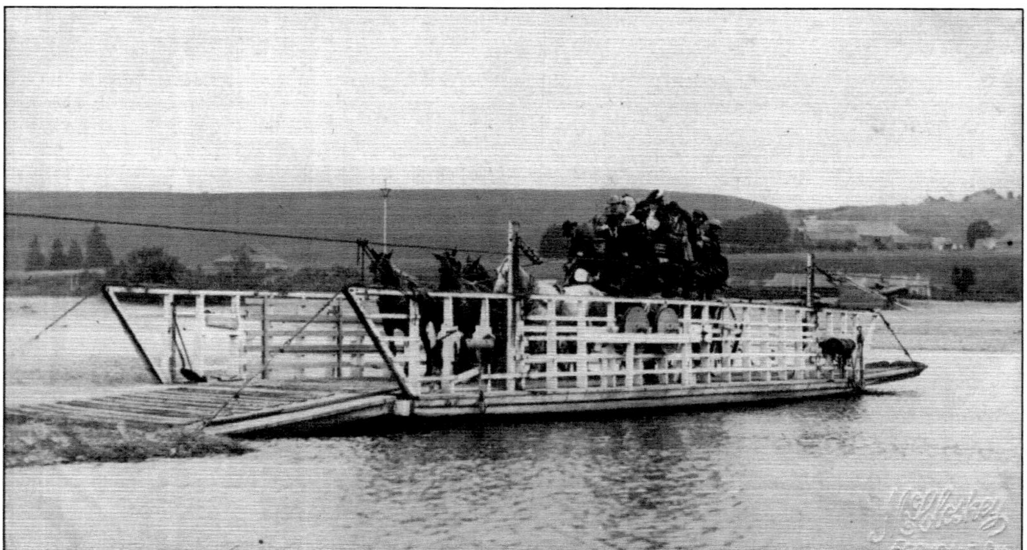

Ferry operators were given a license from the County Board of Supervisors. The board also set the rates that could be charged to passengers. In some locales, the winter ferry was turned into a toll bridge in summer. Ferries operated along the Eel River from the 1860s until the early 1900s when they began to be replaced by bridges.

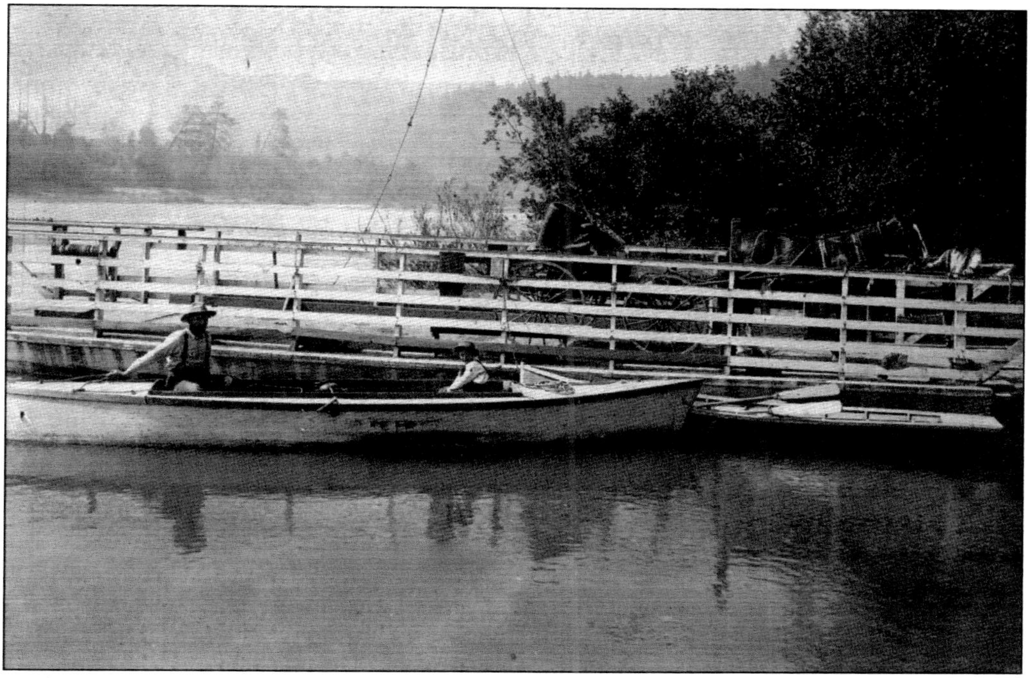

Fred Daggett, in the boat with his son Al, operated the ferry between Rio Dell and Scotia in 1910. He used his big ferry boat for most business, but he also used this small boat to ferry foot passengers. Daggett told the *Humboldt Beacon* he approved of the movement for improved roads, as cars did not fare as well as most wagons when trying to cross the rivers in the summertime.

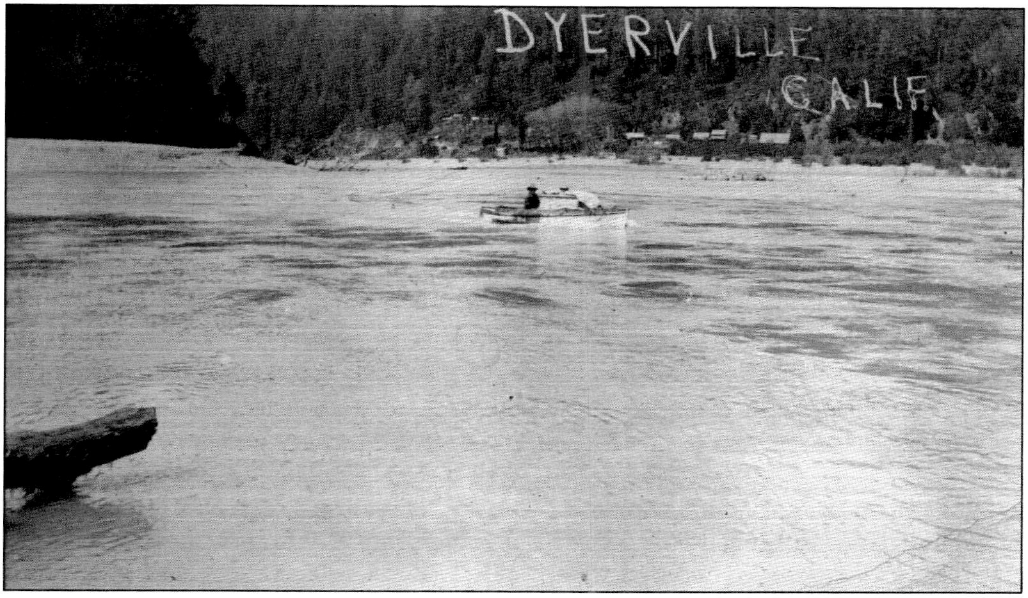

The river also provided a means of transportation in the form of boats that floated from Dyerville to Fortuna. River boats like the *Poison Oak* were flat bottomed and could navigate the river. They hauled produce, such as apples, from Bull Creek to Fortuna. Others, like this boat pictured near Dyerville, were smaller and for personal use. (Courtesy of Bob Lutz.)

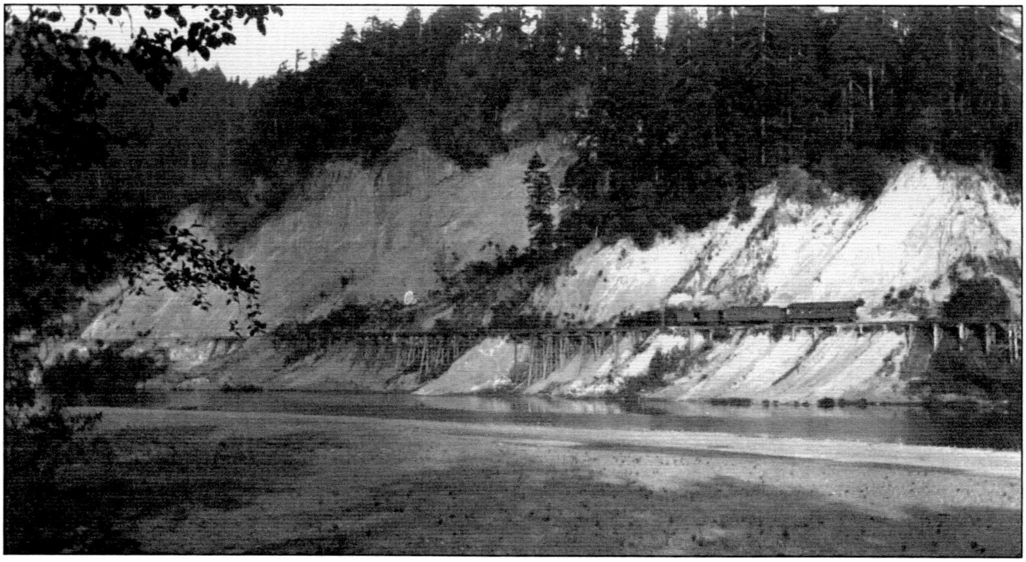

Railroads were another important form of transportation for valley residents. In 1882, the Eel River and Eureka Railroad Company was incorporated, and by 1884, the line was completed to Burnells near present-day Alton. The Pacific Lumber Company originally wanted to build its own railroad to ship lumber from the port at Field's Landing. However, the company decided to utilize the Eel River and Eureka Railroad, extending the line to Scotia in 1885. This train is pictured by the Scotia Bluffs.

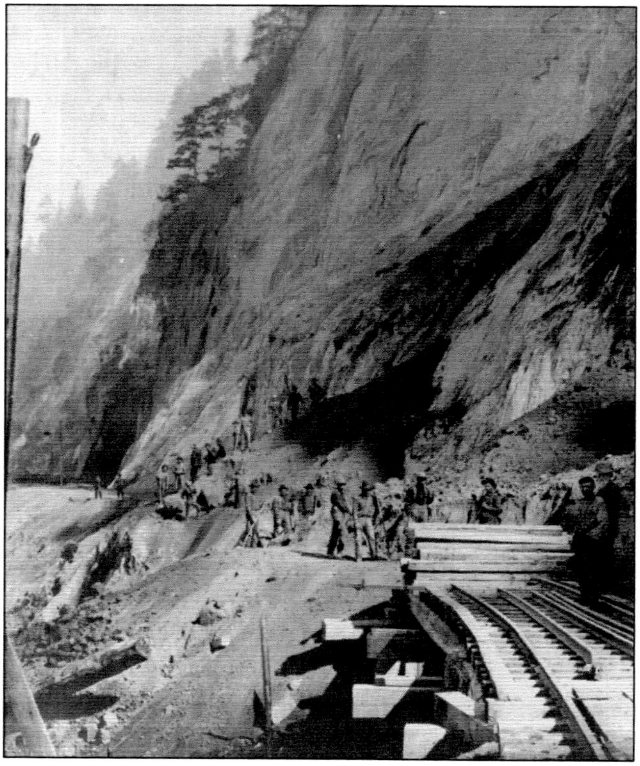

Railroad construction was not easy in Humboldt County. Slides frequently closed or damaged sections. In one such incident, a worker was killed by a landslide near the Scotia Bluffs in 1911. A work train was also damaged. Even with the difficulties in construction, Humboldt County railroads garnered the attention of the large railroad companies Santa Fe and Union Pacific. In 1903, the Santa Fe Railroad acquired ownership of the line from Eureka to Shively.

In 1907, the Santa Fe and Union Pacific Railroads realized it was too costly to build two competing lines. Instead, they combined to form the Northwestern Pacific Railroad. Construction began in the fall of 1907 and lasted seven years. Costing an estimated $25 per inch, work included digging tunnels and building trestles. The line was completed in September 1914, and a golden spike was driven at Cain Rock on October 23, 1914.

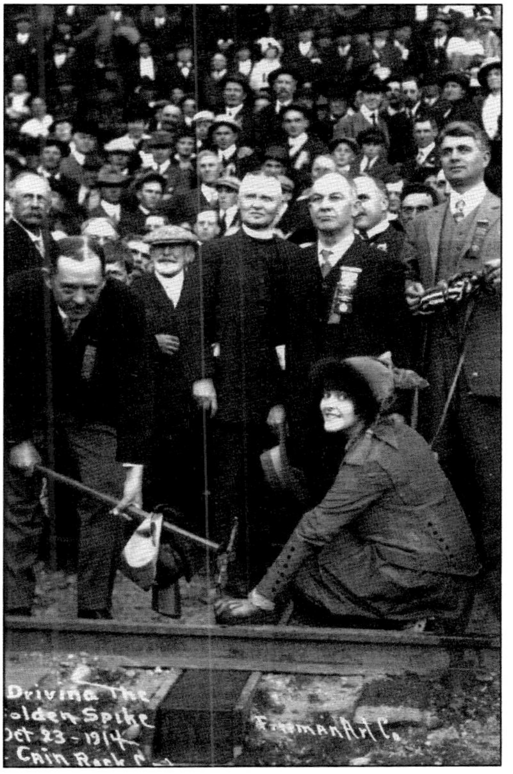

Pictured is the first train to travel the completed road. Henry Allen was the engineer, George Chapman was the fireman, and Bill Johns was the conductor. The brakemen were George Hearvey and Jim McCutchen. The first regular train from San Francisco passed through Fortuna on December 1, 1914. Onboard were Fortuna druggist R.H. Bowman, his daughter Daisee, and local businessman Percy Newell.

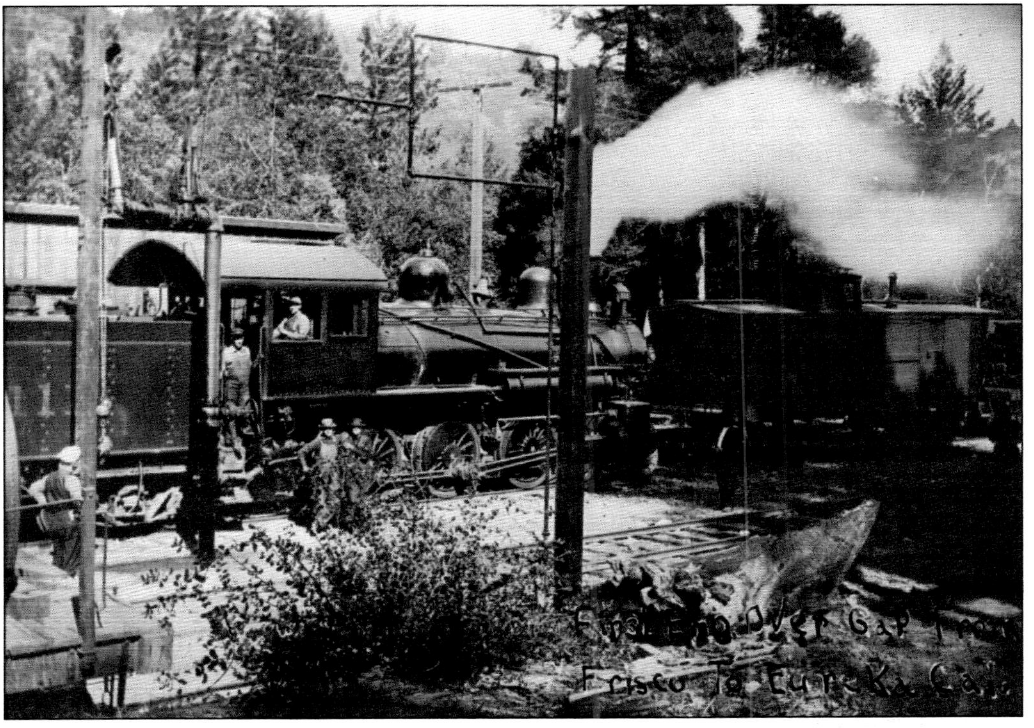

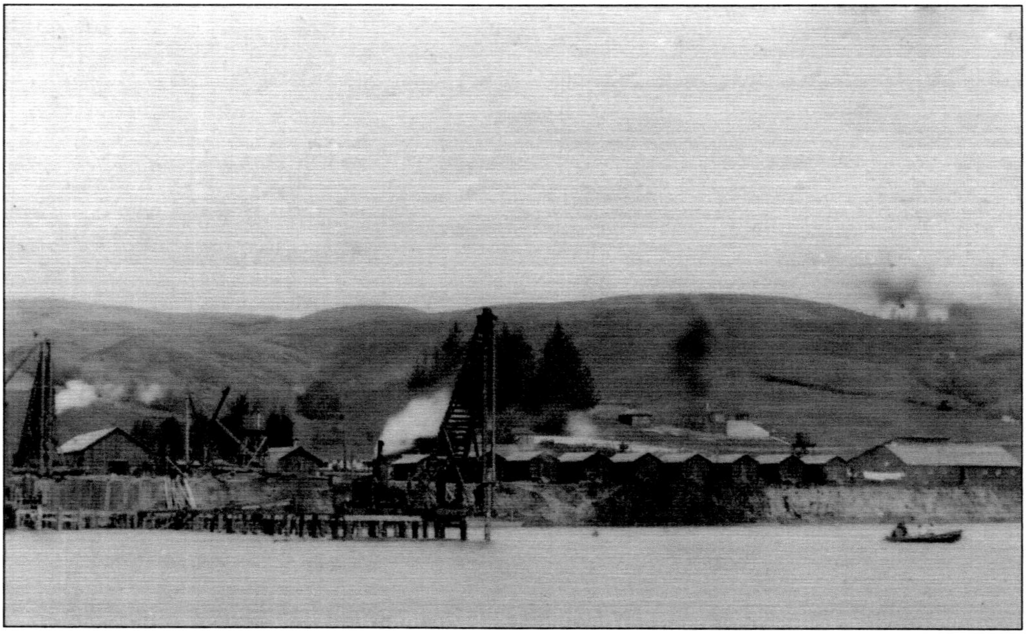

Even with railroads, travel around the valley could be difficult. Beginning in 1893, residents began circulating petitions to have the county build a bridge across the Eel River at Singley, connecting the town of Ferndale with the rest of the valley. By 1911, the Humboldt County Board of Supervisors, led by District 1 (Ferndale vicinity) supervisor George Hindley, agreed to build the bridge; it cost $245,967.

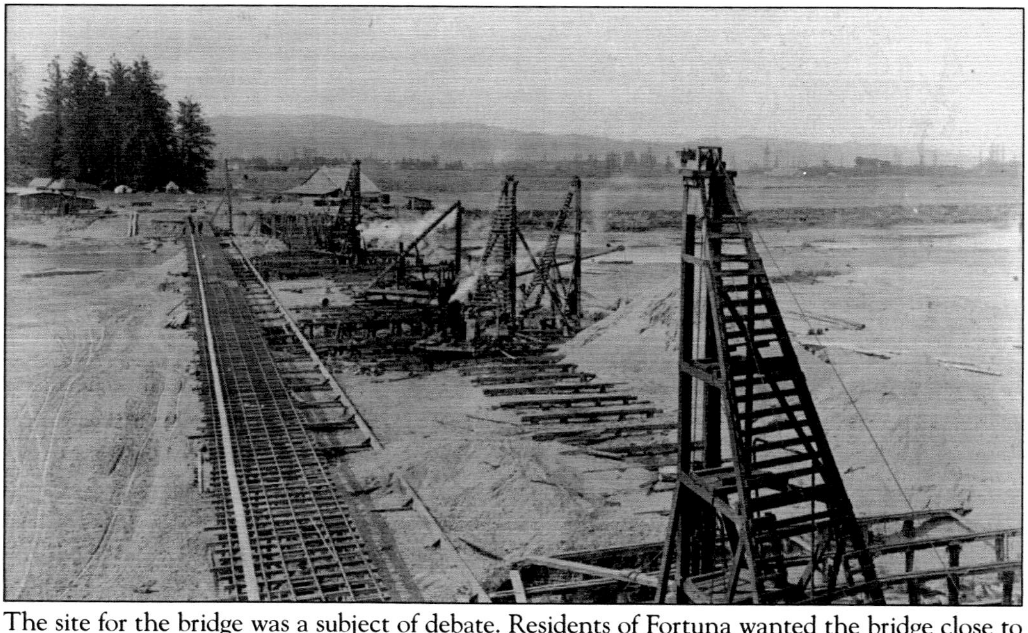

The site for the bridge was a subject of debate. Residents of Fortuna wanted the bridge close to town for business reasons, while others advocated for a site near Alton or Sandy Prairie. The site selected was picked because the river showed little erosion of the banks. The contract for the job was awarded to the Pacific Construction Company of San Francisco.

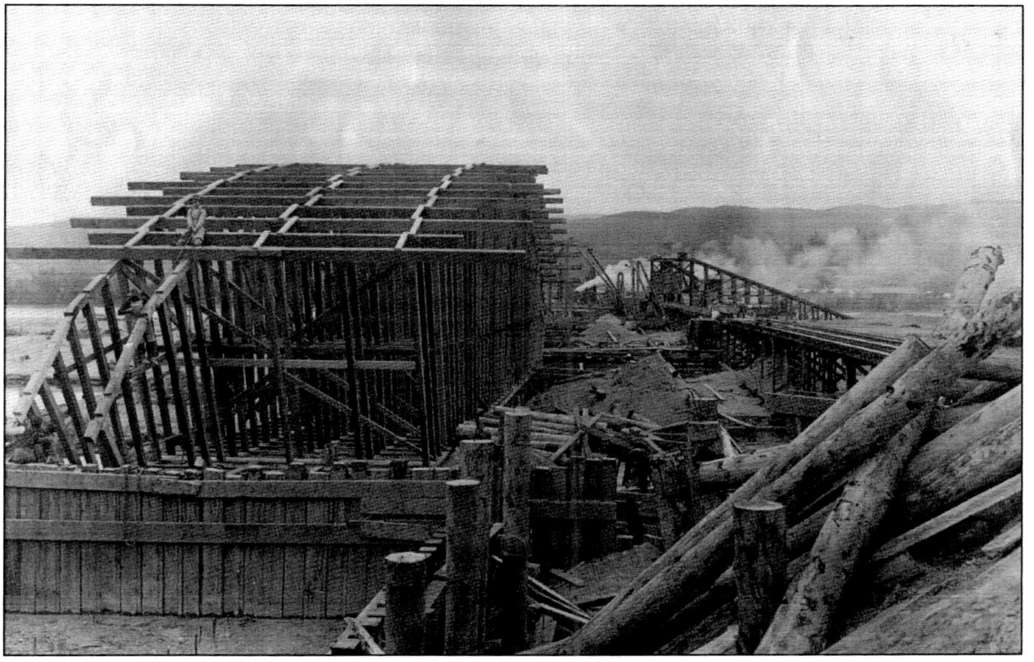

The architect for the bridge was Humboldt County surveyor George W. Conners. Construction created many jobs; the *Humboldt Beacon* reported that 200 men would be employed since a concrete bridge required more labor than one made of steel. The portland cement for the concrete was brought from Humboldt Bay in steamers. The *Humboldt Beacon* enthused over modern construction methods, including the use of a machine to ensure that cement was thoroughly mixed.

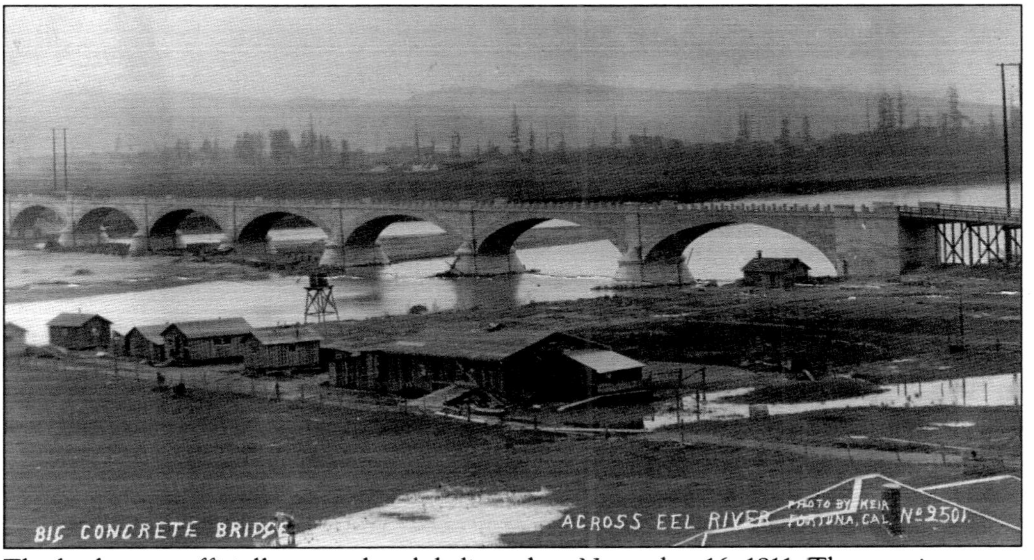

The bridge was officially opened and dedicated on November 16, 1911. The opening was a county-wide celebration, with the railroad running a special train from Eureka for the event. Crossing the bridge was also cause for celebration. In 1912, Jane Burns wrote on this postcard to her friend Grace Eagle, "How does this look to you, I have crossed this bridge." Fernbridge was the longest reinforced concrete structure of the time.

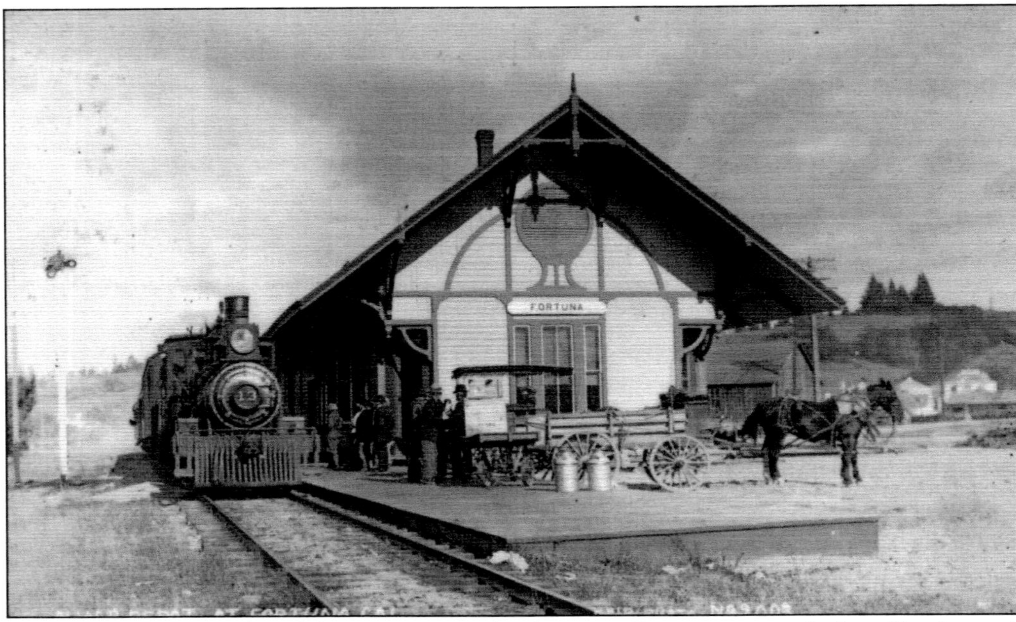

In the late 1880s, a railroad depot was erected in Fortuna. Running twice daily to Eureka, with a fare of $1, passenger trains stopped at South Bay, Salmon Creek, Loleta, Singley (near the later Fernbridge), Fortuna, Alton, and Scotia. In addition to passenger service, a twice-daily freight train also used the track.

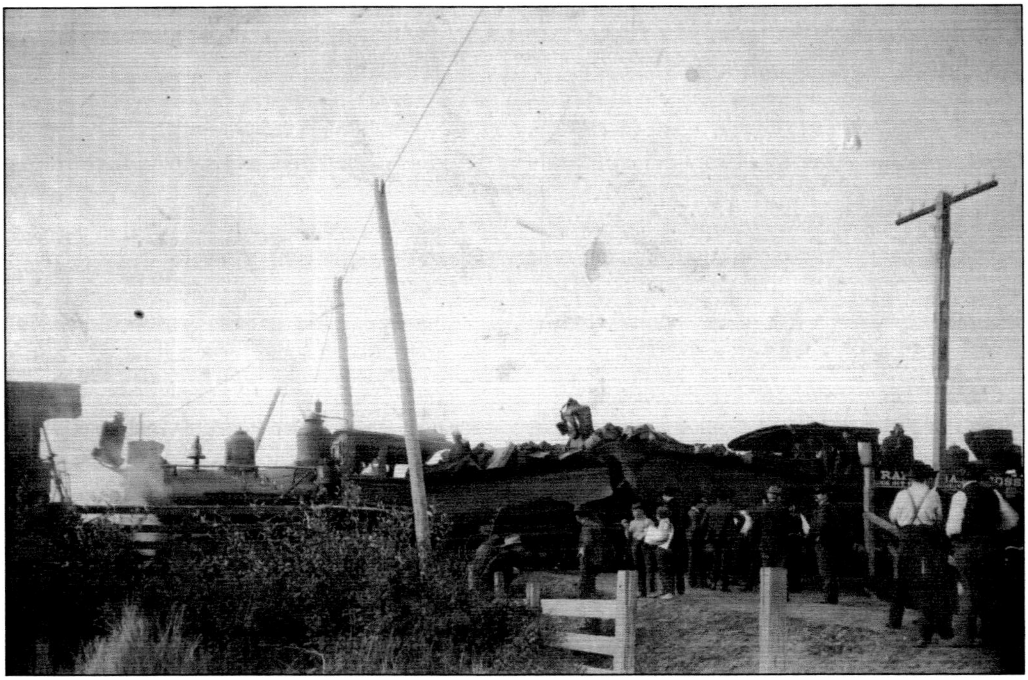

On October 5, 1903, one of the daily trains wrecked north of Fortuna. Any derailment at the time was a crisis, as it took several days to right the train. Note the large wood boxes for hauling firewood that provided heat for the steam engine to operate.

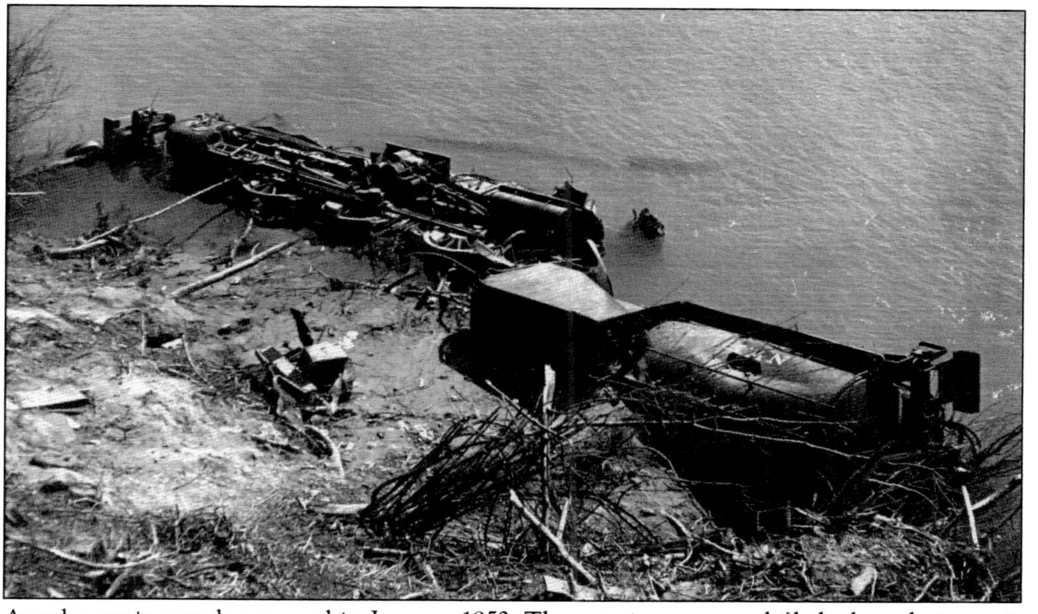

Another train wreck occurred in January 1953. Three trainmen were killed when their repair locomotive was swept into the Eel by a landslide south of Scotia. The men had been sent to repair damages that were a result of flooding along the Eel. The men killed were D.G. Liscom, engineer; T.R. Porter, fireman; and H.J. Aure, brakeman. A memorial to these men now stands in front of the Fortuna Depot Museum.

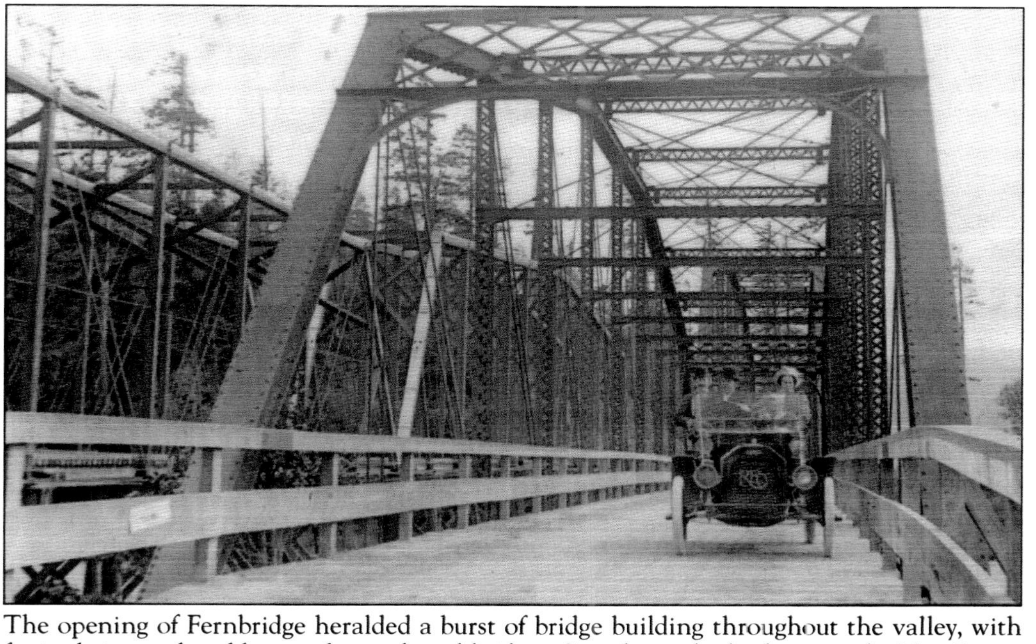

The opening of Fernbridge heralded a burst of bridge building throughout the valley, with ferries being replaced by wooden and steel bridges. Seen here, the bridge over the Van Duzen was constructed of both wood and steel, as were many of the bridges in the region. Adding to the impetus to replace the ferries with bridges was the arrival of affordable automobiles and an increase in car ownership.

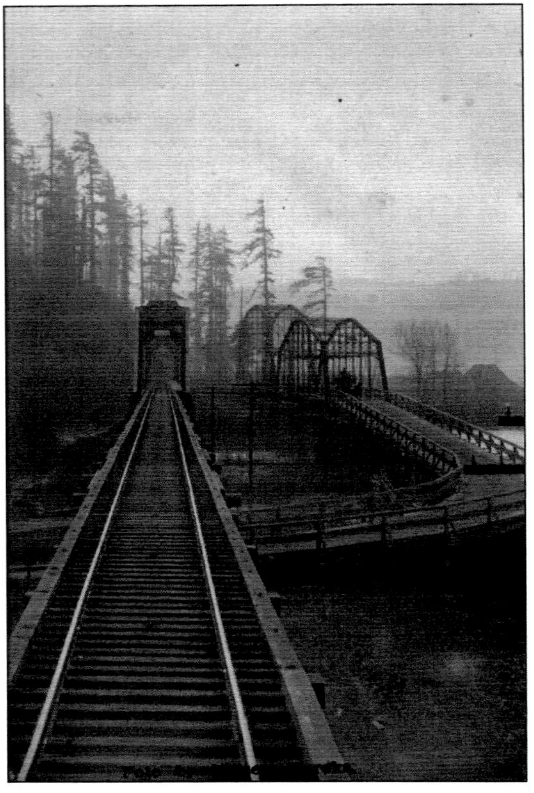

The County Board of Supervisors was petitioned in 1918 to build a vehicle bridge across the Van Duzen. Paralleling the railroad bridge, it crossed the river in a straight line, requiring sharp turns to access the bridge. Note the horse and wagon crossing the bridge, as well as the power lines marking the advent of another technological advance.

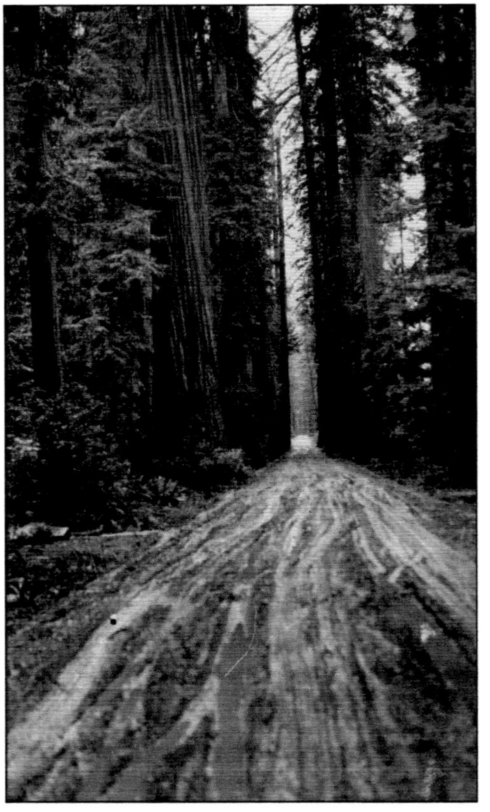

Early road systems in Humboldt County were based on Native American trails and the initial mule trails. These trails were widened to accommodate wagons and cars. Roads were often muddy and impassable in winter. In summer, roads were covered in thick layers of dust. In some places, logs were placed crossways in the roadbed. These corduroy roads were bumpy but less difficult to cross than the muddy roads.

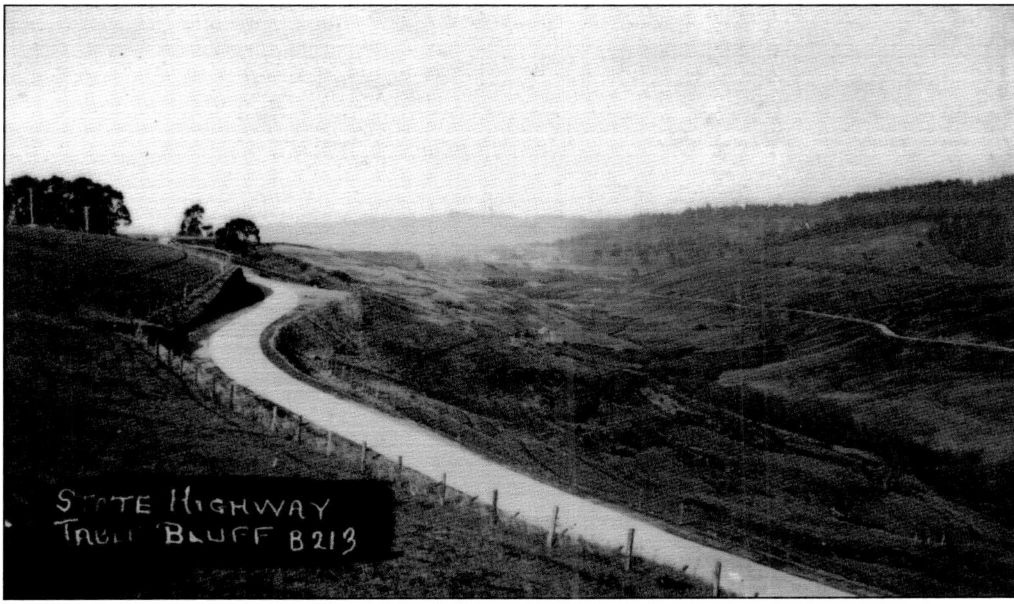

Coinciding with the railroad's completion was a rise in automobile ownership. This led to an interest in completing a roadway for cars. Beginning in 1912, wagon roads and existing county roads were connected and improved. By 1926, this road system was connected to those in other regions and became designated as US 101. The road was often narrow and winding.

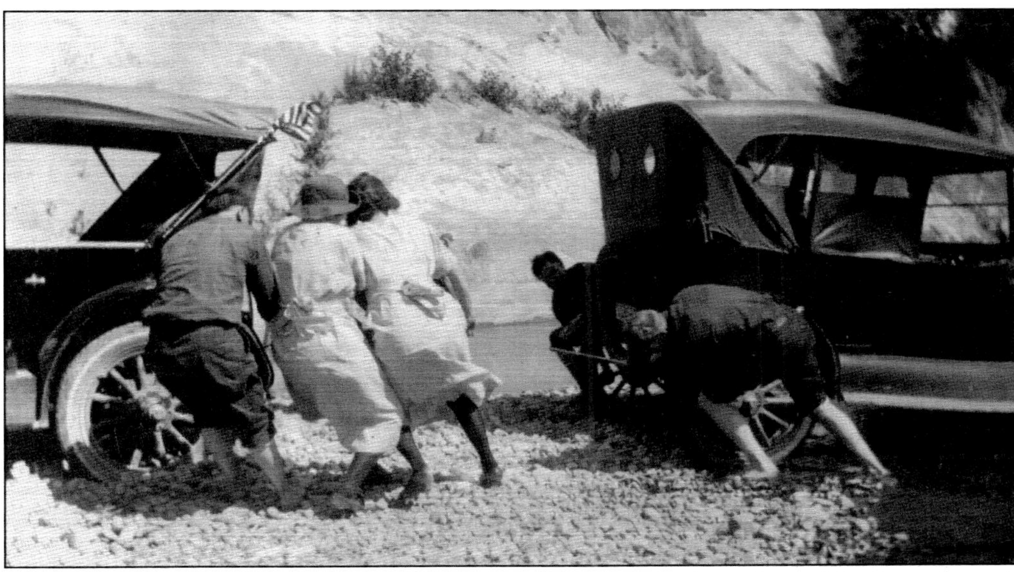

Cars allowed residents to travel around the county for picnics and socializing. Travel on the early road systems was always an adventure, as seen in this photograph from the Hellard family's album. Tires could be punctured, or the car could get stuck in muddy ruts in winter. Car owners brought spare parts and tires with them to repair their cars.

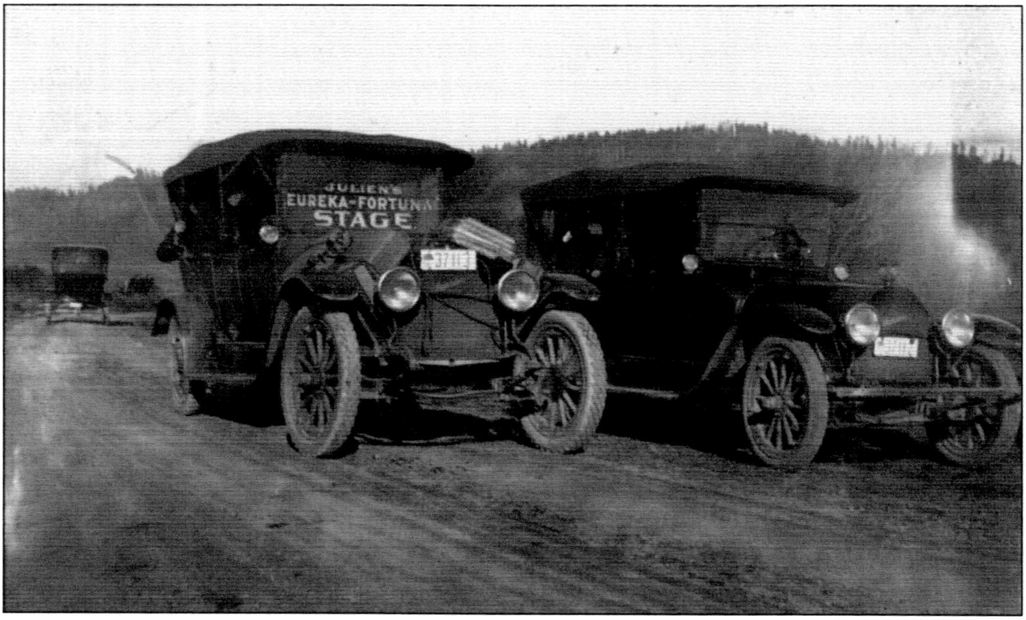

As early as 1908, auto stages began to replace horse stagecoaches. Julien's Eureka-Fortuna Stage is one example. Additionally, the *Humboldt Beacon* reported in 1910 that Fred Daggett had purchased a five-passenger Rambler he planned to use as a stage as soon as he became "thoroughly proficient in driving his car." Auto stages permitted passengers to travel more quickly without having to stop at all the small towns on the route as the railroad did.

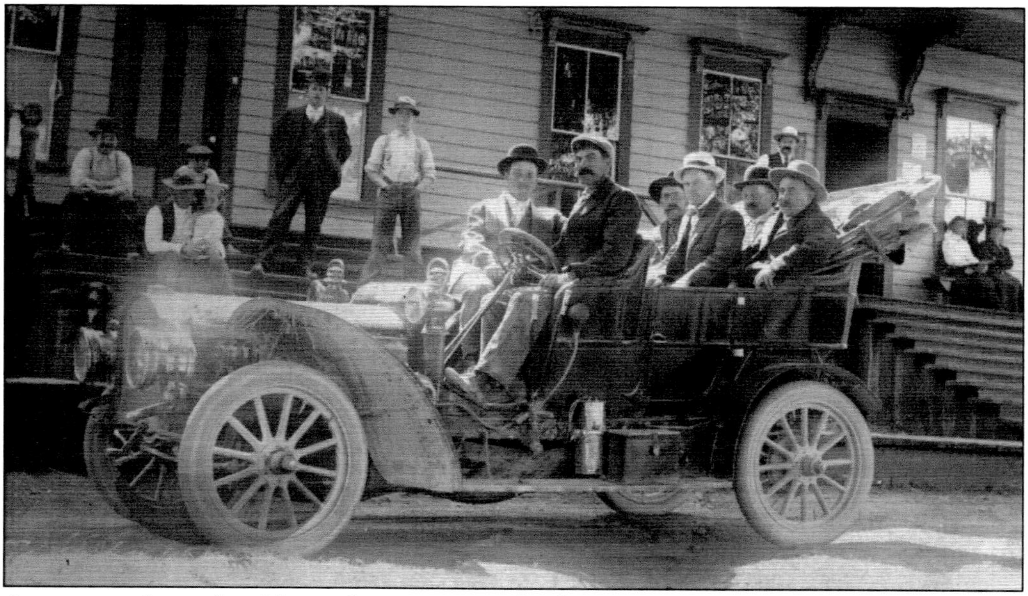

Auto stages also replaced horse-drawn stagecoaches between Scotia and Willits. Fred Smythe of the Overland Auto Line operated six cars and reported in 1910 that the auto stage would begin operations in May. The fare to San Francisco by automobile and train was $20. Smythe estimated that by July, the train would be to Dyerville, and the auto stage would leave from there. (Courtesy of Bob Lutz.)

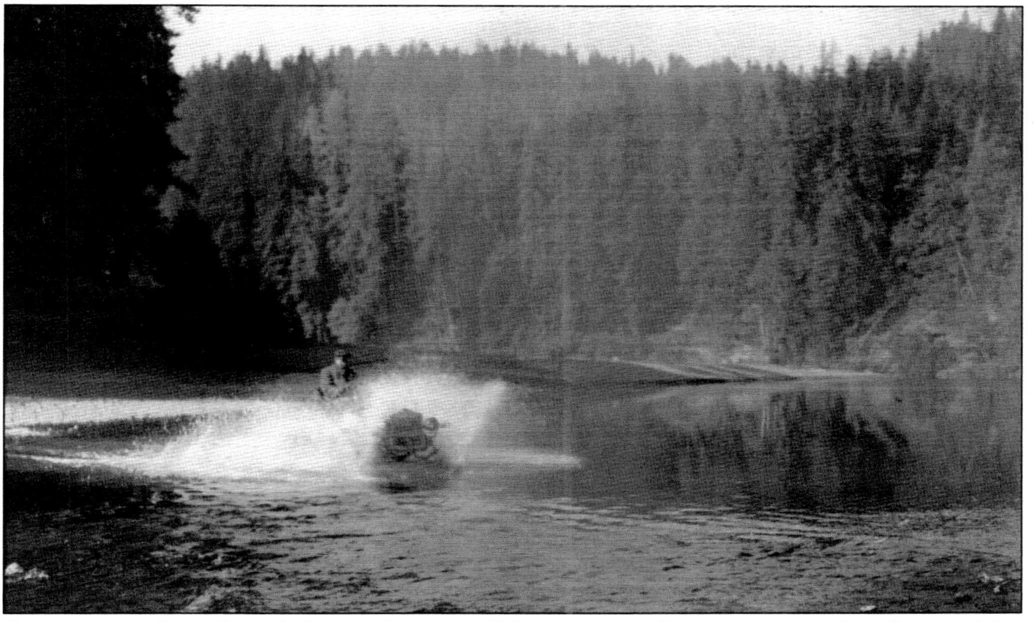

Private ownership of cars led to exploration of the region, and soon cars were found around the county. In 1909, a photographer captured this automobile crossing of the South Fork of the Eel at Dyerville. Many chose to take the toll bridge made by placing the winter ferry across the river. Others, however, risked the damage of a water crossing. (Courtesy of Bob Lutz.)

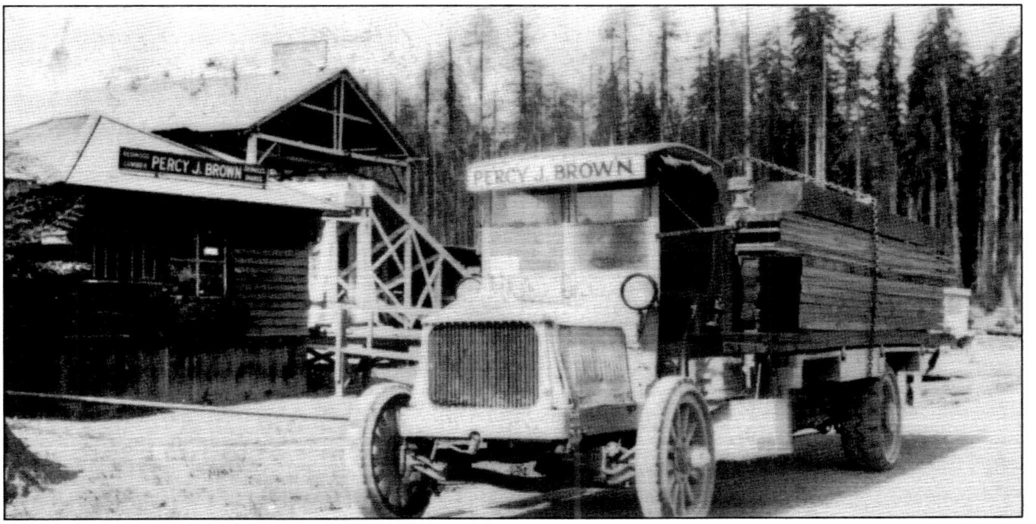

Changes in how people did business brought about by the technological advances of the car are reflected in this photograph of Percy J. Brown's lumber delivery truck. Brown had a lumber store in Stafford, and he delivered lumber, sashes, doors, and building materials "to points accessible" by trucks.

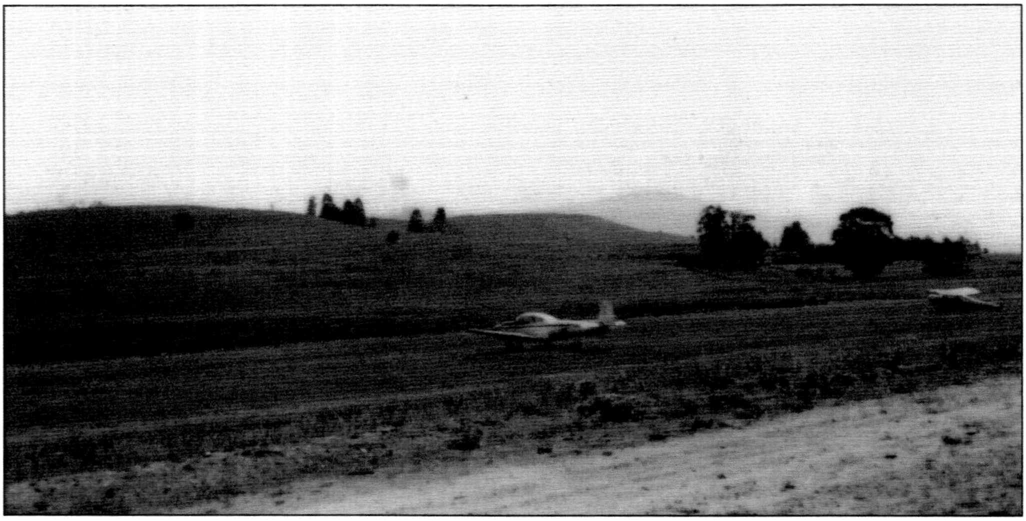

In 1945, Fortuna entered the aviation age with construction of the Rohnerville Airport. Built by LeRoy Gates and Jim Mead, the airstrip was first a dirt runway that had been leveled with a grader borrowed from the city. Around 30 planes used the field when it was first opened. By 1949, the runway was paved. In 1964, the California Division of Forestry opened an air attack base at the airport for retardant bombing of forest fires.

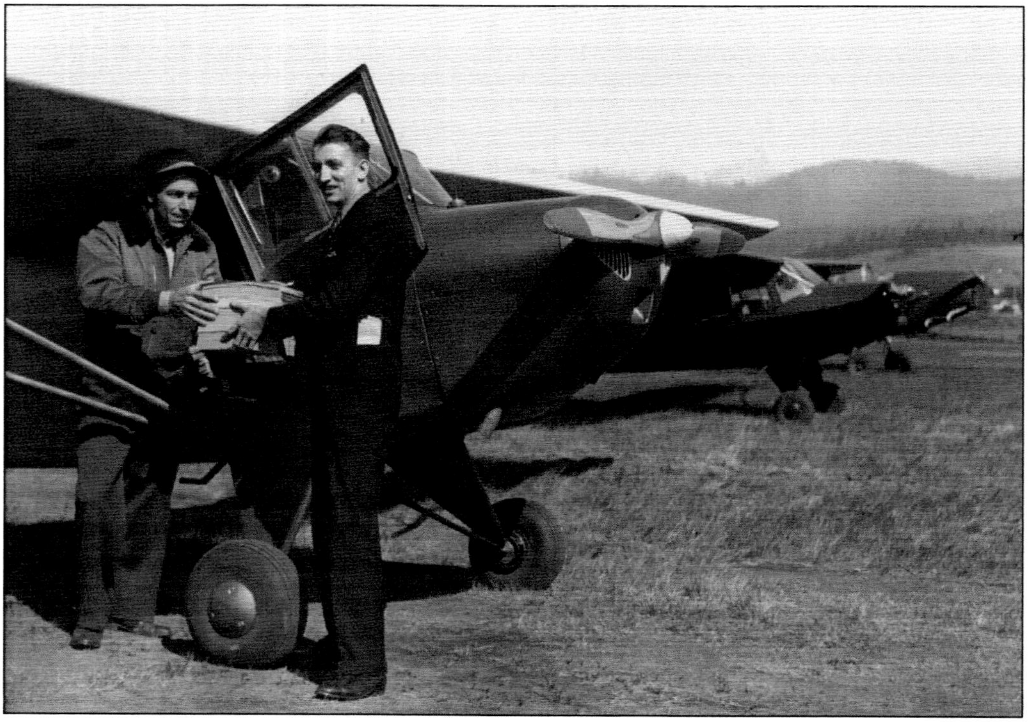

LeRoy Gates (left) is shown with Fortuna Theater manager Ted Roberts in the late 1940s. Gates was a World War II pilot who gave flying lessons and had a charter service. As a promotion for his theater, Roberts had Gates drop movie advertisements over Fortuna, Scotia, Ferndale, and Fernbridge.

Six

Fires and Floods

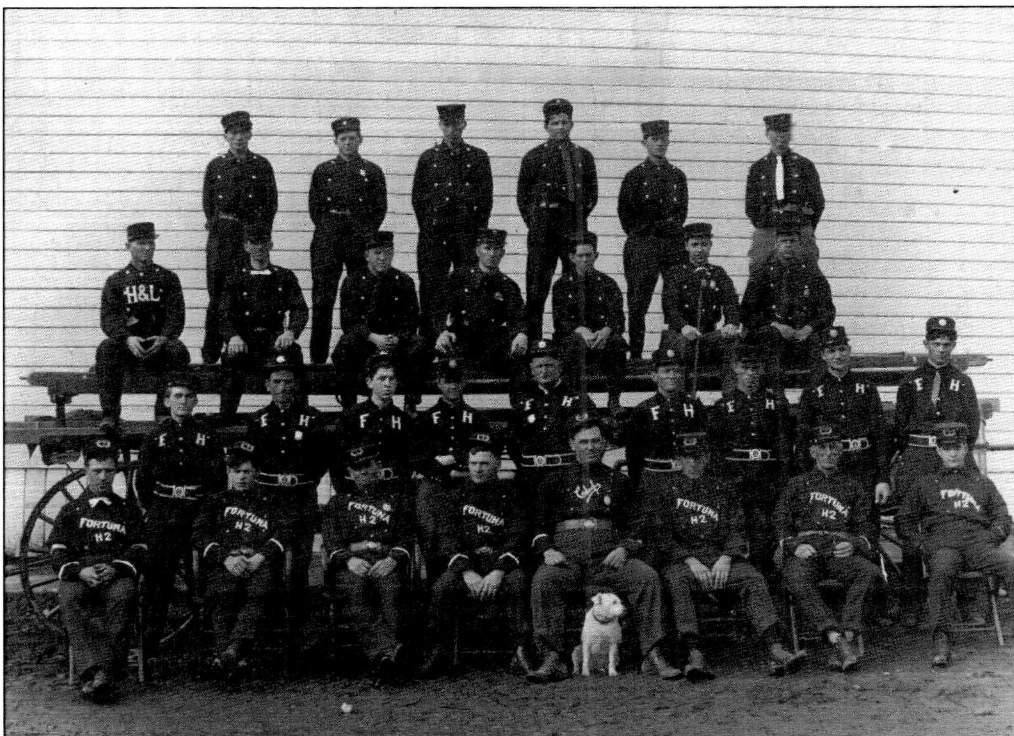

The Fortuna Volunteer Fire Department (FVFD) was created in response to a large fire in November 1902. An early morning blaze destroyed a significant portion of the buildings on Main Street. Concerned citizens met after the fire, and in June 1904, the FVFD was formed. Harry P. Monroe was named the first fire chief. (Courtesy of FVFD.)

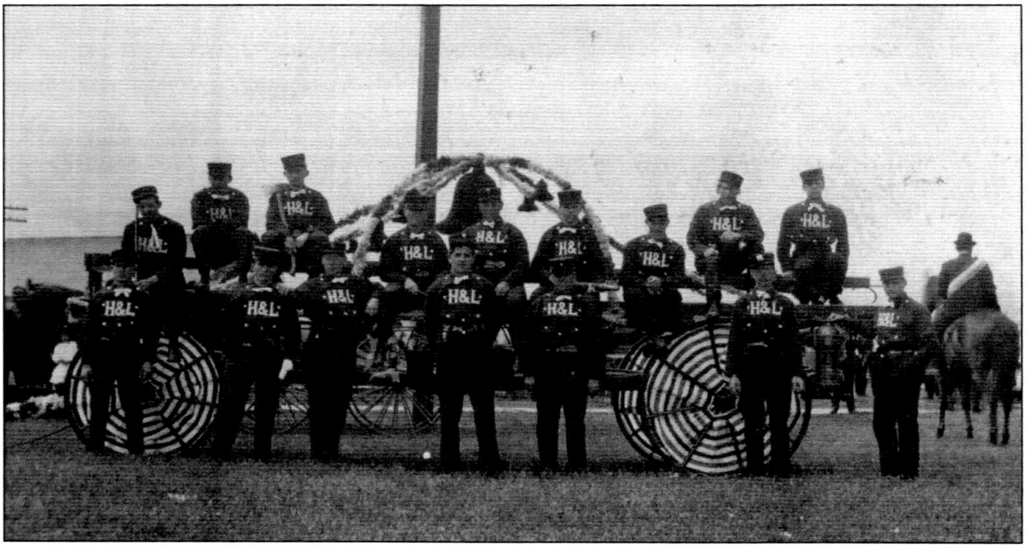

At the fire department's initial meeting, hook and ladder and hose companies were formed. In this 1909 photograph is the hook and ladder company with its equipment. The department raised funds for equipment and uniforms through sponsoring an annual firemen's ball. The first ball was held four months before the formation of the fire department in 1904. (Courtesy of FVFD.)

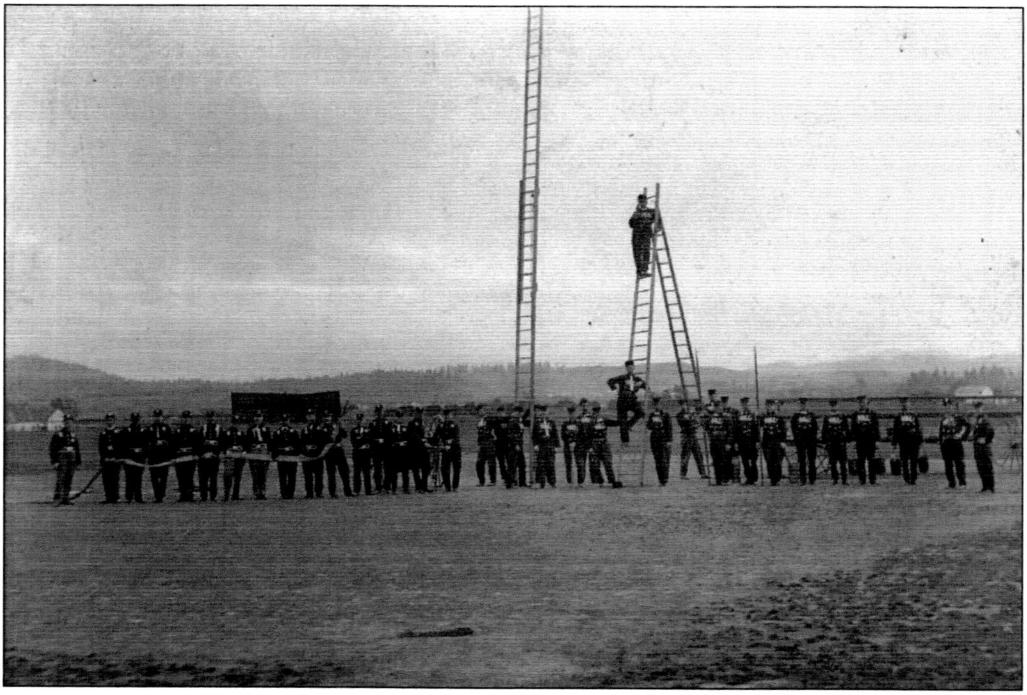

By 1913, the fire department had 65 members and boasted both the hook and ladder company and two hose companies. L.L. Bryan was now chief, and E.J. Hunter was the assistant chief. The tall ladders seen in the photograph were necessary firefighting equipment given the many multistory wooden buildings in Fortuna at the time. (Courtesy of FVFD.)

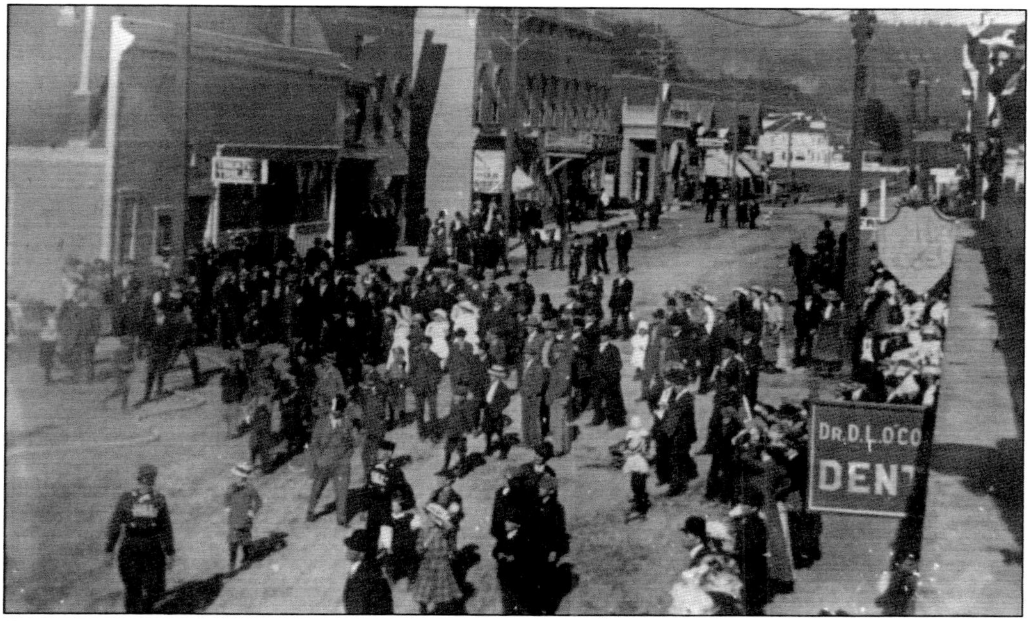

On June 12, 1911, the fire department was called to put out a large fire, again on Main Street. Fire raged through the Fortuna Merchandising Company building. The firemen successfully combated the blaze, aided by the equipment they had purchased. The department had a hook and ladder chemical engine, two hose carts, one hook and ladder cart, one two-wheeled chemical cart, and 2,000 feet of hose.

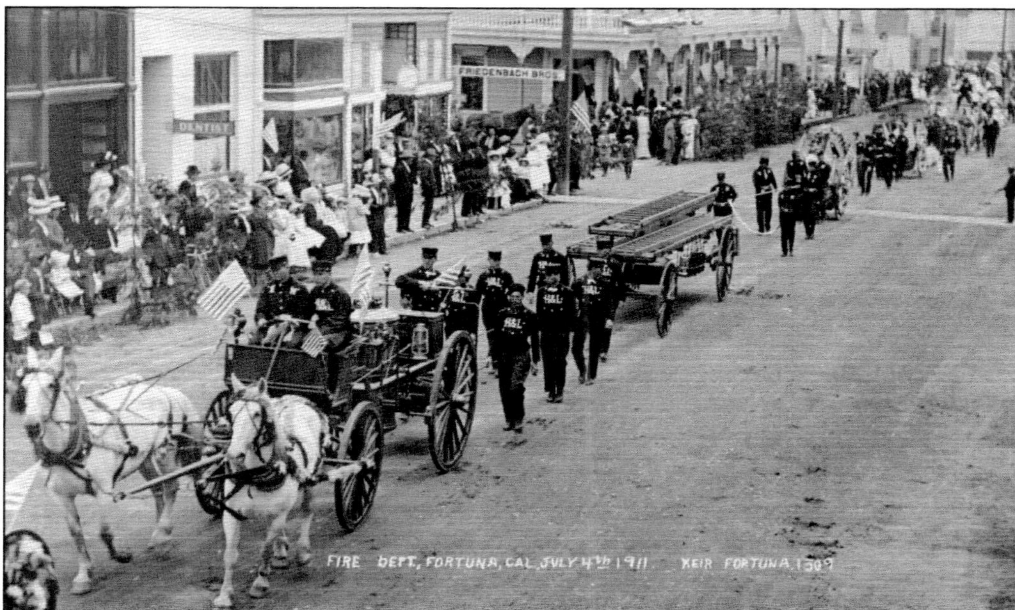

In the 1911 Fourth of July parade, the fire department proudly displayed all of its firefighting equipment. The chemical engine had been purchased in 1906 and had been shipped on the steamer *Vanguard*. E.J. Dodge, president of the Eel River Valley Lumber Company, paid for the shipping. (Courtesy of FVFD.)

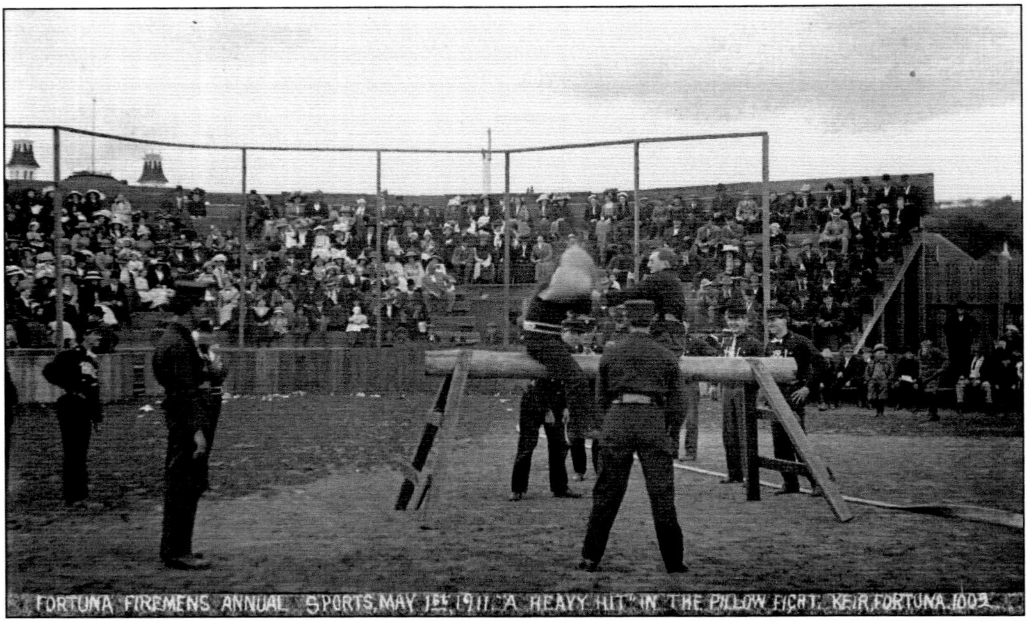

Fundraising was an ongoing requirement of the fledgling department, and the May 1st Sports Day became an annual event. In 1911, the events included a pillow fight between the two companies. The hook and ladder company won the event, three to one. (Courtesy of FVFD.)

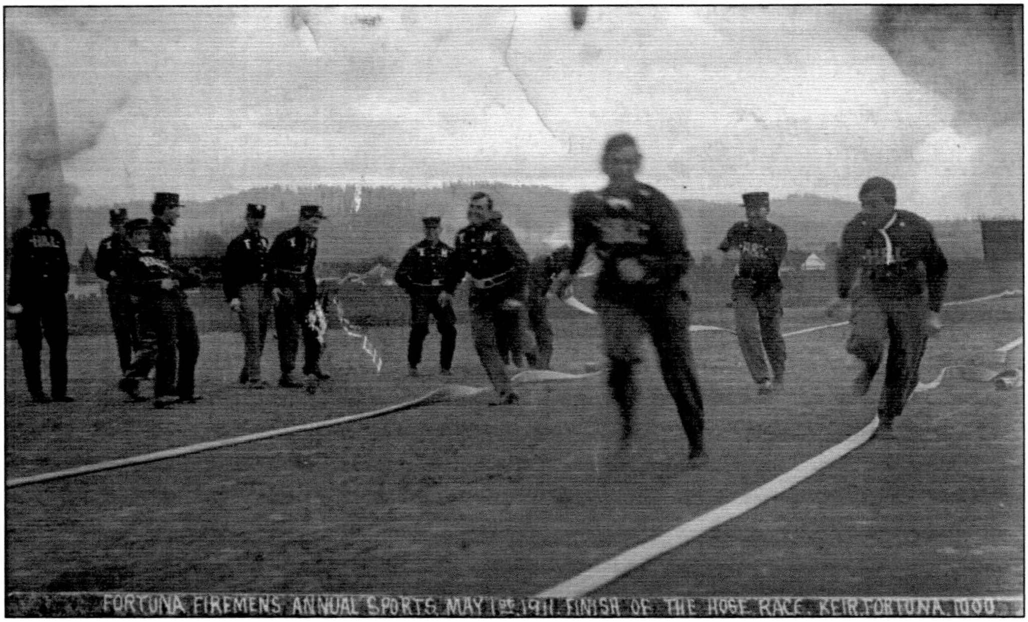

Another event in the 1911 Sports Day was the hose relay race. The hose coupling contest was won by Clyde Johnson and Paul Jasper. In addition to the relay race, the hose companies also did a demonstration downtown, laying hose up and through the Star Hotel, and according to the *Humboldt Beacon*, "showing what the companies could do when called on for quick action." (Courtesy of FVFD.)

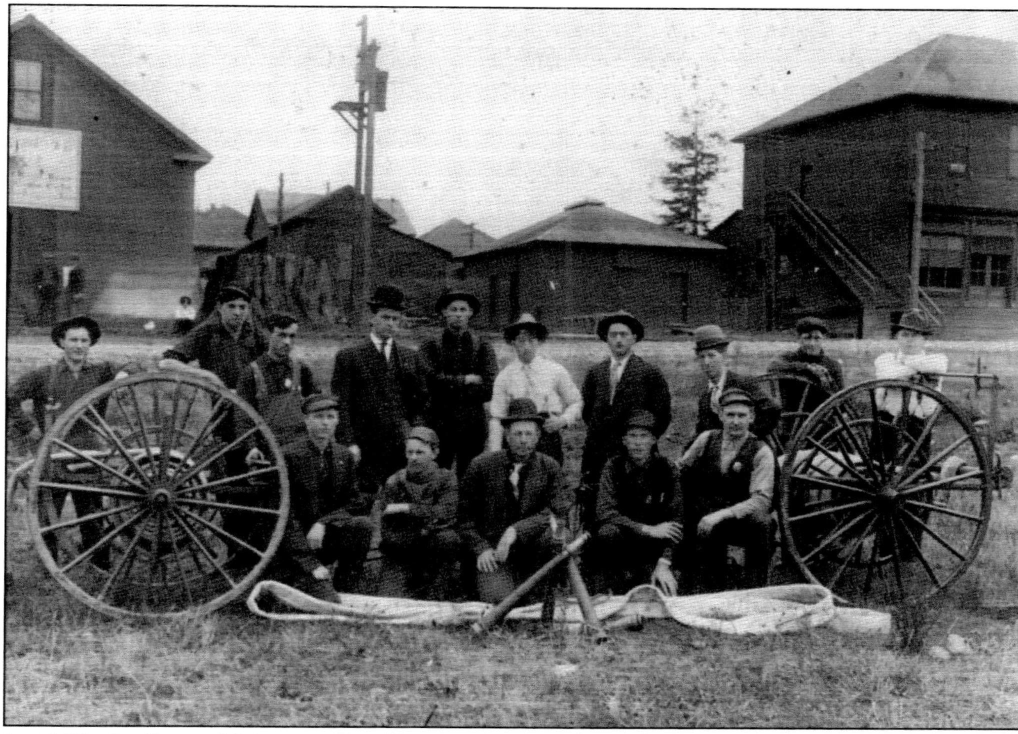

In 1908, the Scotia Volunteer Fire Department was formed to protect the town of Scotia and T.P.L. Co.'s mill. The first fire chief was E.A. Blocklinger. Hose cart races were a popular activity near the turn of the century; pictured is Scotia's hose cart team in 1908.

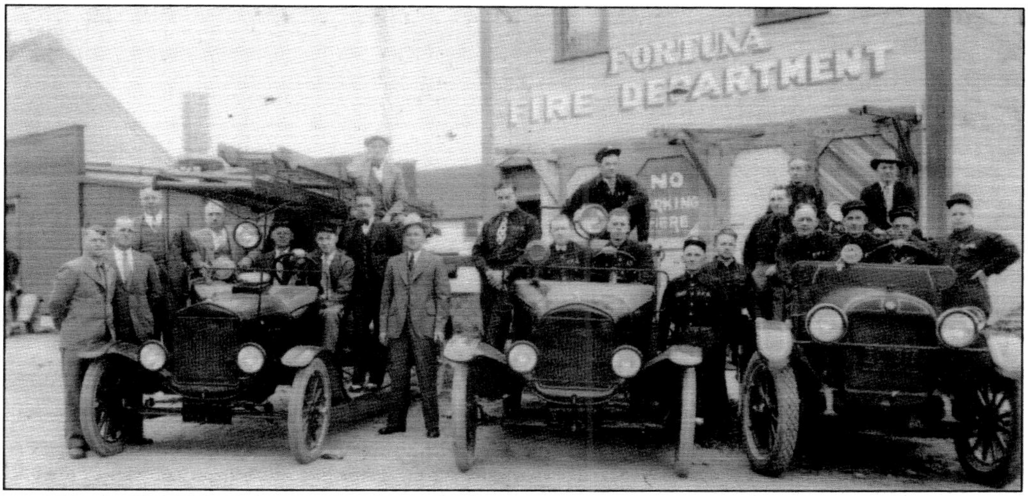

In 1930, the FVFD had three companies: the hook and ladder with 20 members, the hose company with 25 members, and the chemical company with 20 members. Art Chandler was fire chief. The fire department's area of responsibility extended to Singley Road on the west, Rio Dell-Scotia Bridge to the south, and Cuddeback to the east.

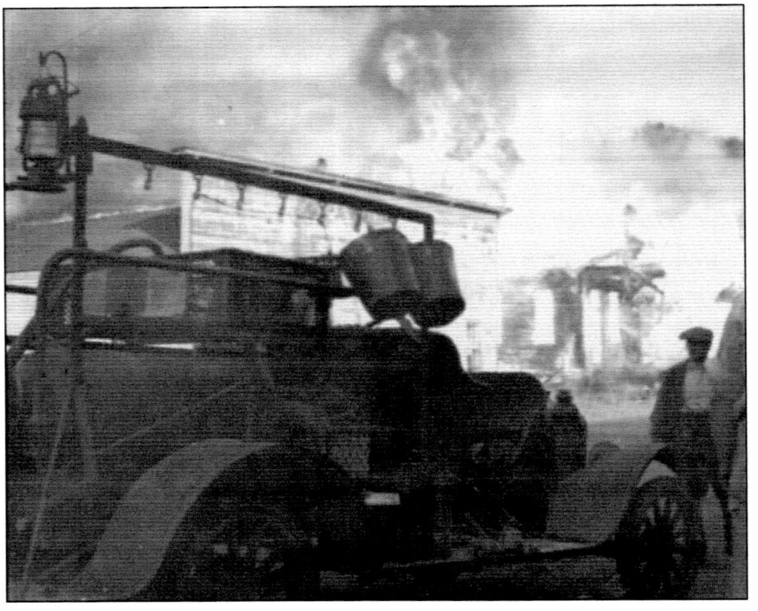

The disastrous fire in Rohnerville on July 4, 1940, destroyed much of the business section of that town, including George Patmore's furniture store, the Grange, and the hotel. Started by firecrackers thrown behind the structures, the dry redwood of the buildings quickly caught fire. The Fortuna, Loleta, and Ferndale departments fought the fire, as did state trucks from Dyerville. (Courtesy of FVFD.)

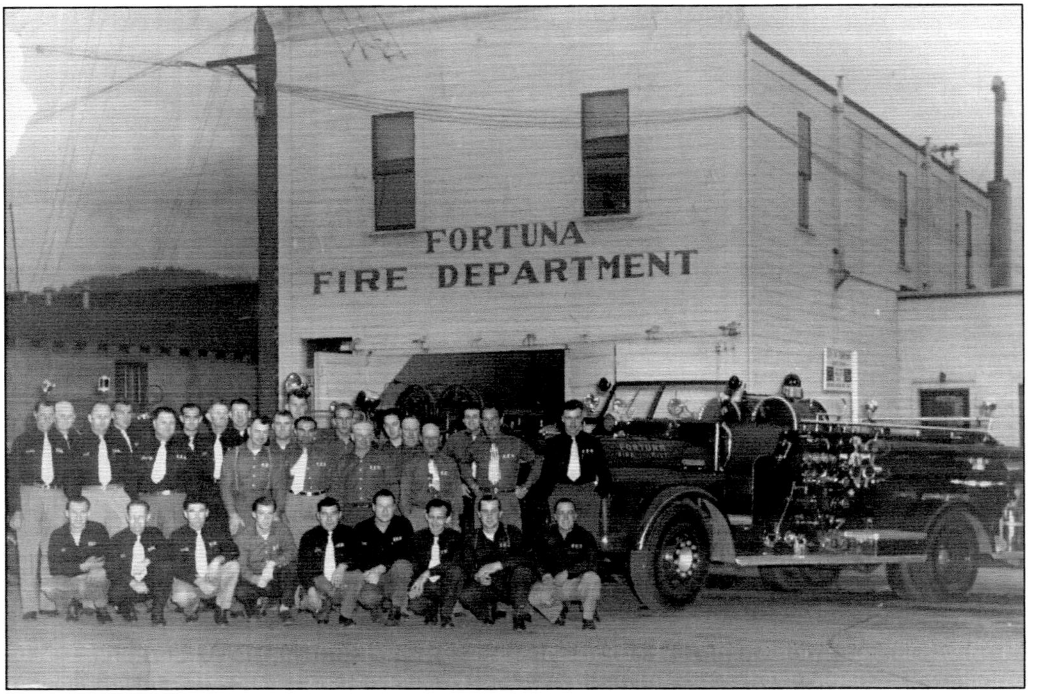

The FVFD is pictured in front of their fire hall in the 1940s. Another tool of the department was the siren. One long call meant a fire in the city limits, while one long call followed by two short calls was the signal for first aid. (Courtesy of FVFD.)

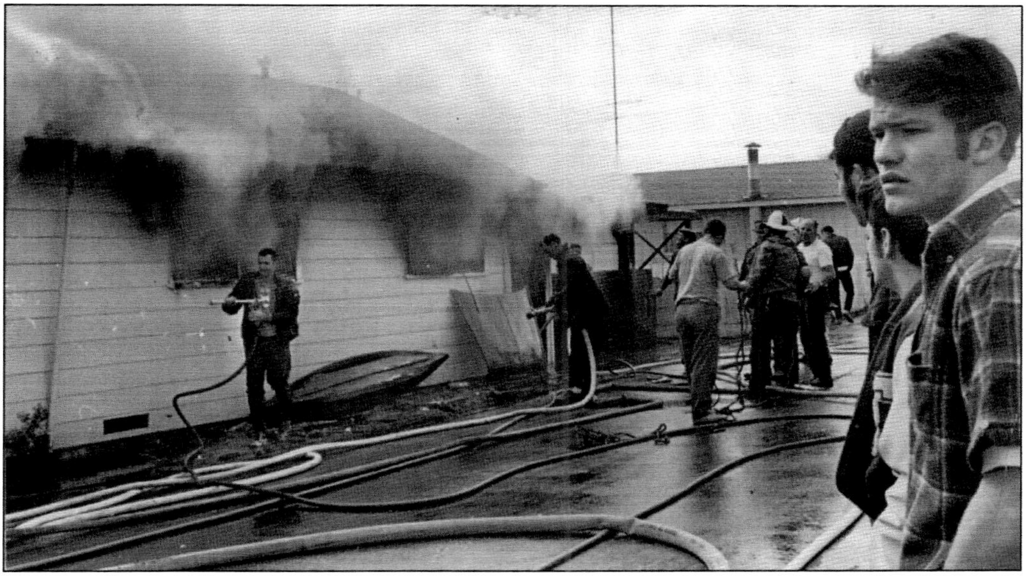

In the early 1950s, a house fire behind Pam's Restaurant on Main Street was a cause of great concern. Shown fighting the fire are Don Carter, Dave Adamson, Bob Durfee, and Bud Wescott. (Courtesy of FVFD.)

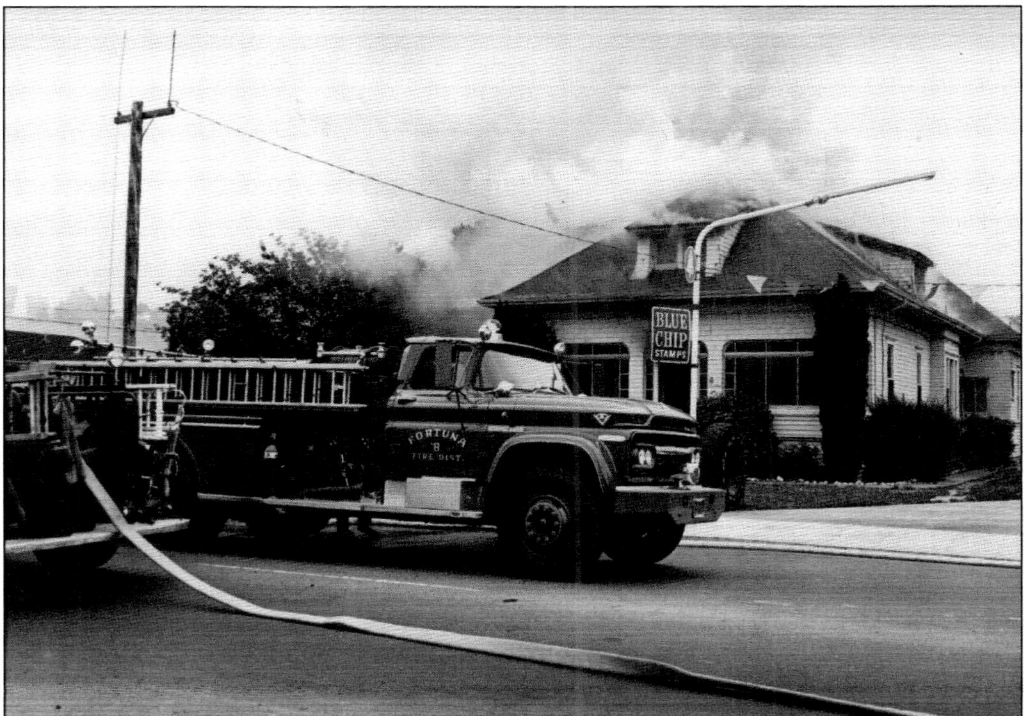

The Elizabeth Rohner Barcus house near Rohner Park burned in the early 1960s. This fire truck was acquired by the FVFD in 1962. Truck No. 8 was used as a primary attack vehicle until 1980 but continued to be used as a hose truck until it was replaced in 1992. (Courtesy of FVFD.)

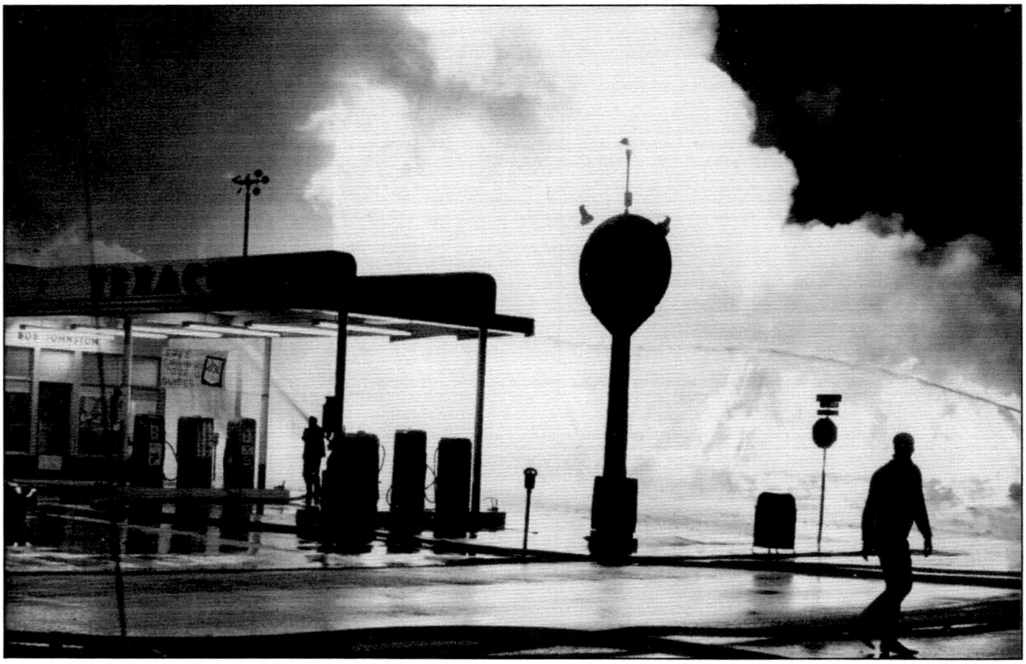

One of the most devastating fires in Fortuna occurred October 12, 1962. The Fortuna Paint Store stood at the corner of Twelfth and Main Streets in a building constructed in 1904. One ton of ammunition in the Fortuna Hardware Store exploded as paints and oils in the paint store burned during the fire. Other businesses damaged included Wycoff Plumbing and Fortuna Construction. (Courtesy of FVFD.)

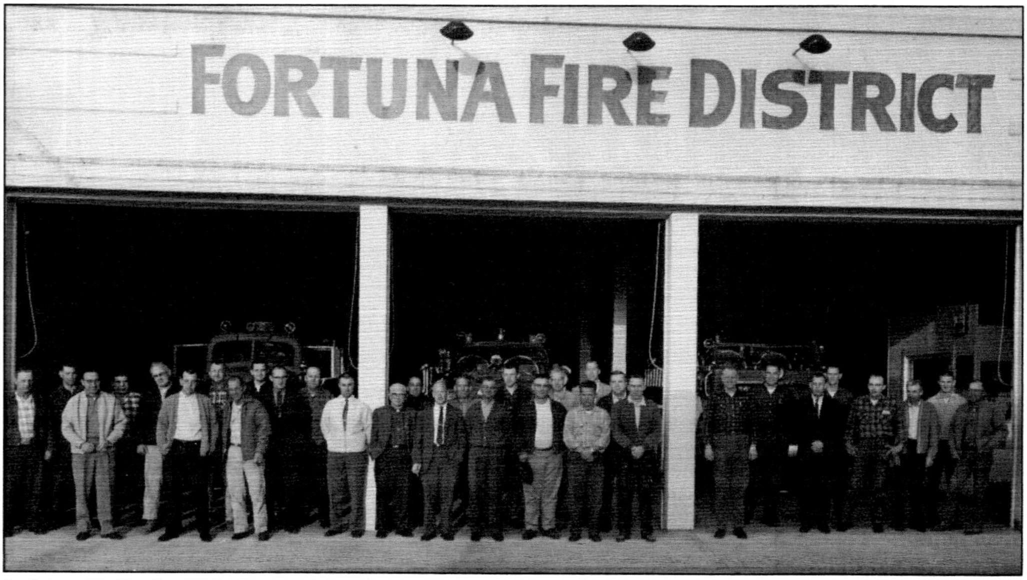

In May 1963, the FVFD posed for this group portrait. The department was still divided into three companies, and Bud Wescott was chief. Paul Jadro and Ken Newell were assistant chiefs. The department had recently moved into the building that had been the Safeway store in Fortuna. (Courtesy of FVFD.)

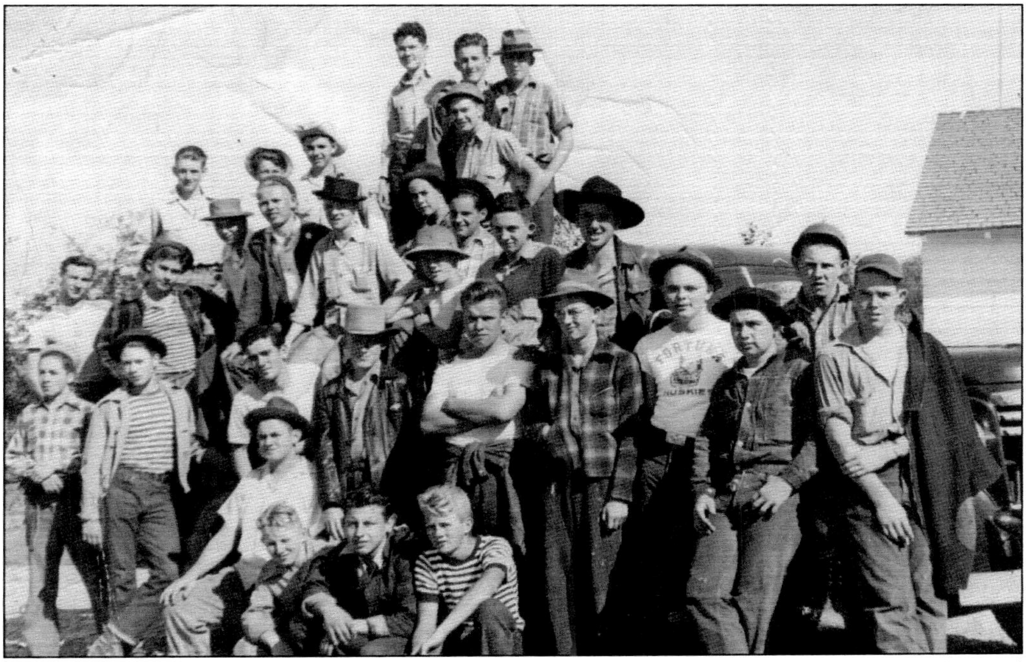

In addition to the threat of fire in the city, there was always the threat of wildfires in the land around the town. Responding to the need for fire protection near the end of World War II were the Fortuna High School Firefighters, pictured here in 1944. (Courtesy of FVFD.)

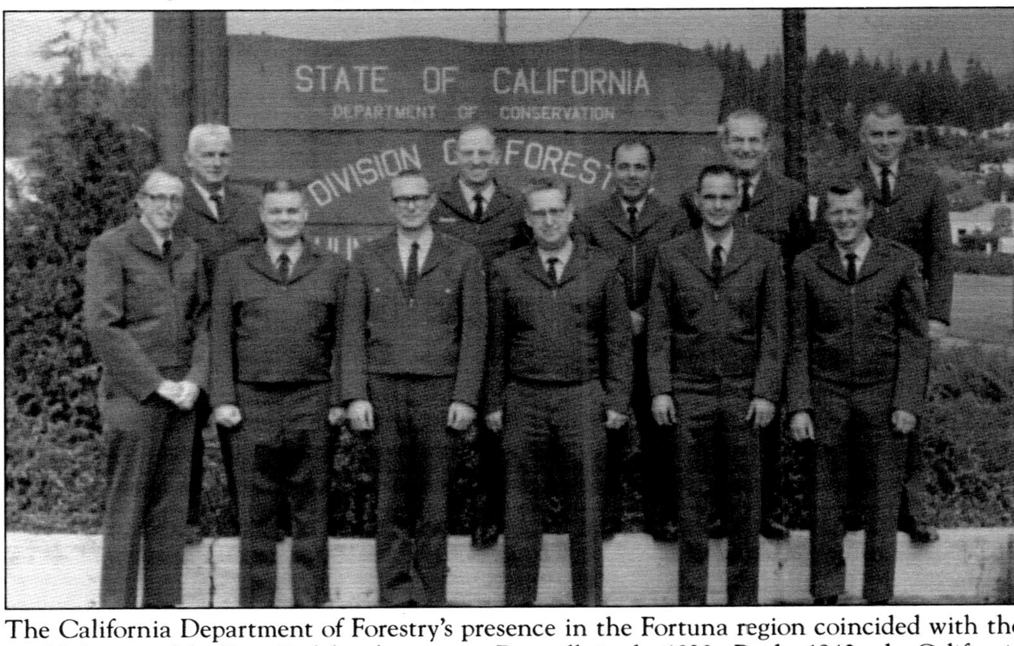

The California Department of Forestry's presence in the Fortuna region coincided with the establishment of the State Park headquarters at Dyerville in the 1930s. By the 1940s, the California Division of Forestry headquarters were moved to Fortuna. In 1967, the forest rangers for the Humboldt-Del Norte Operational Unit posed in front of the Division of Forestry sign. Standing third from the right in the first row is Harry Pritchard, who later became county supervisor.

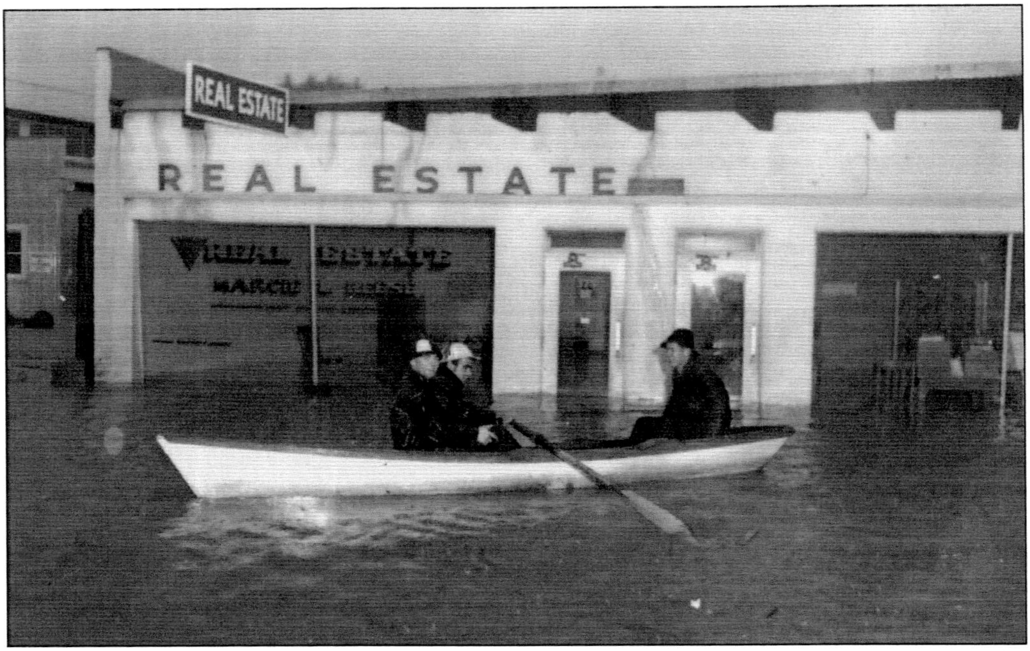

On the Eel River, high waters (or freshets) were a common occurrence during the winters of the 19th and 20th centuries. The men in the boat in this 1946 photograph are in front of what used to be Johnny's Cookhouse on Fortuna Boulevard.

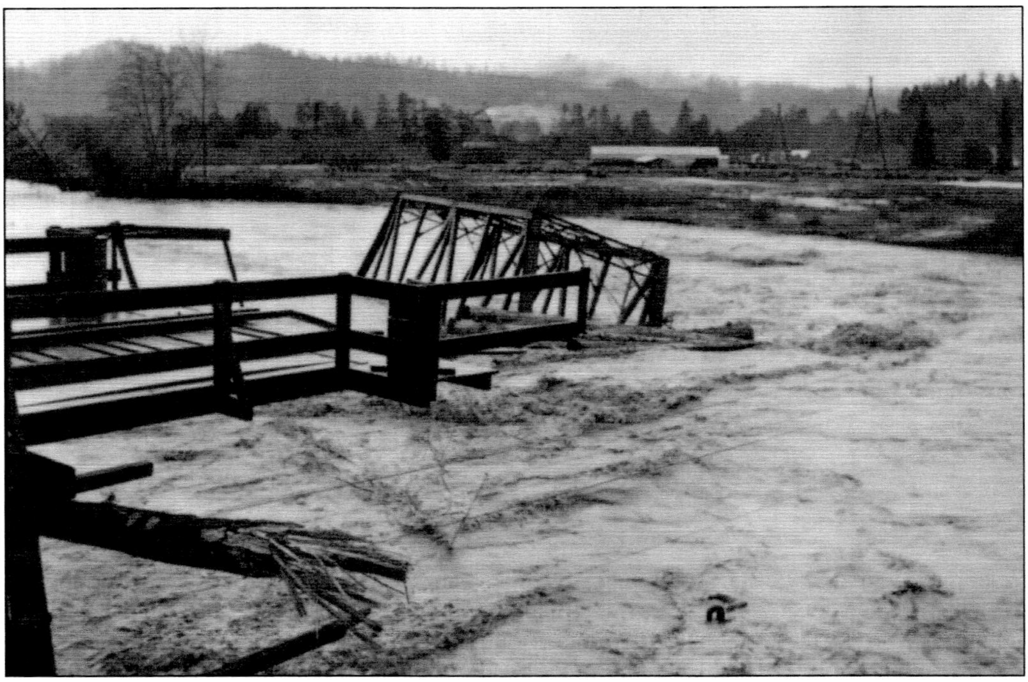

Shown is damage to the Carlotta bridge over Yager Creek after high water in the mid-20th century. Bridges were frequently damaged during floods, including the flood of 1955. At that time, the Eel River rose higher than in any previously recorded flood.

The December flood of 1964 became indelibly marked as the worst high-water event along the Eel. A December 23rd newspaper account of the flood reported that "the devastation was indescribable—A nightmare!" The heavy rains began a few days before and melted the snowfall of the previous week. The river began to rise quickly on the 21st and soon passed levels marked in the 1955 flood.

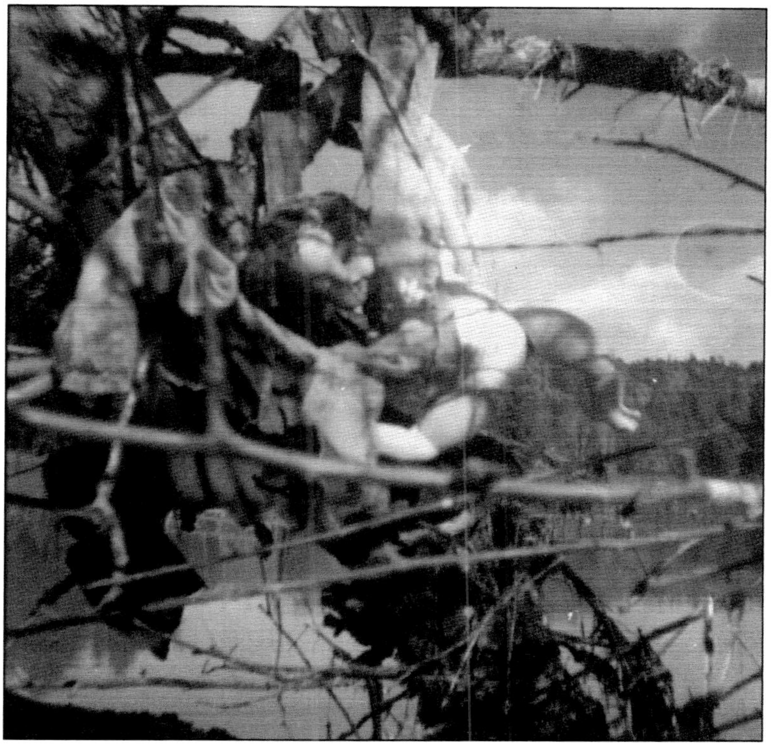

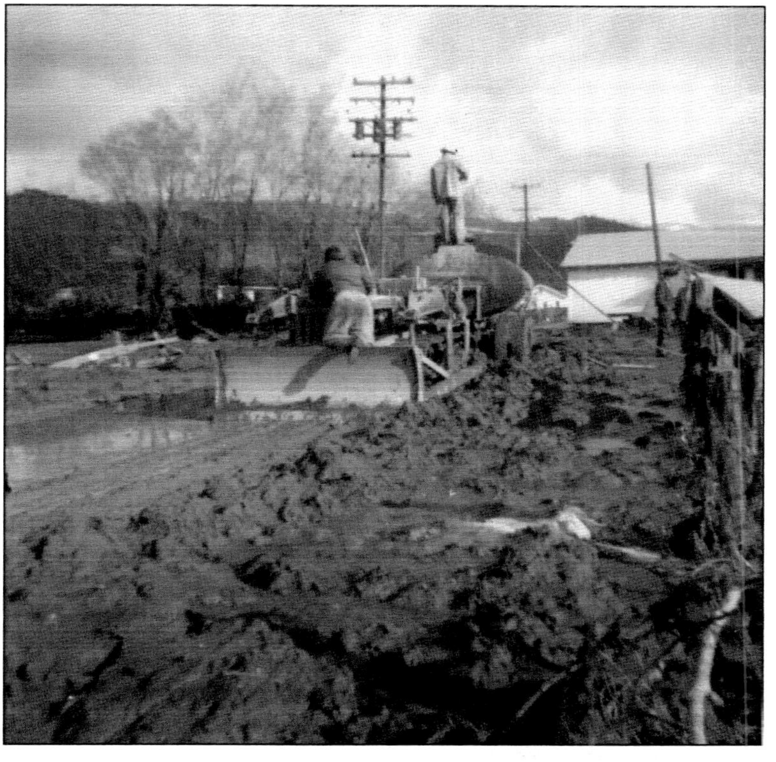

After the water receded, the cleanup efforts began. The highways, bridges, and railroad all needed massive repairs. The heavy silt left behind needed to be removed as well. Cleanup lasted for months. The Future Farmers of America students at Fortuna High were involved, having been asked to help clean moldy hay out of barns that had been inundated by the floodwaters.

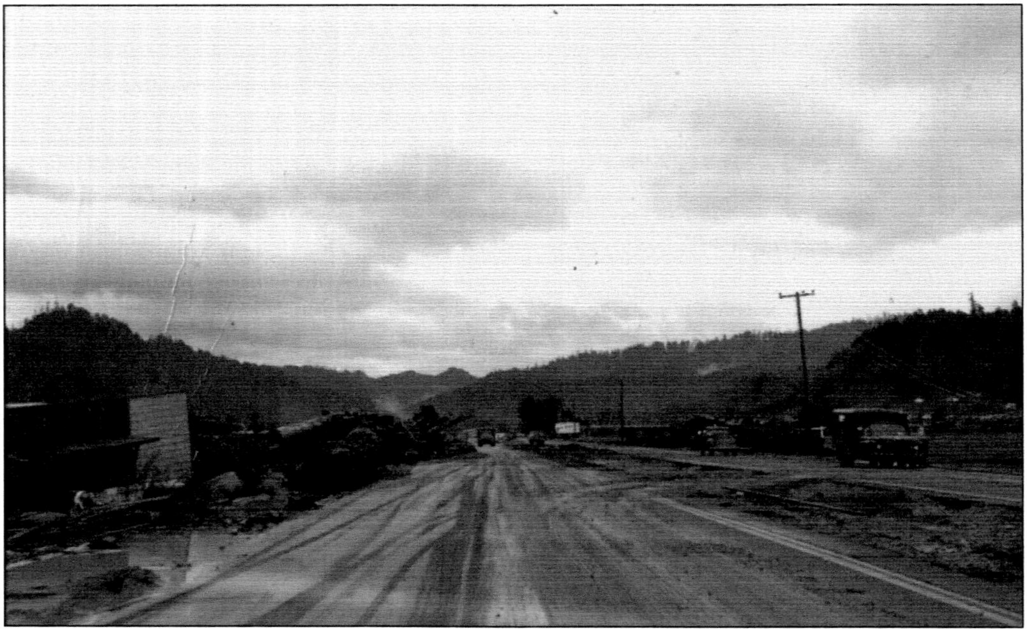

The logs, lumber, and other debris washed away by the high water covered the silt in many places. Although the Dyerville Bridge and Fernbridge survived, all other bridges along the Eel River were washed away and needed to be rebuilt. Most of the damage was from logjams that formed at the bridges.

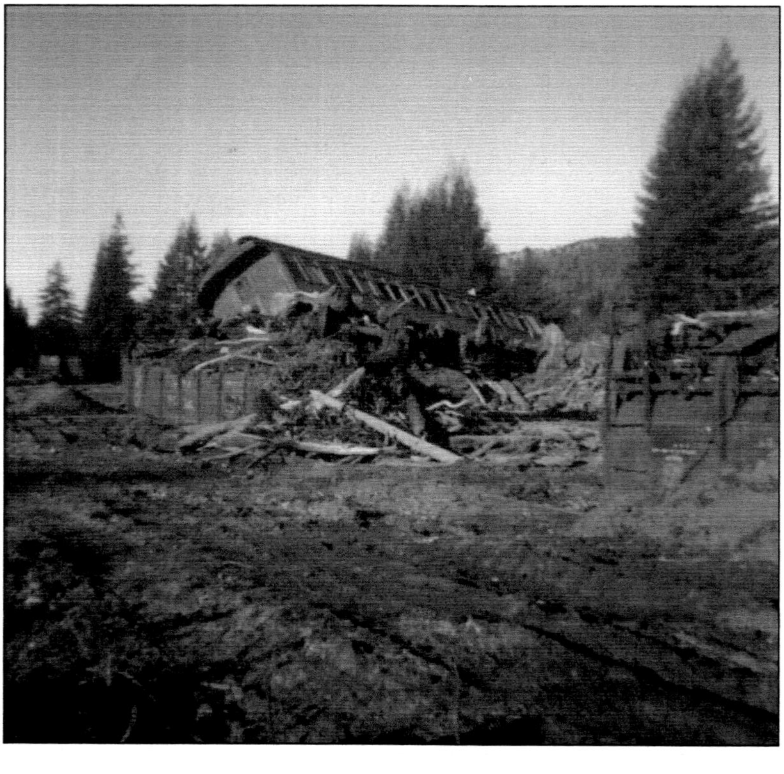

At South Fork, the power of the floodwaters moved around and stacked the railroad cars as if they were children's toys. High water and floods continue to impact the lives of valley residents as the river reshapes the environment.

Seven

EDUCATION

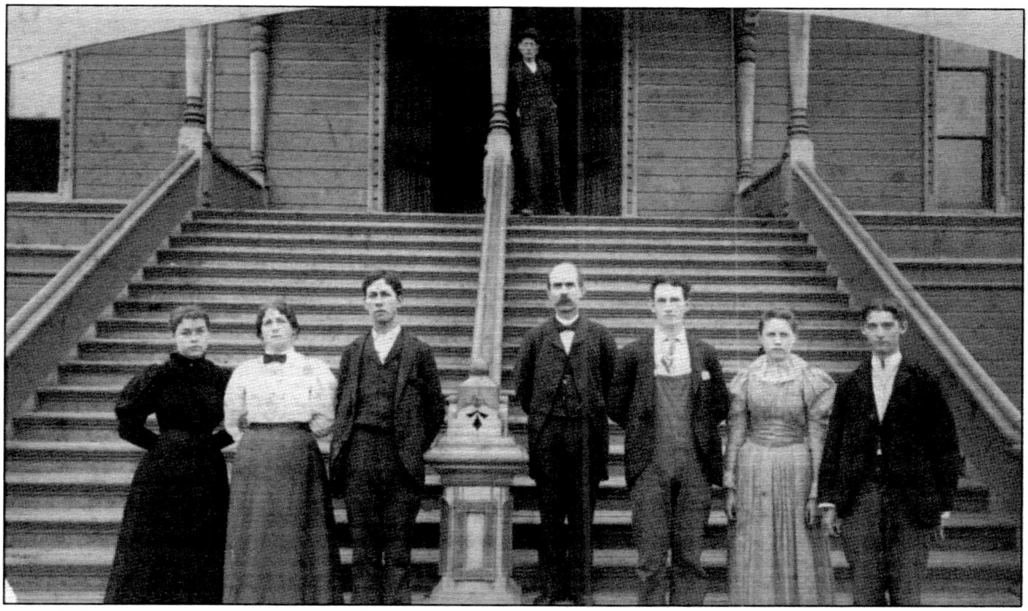

Population growth in the Eel River Valley led to a demand for teachers. In 1896, the 86 school districts employed 140 teachers in Humboldt County. Prospective teachers were trained at the grammar school building in Fortuna. This photograph of the 1900 class listed the participants' nicknames. The student teachers and instructor are, from left to right, Edna "Sally" Swortzel, Emily "Em" Morris, Frank "Rue Jay" Swortzel, Marion "Mike" Chidester (instructor), Lawrence "Boss" Morgan, Matilda "Mattie" Pierson, and Harry "Nibs" Leslie. Shown at the top of the stairs is J.R. McAtee, the janitor.

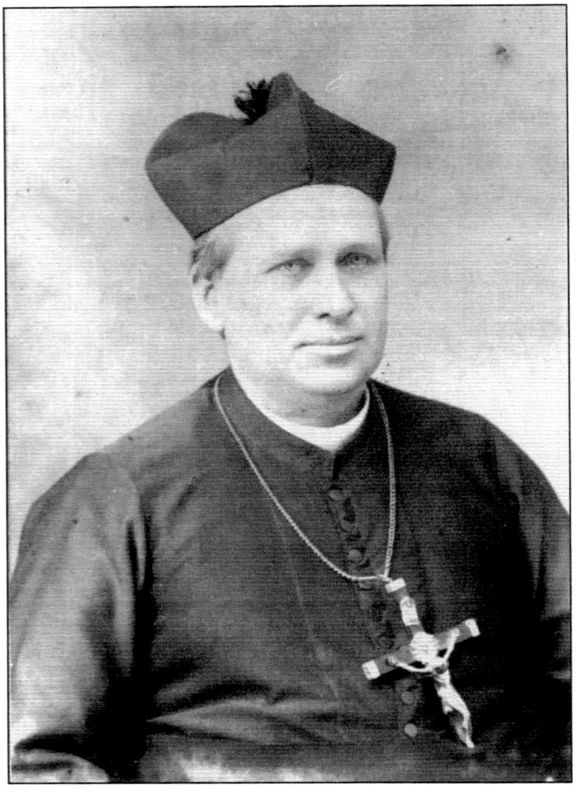

One of the earliest sites of higher learning in Humboldt County was in Rohnerville at the Mount St. Joseph College opened in 1871 by Father Henneberry, a pastor of the Catholic Church. He wanted to create a college to bring education and culture to frontier communities. In 1872, the college had more than 100 day and boarding students and attracted students from as far away as Santa Barbara.

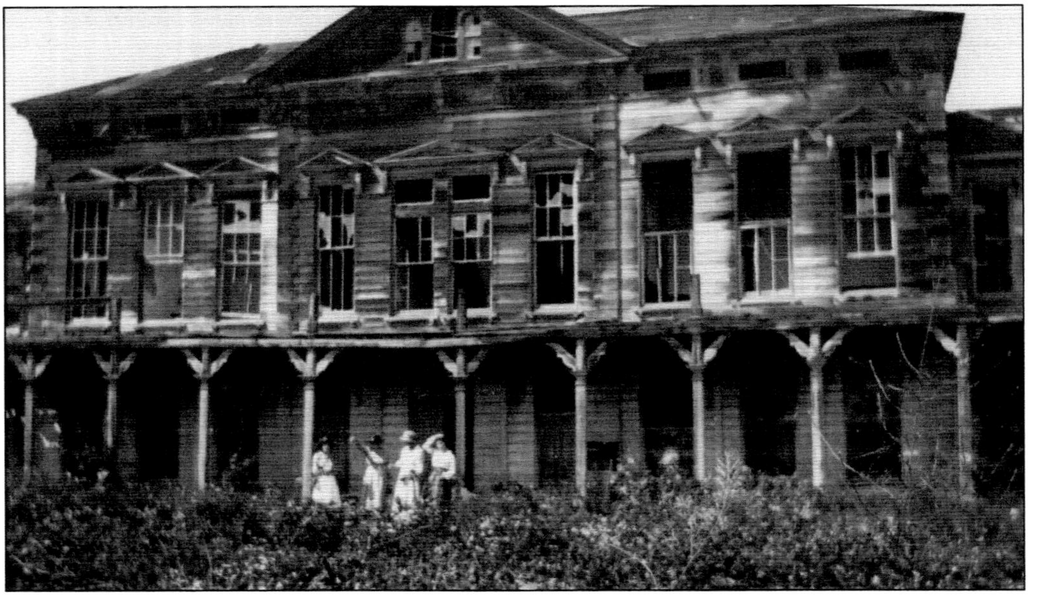

Mount St. Joseph College offered courses in English, Latin, German literature, mathematics, and natural philosophy. However, it struggled with financial difficulties. The college closed in 1879 and was briefly reopened in 1886, only to close permanently in 1889. The building fell to ruin in the 1920s.

Built in 1891, the two-story Fortuna Grammar School building on Main Street was the second grammar school to serve the community. In 1896, the *Humboldt Beacon* reported that 250 students attended school, the principal was Marion Chidester, Eva North taught the grammar grade, and Eola Armstrong and Lizzie Bailey taught in the primary department. (Courtesy of Clarke Historical Museum.)

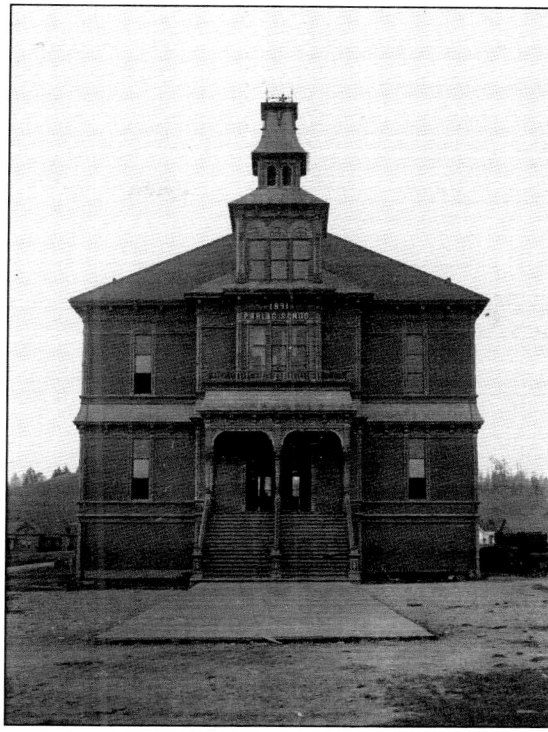

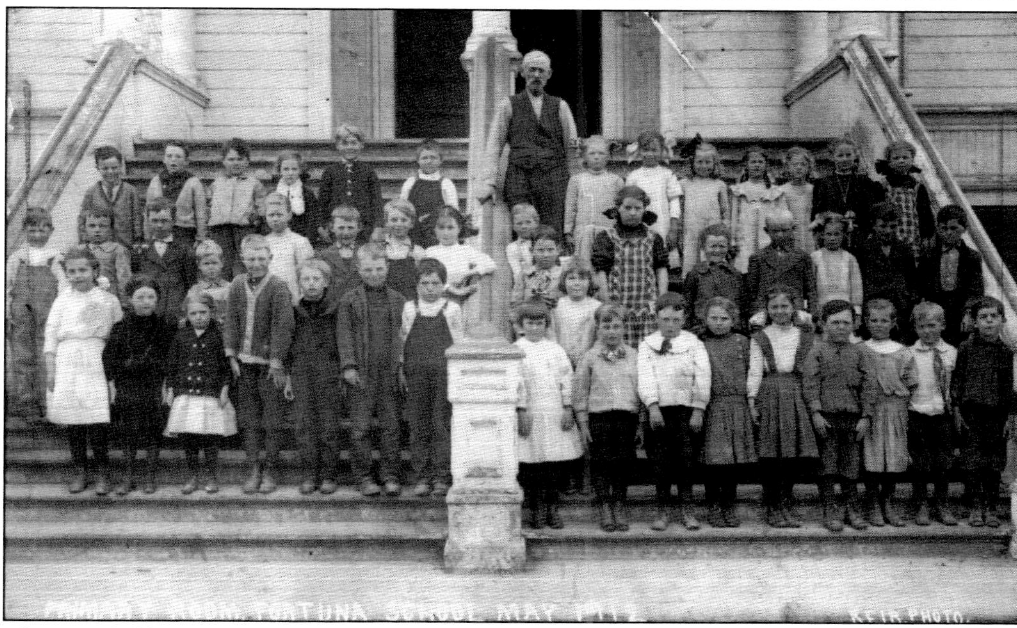

The *Humboldt Beacon* described Fortuna in 1913 as "rich in the conditions that make a good school." It continued, writing that the town had "graded schools equal to those of the city." One of the reasons for the excellent schools was Professor Inskip, the first principal of the high school. Pictured with grammar school students in 1912, he helped to found Fortuna High School in 1903.

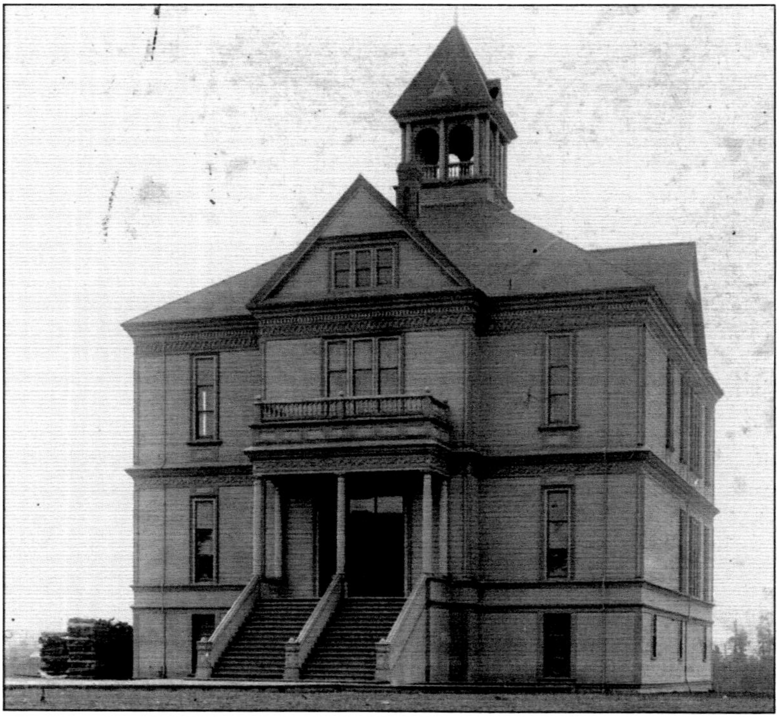

Professor Inskip taught in a private high school in Fortuna from 1900 to 1903. College-bound students needed proof of attending a school of higher learning. After becoming a public school in 1903, the first class to graduate (1905) consisted of Charles Edson and Delbert Swortzel. The high school received accreditation from the state in 1907, at which time three teachers were employed.

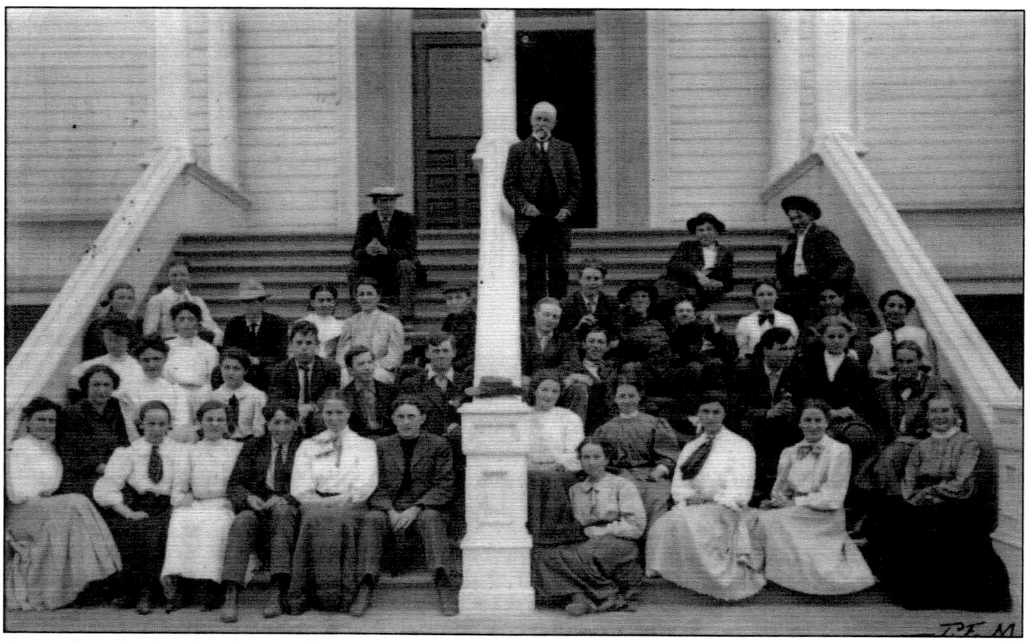

Attending high school was a luxury few could afford in the early 1900s. Many went to work in the logging or farming industries instead of going to high school. Those who did attend encountered rigorous course work, including four years of English and Latin, two years of algebra, a year of geometry, and a year of trigonometry. Courses in chemistry, physics, and ancient and modern history were also required. Professor Inskip and students are pictured here around 1906.

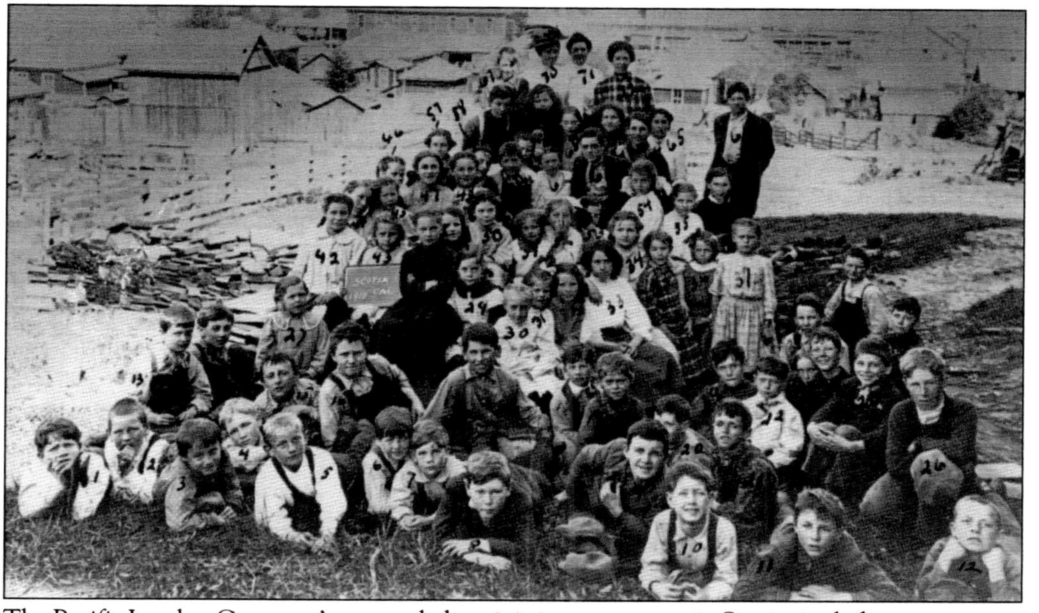

The Pacific Lumber Company's success led to civic improvements in Scotia, including a two-story school built in 1914. The students in this 1910 photograph are shown with their principal, Alice Clancy (at right in the back row). Taught in large groups, students most likely learned to read with the benefit of McGuffey readers. Those wanting education beyond the eighth grade would have gone to the high school in Fortuna.

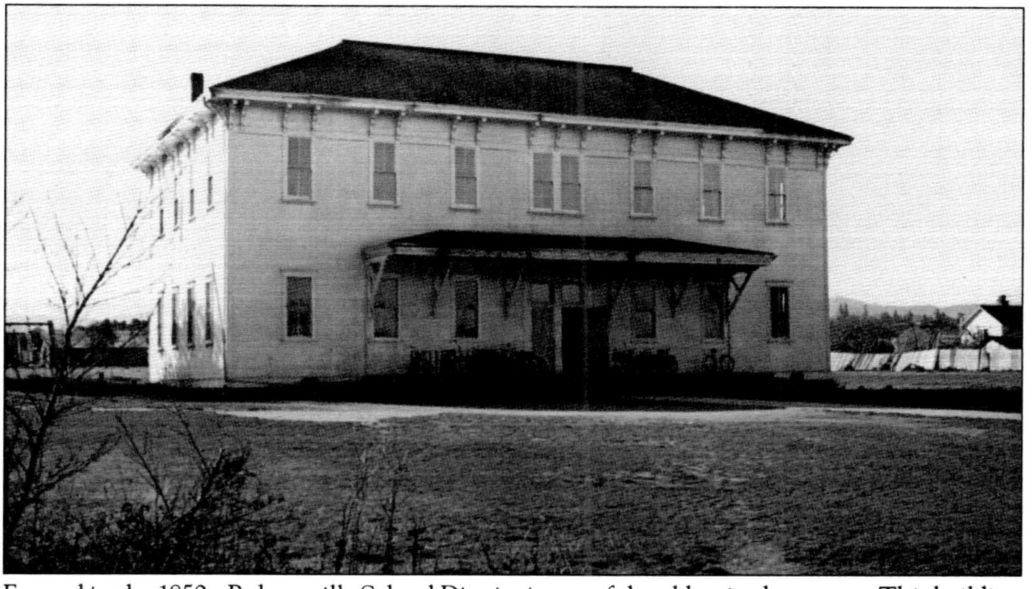

Formed in the 1850s, Rohnerville School District is one of the oldest in the county. This building located on School Street was the second Rohnerville school to be constructed. Built in 1889, it was the first of the improved schoolhouses in the valley. In 1913, the *Humboldt Beacon* described the improvements, including "arranging and furnishing of an assembly hall, where the entire school may be gathered for instruction or pleasure." (Courtesy of Humboldt County Office of Education.)

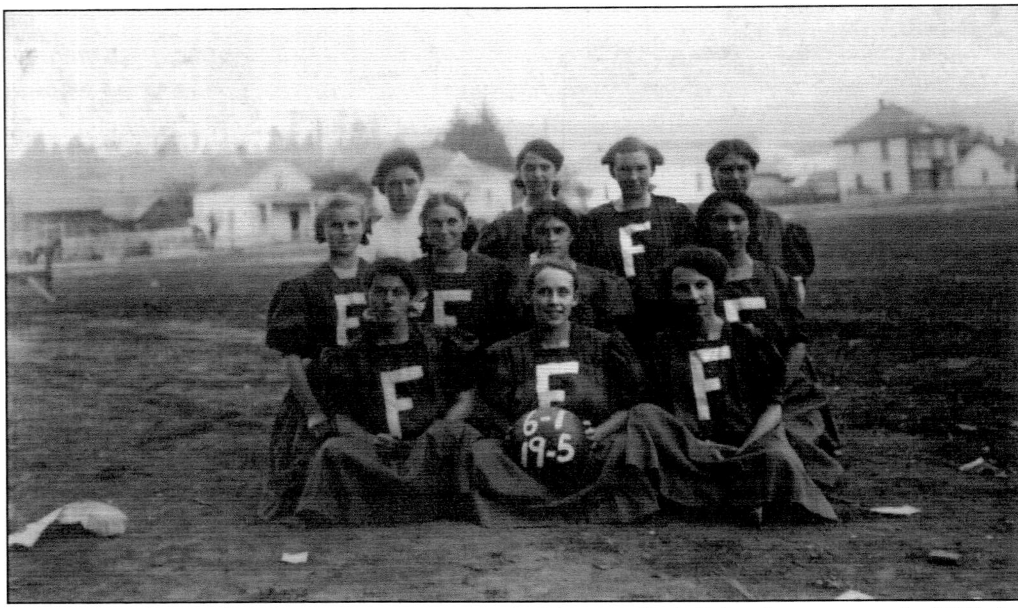

Sports have always played an important part in the Fortuna High School experience. In 1907, the girls' basketball team won the championship game. One of the players, Hazel Jarvis (holding the ball), wrote to her friend James Belloni, a 1906 graduate, that the photograph shows "the bunch that horned the other H.S. coeds." The scores are shown on the game basketball.

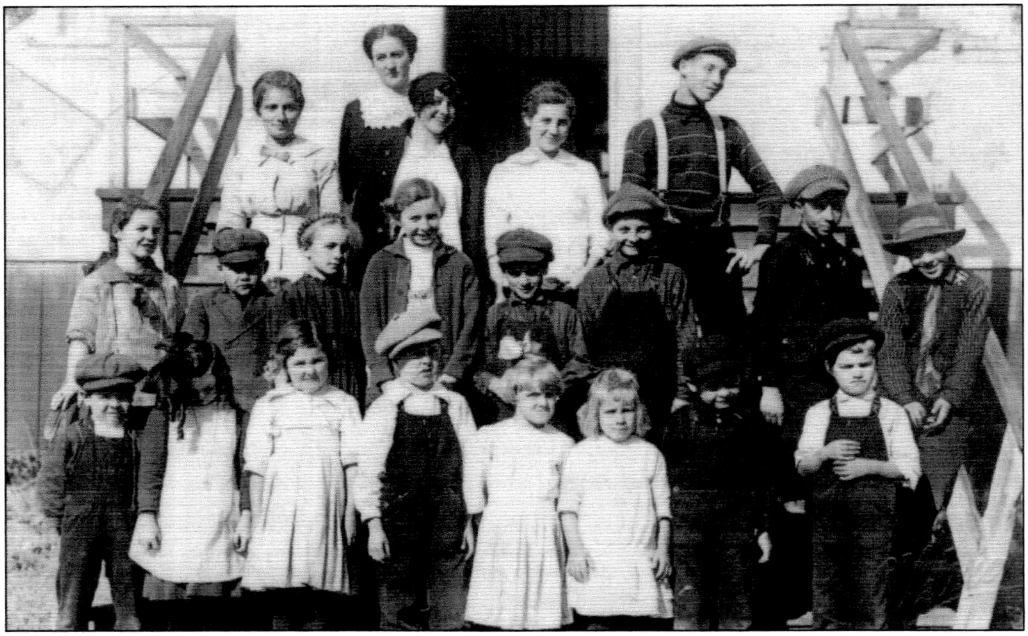

The town of Newburg, site of the E.J. Dodge Lumber Company, had its own school, pictured here in 1915. Children of the lumber company employees attended, their surnames (Koskela, McCaughan, Cronin, Kiefer, McKale) representing the different heritages of the mill town residents. Their teacher, Angeline Davis, most likely earned her teaching credential in Fortuna.

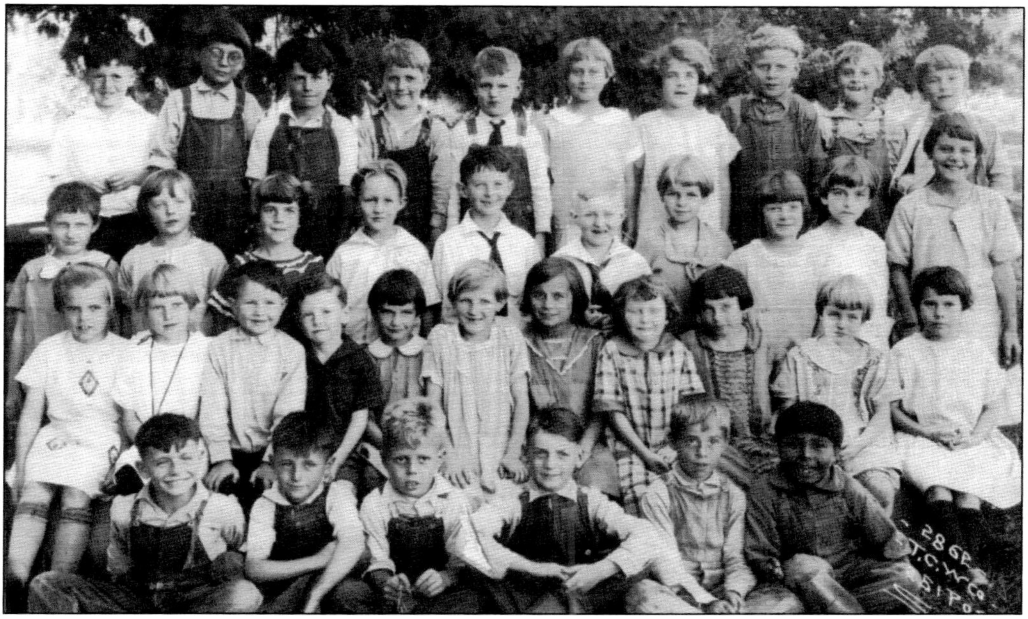

This 1926 photograph of the Fortuna Grammar School's second grade includes Helen Friedenbach (third from right, second row), who later became one of the teachers at the school. At the far right in the first row is thought to be Lloyd Brenard, a member of one of five Fortuna families identified as Indian in the 1920 US Census. His father, Smith Brenard, was a farmworker and a World War I veteran.

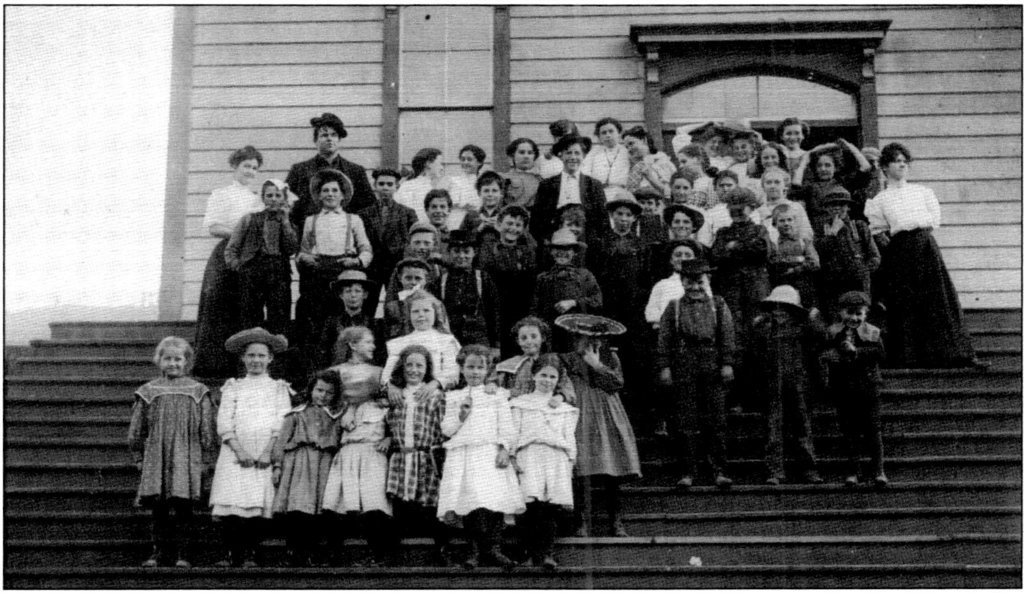

Taken on the steps of the new Scotia School building, this photograph is of one of the classes in the 1910s. Mickey McKay attended Scotia School from 1918 to 1926. He recalled that the school consisted of two buildings: one for the first through fourth grades and a two-story structure for the fifth through eighth grades. On rainy days, boys would play in one of the basements, the girls in the other.

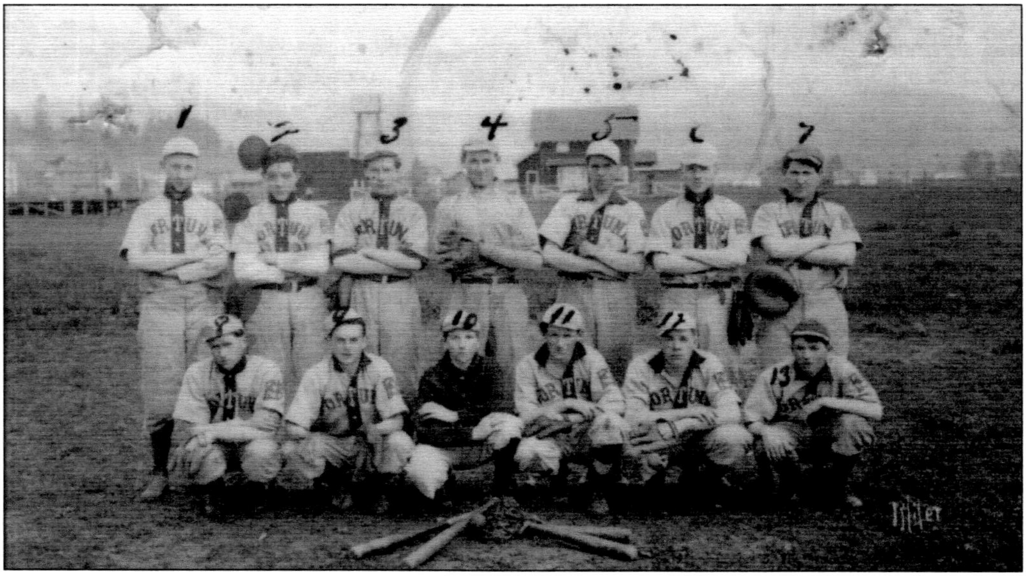

The 1915 Fortuna High boys' baseball team was league champion. Launcelot Beacom, kneeling second from the left, was a popular student, captaining the debate, basketball, and tennis teams. He participated in baseball, football, track, glee club, and was also part of the yearbook staff. He died of Spanish influenza while in the Army in World War I, the first Fortuna boy to die during the war.

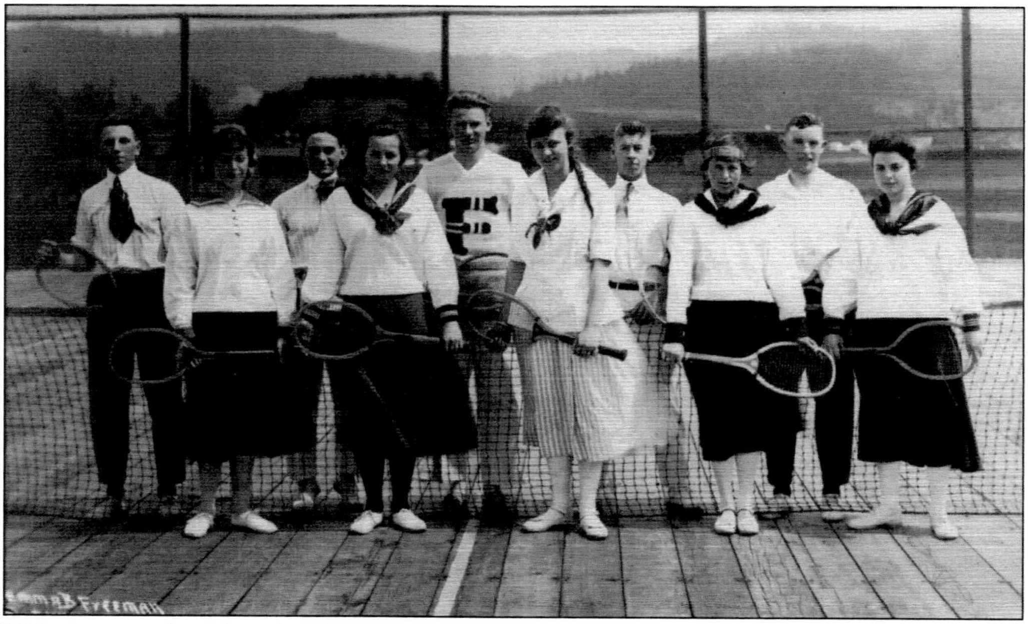

This photograph of the school's tennis team was taken for the 1918 Fortuna High yearbook. The team participated in several tournaments and won against Ferndale. The team members are, from left to right, J. McNeill, Daisee Bowman, Robert Fisher, Della Langin, Ralph Taylor, Mary Fleming, Belford Williams, Constance McKee, Edmund Starks, and Mildred Petersen.

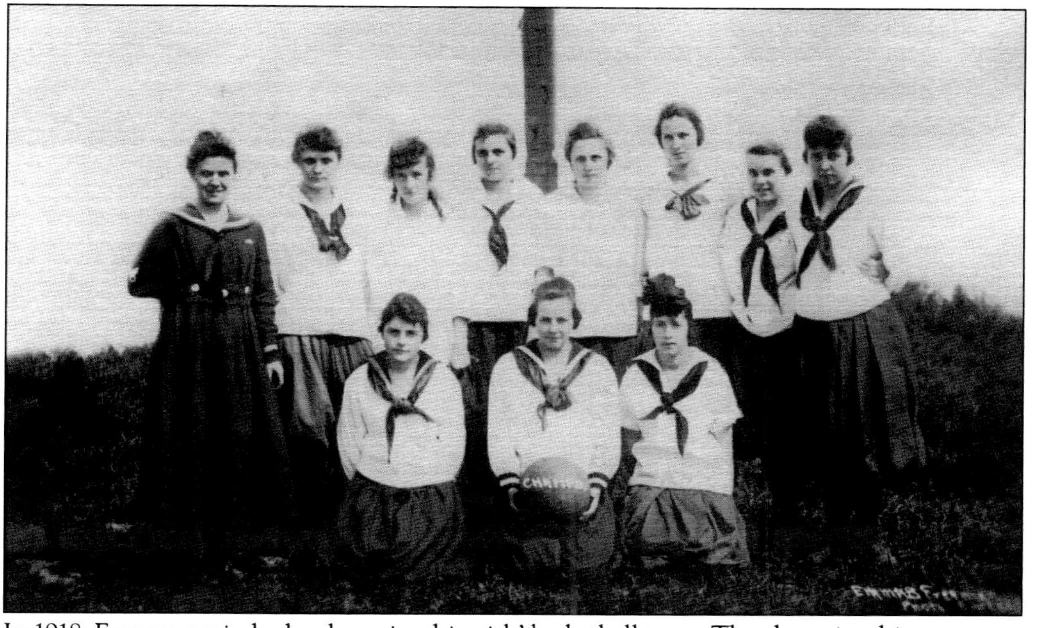

In 1918, Fortuna again had a championship girls' basketball team. The championship game was played on October 20, and according to the yearbook, it "was a great day for Fortuna when the Eureka team for the first time in four years lost the championship. Fortuna was there to play the game, and by its speed and accurate teamwork together with its strong defensive, Eureka was outclassed in every way."

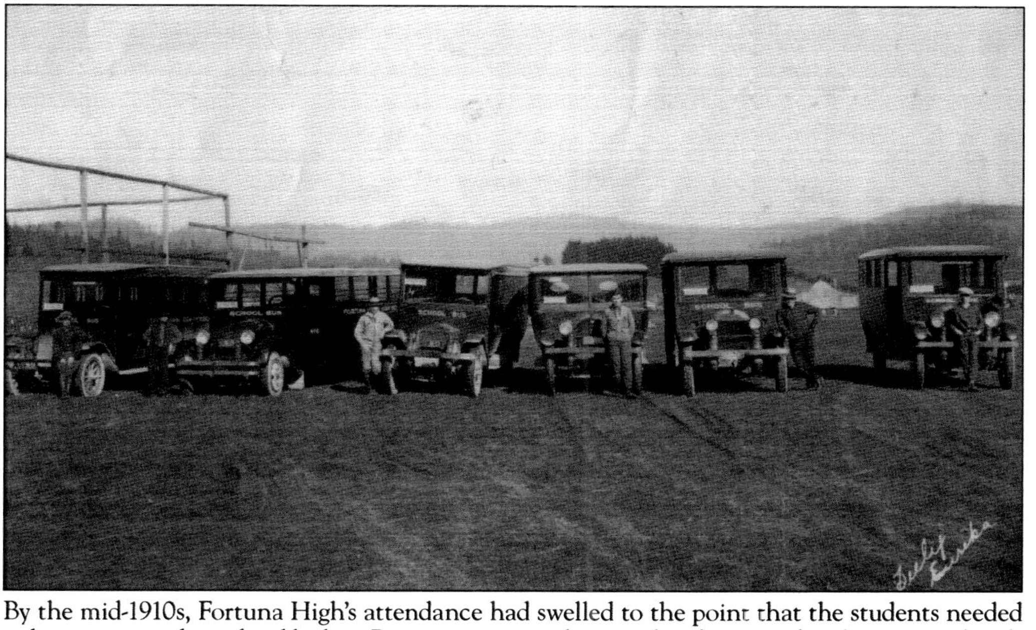

By the mid-1910s, Fortuna High's attendance had swelled to the point that the students needed to be transported to school by bus. Buses were privately owned and operated and contracted with the school. Then, as now, Fortuna High's district students came from Loleta, Alton, Hydesville, Cuddeback, Rio Dell, and Scotia. Mr. Briggs and Herbert Hill are identified as two of the drivers in this 1927 photograph.

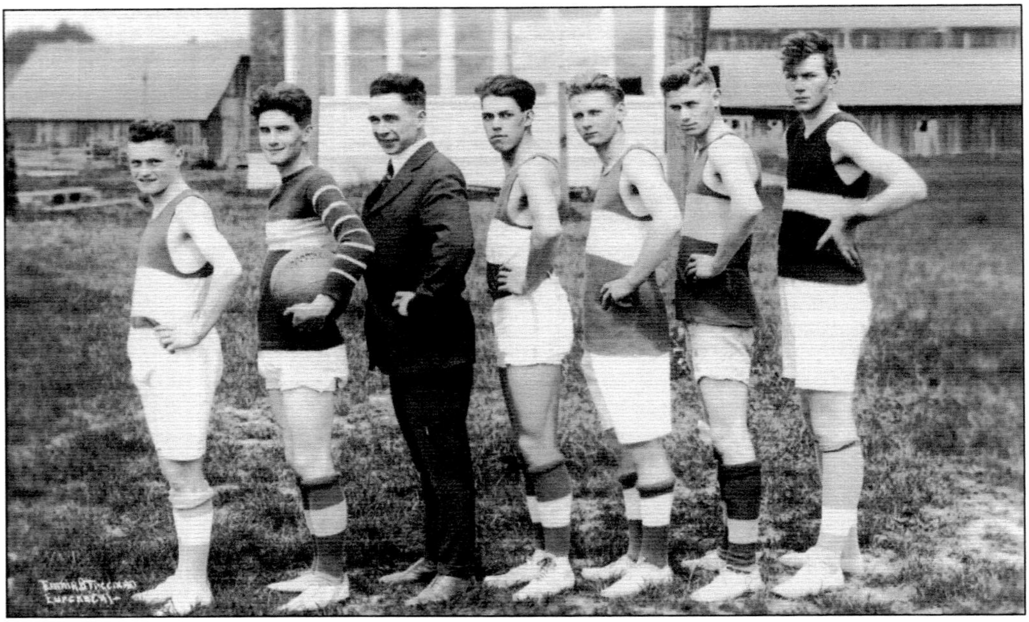

The 1918 Fortuna High boys' basketball team, coached by Ray Goble, did not fare as well as the girls' team. The writers of the yearbook felt that "although the Boy's squad did not bring any points for the County Championship Banner . . . hard luck, in the line of fouls and referees . . . was the cause of the defeat. The individual playing and teamwork was recognized by the other schools of the county."

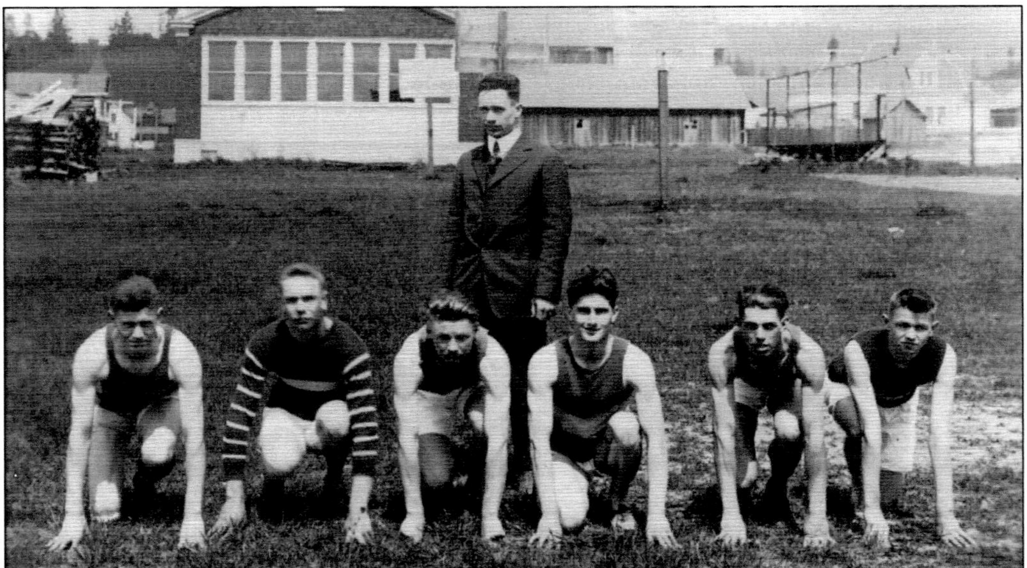

Ray Goble also coached Fortuna High's track team in 1918. An annual track meet was held at Ferndale, where Starks of Fortuna set a county record for the mile at 4.56 minutes. Edmund Starks, Paul Boren, and Harry Hanson were the point winners for Fortuna. This was the first time that all four of the county's high schools—Ferndale, Eureka, Arcata, and Fortuna—participated in the event.

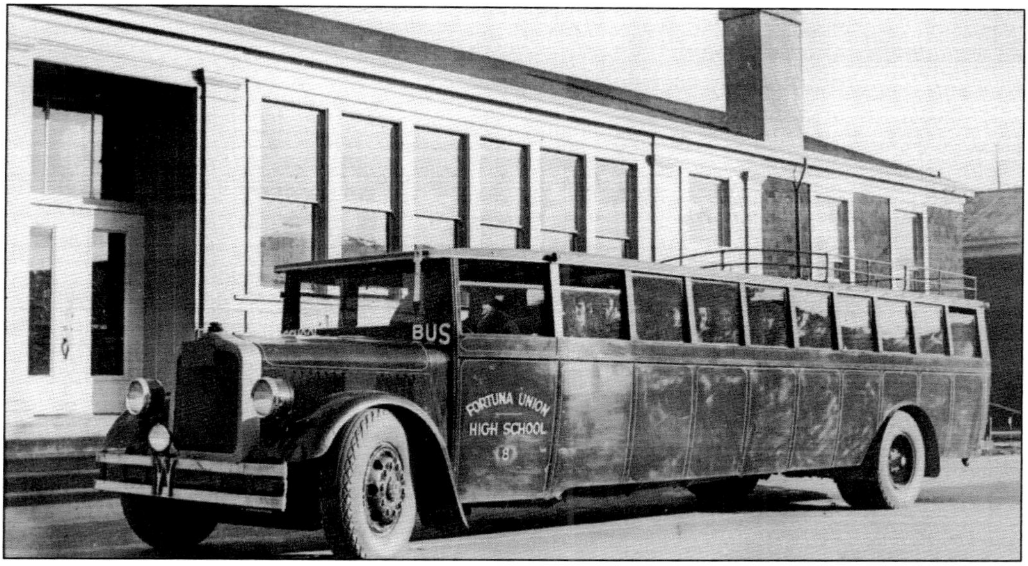

This 1930s school bus, photographed in front of Fortuna High, provides a glimpse of students' faces in the windows. The all-metal construction of the bus was a safety invention incorporated during the 1930s. Prior to this, the wooden frames used would splinter and cause injuries during crashes.

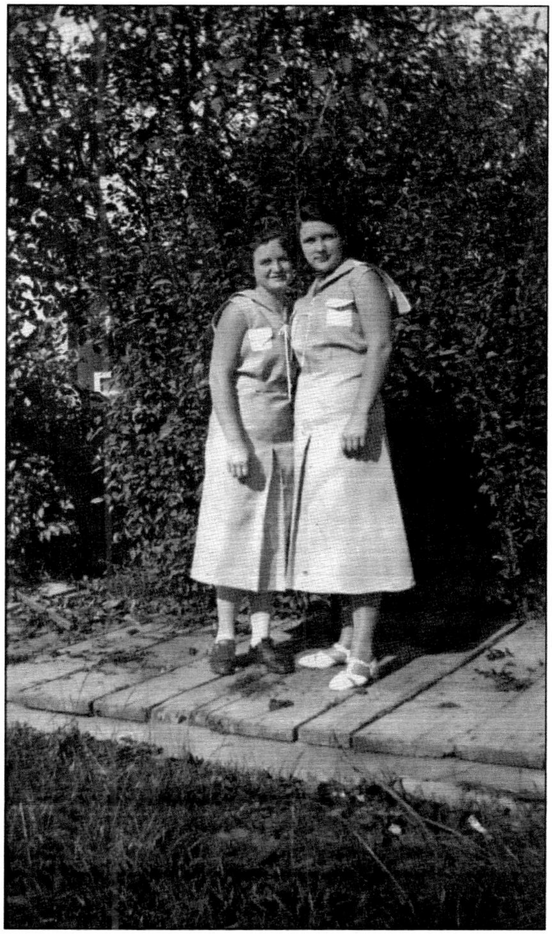

During the 1930s, girls who attended Fortuna High were required to wear blue uniforms with white pockets. Pictured in 1933 are Effie (left) and Elva Patton. They were en route to Eureka to participate in the National Recovery Administration's parade on November 11, 1933. The *Megaphone* reported that 400 Fortuna High students marched in the parade. (Courtesy of Marguerita Nichols.)

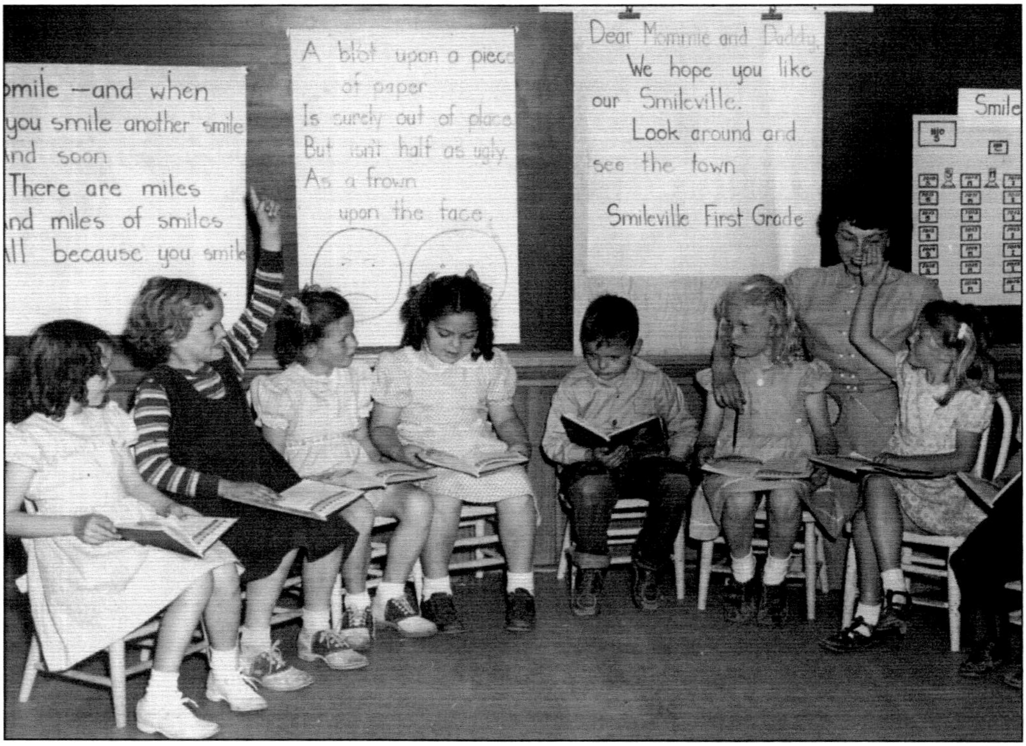

Pictured is Helen Friedenbach's first grade classroom in the 1950s. Friedenbach attended local schools and returned to serve as a teacher, following in the footsteps of her aunt Anna Friedenbach, who became a Fortuna Grammar School teacher in 1904. In 1920, the *Humboldt Beacon* praised Anna Friedenbach as a dedicated teacher who gave her students a "good start along the path to knowledge and citizenship."

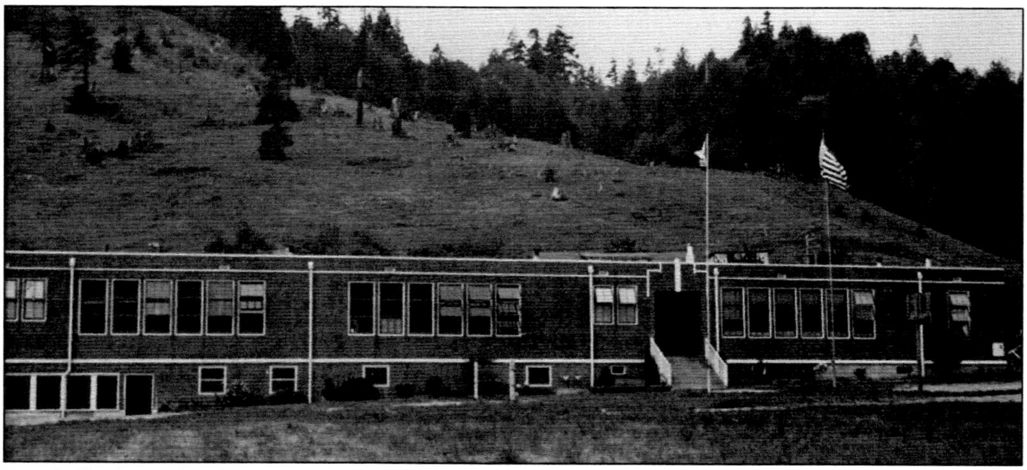

Rio Dell's first school was constructed in 1874. This building is the third to serve Rio Dell. It was located near the present-day Rio Dell City Hall. It was insulated with redwood bark, which was used for its fire-retardant qualities. During the 1950s, the first story of this building was moved to the school's current location, serving as the main wing. (Courtesy of Humboldt County Office of Education.)

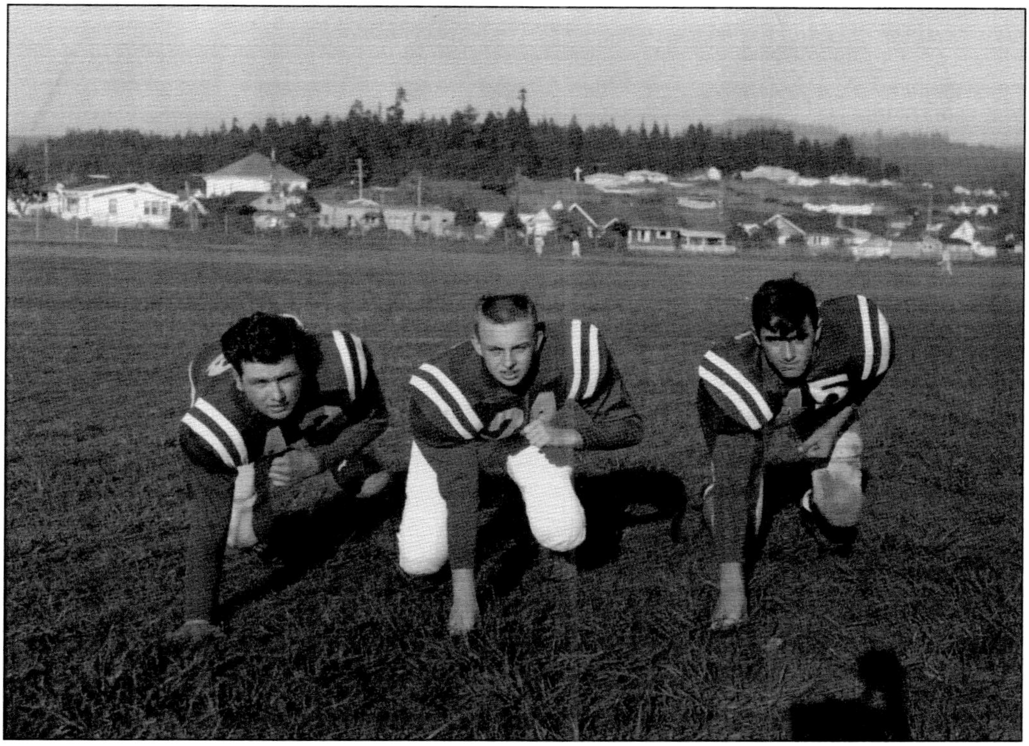

Today, the Fortuna High Huskies and football are closely identified. However, from 1929 to 1945, no football was played at Fortuna High. A player was killed during a game in 1928, and the following year, the student body voted to have golf replace football as the fall sport. Husky football was reinstated as the fall sport in 1945. Pictured from left to right are 1957 football players Dewey Davis, Jim Munz, and Dick Schwartz.

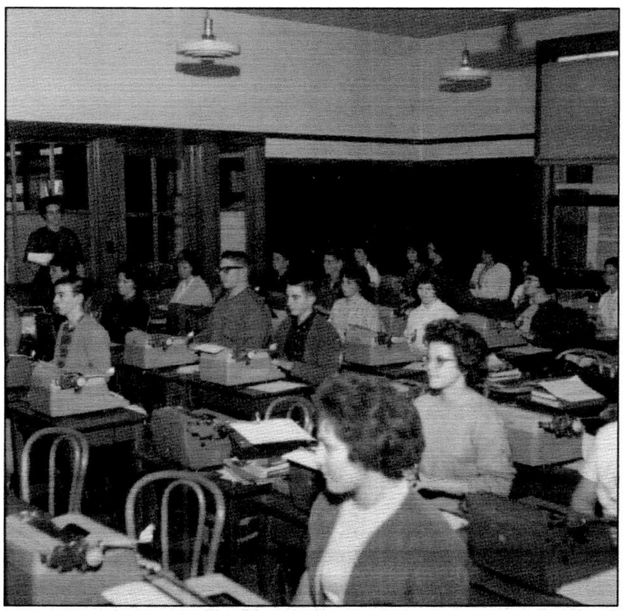

By the 1960s, the Fortuna High School curriculum had expanded to include vocational classes. Typing was part of the business courses and helped prepare students for careers as secretaries. At this time, all the girls had to wear dresses or skirts to school, even to the football games.

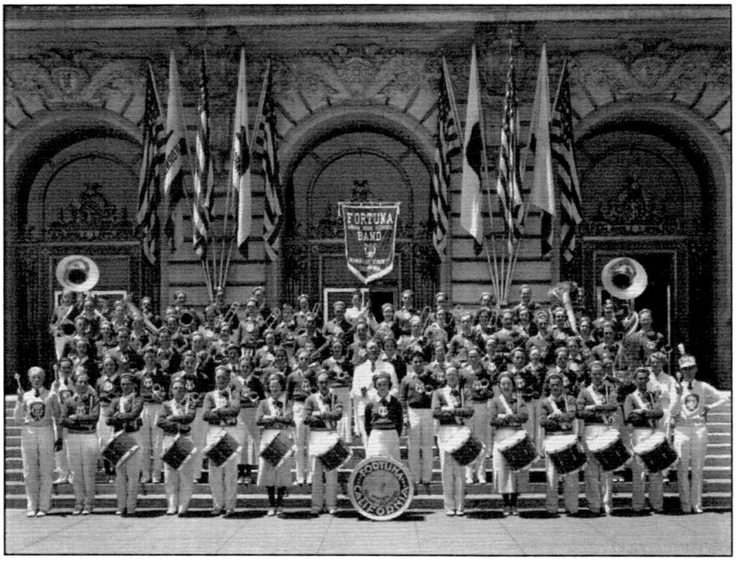

In 1937, the Fortuna High School marching band participated in the parade marking the opening of the Golden Gate Bridge. They won an award for their prowess. It was a long-remembered honor for the band to participate. The opening of the Golden Gate Bridge also signaled the connection of the northern coast with the San Francisco Bay area. Lloyd Anderson was the bandleader.

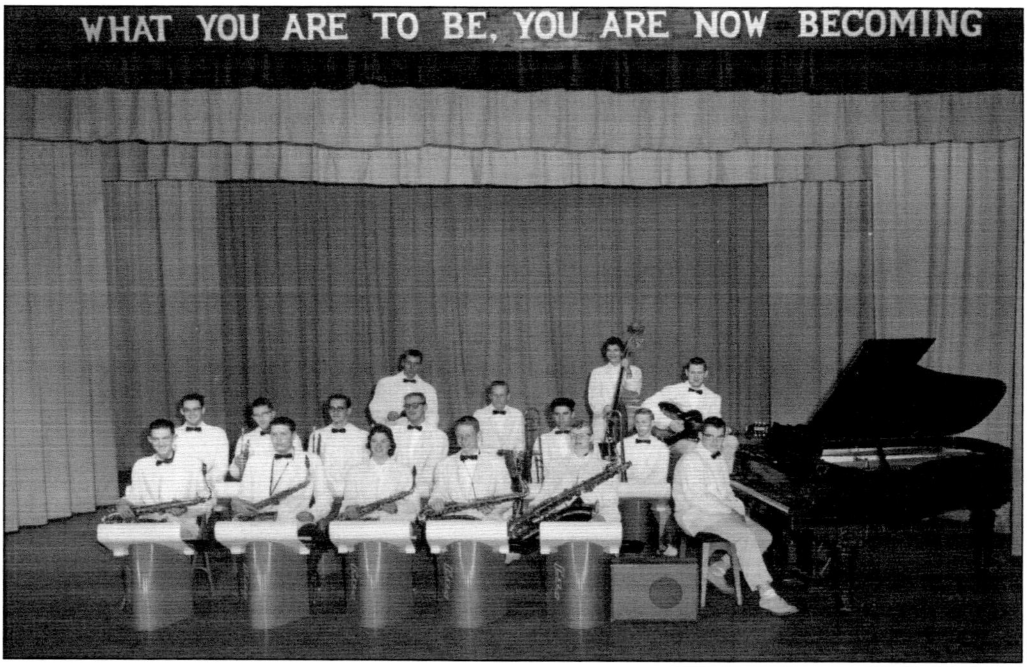

The Fortuna High Dance Band, formed in the 1940s, gave students experience playing at dances. According to the 1955 yearbook, the band "was in great demand, [playing] music in the style of Glenn Miller, Woody Herman, Les Brown, Benny Goodman, and Tommy Dorsey." "What you are to be, you are now becoming," included in a speech given to students by economist Cameron Beck, became the school motto. A senior class donated the sign above the stage.

Eight

Celebrations and Recreation

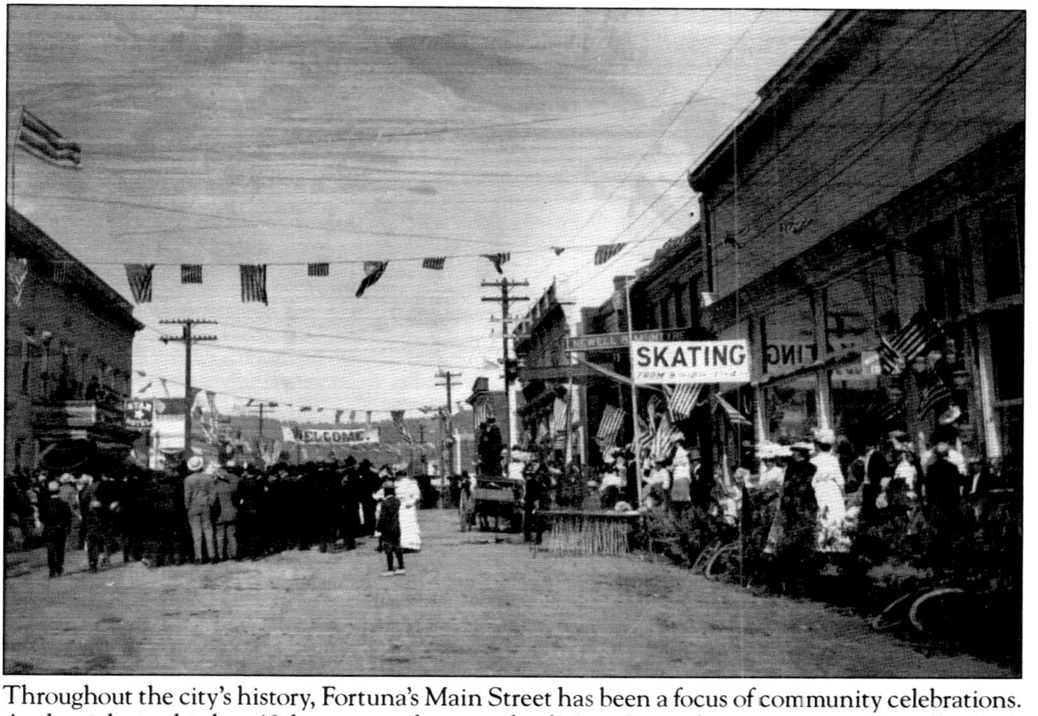

Throughout the city's history, Fortuna's Main Street has been a focus of community celebrations. At the right in this late-19th-century photograph of Main Street festivities is Hunt's Hall, which was built by Wilson Hunt as a skating rink in 1886. The *Eel River Valley Advance* reported in 1896, "when the love for that class of amusement waned, it was converted into a hall for theatrical, concert, and dancing purposes."

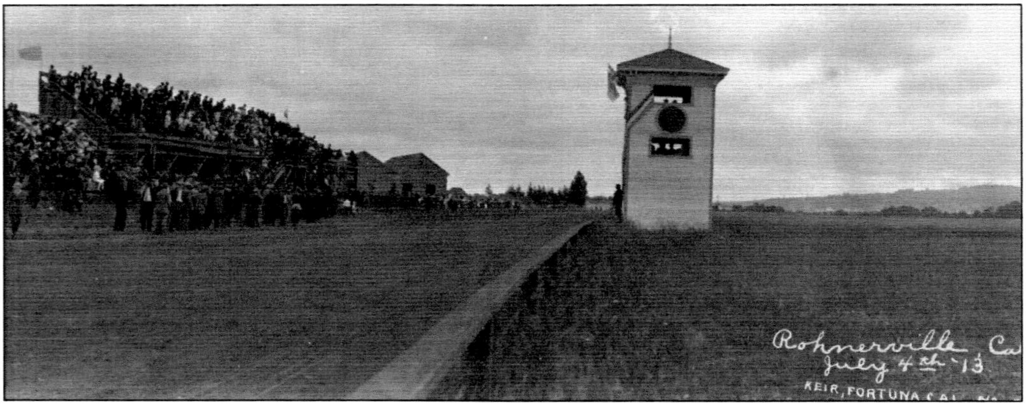

Rohnerville Racetrack was built in 1866, and from the 1860s until 1896 it hosted the county fair. Traces of the long-vanished racetrack can still be seen, as the curve in Kenmar Road follows a corner of the old fairgrounds. Two water towers were used to keep down the dust on the mile-long oval racetrack. Sulky buggy races, such as the one pictured, were the biggest events of the fair. They ran for three heats, the winner having the best times of two heats. The racetrack was operated by the Eel River Jockey Club, whose members included some of the community's leading businessmen. Shown below with racehorse Sam Adams are, from left to right, Charles Perrott (seated), Will East, Kimball Hatch, and Ed Dougherty. The man holding the horse's bridle is unidentified.

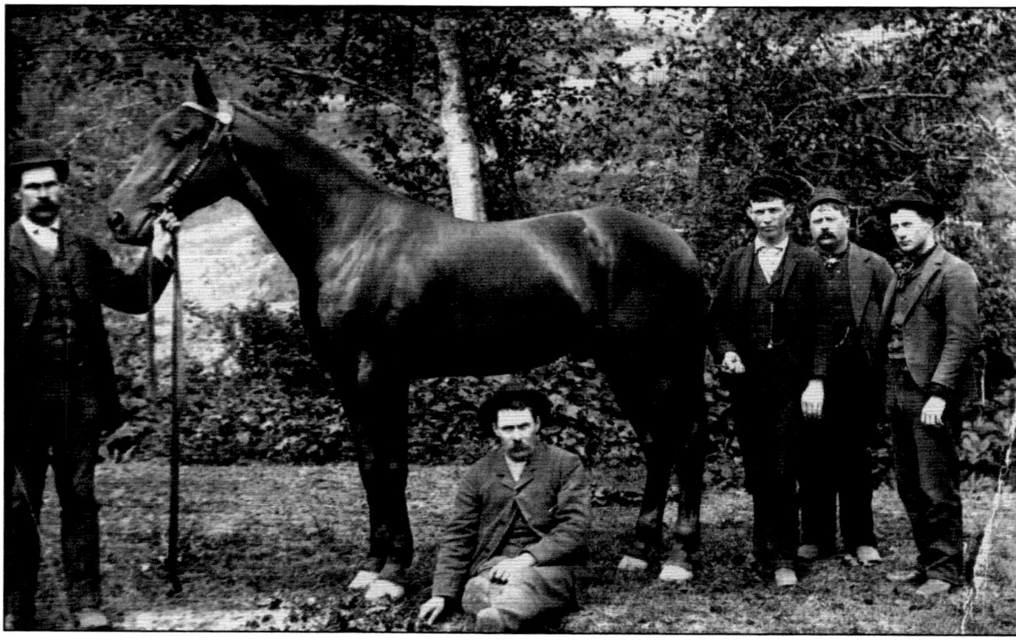

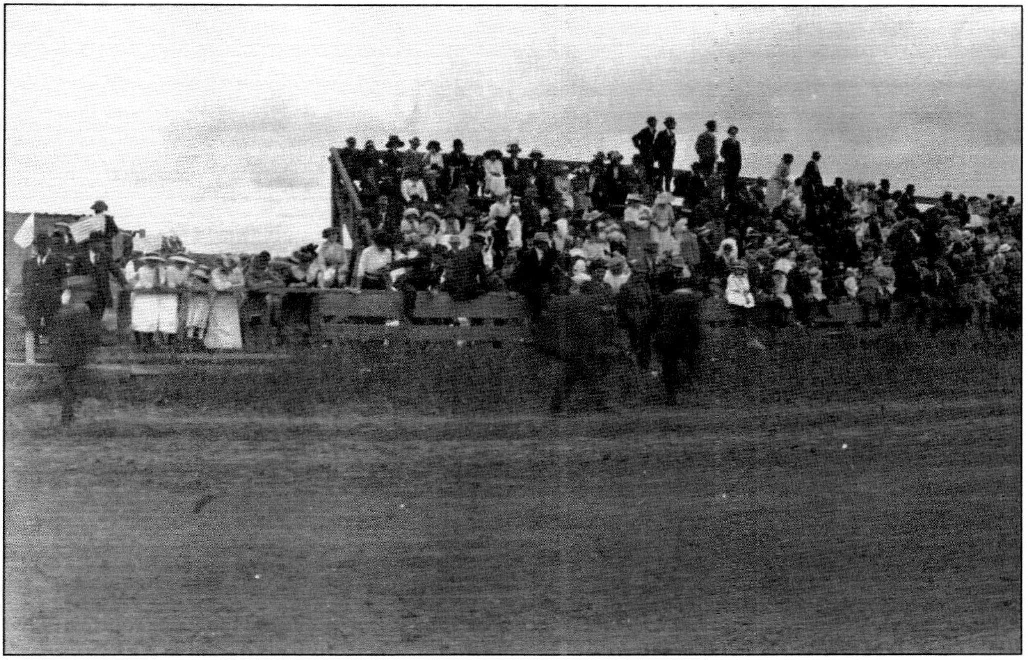

As forms of transportation evolved, Rohnerville Racetrack kept up with the times. On July 4, 1914, a particularly celebrated contest at Rohnerville pitted Ernest Hagman's roadster against Frank Brelle's Model T. The 10-mile race ended with Frank Brelle crossing the finish line just ahead of his opponent, despite the fact that Brelle had to change a tire during the race. Another view of the Rohnerville Racetrack shows a barnstorming event, decades before the creation of Rohnerville Airport. Beginning in the 1920s, two decades after the Humboldt County Fair moved to neighboring Ferndale, the racetrack and fairground structures were dismantled.

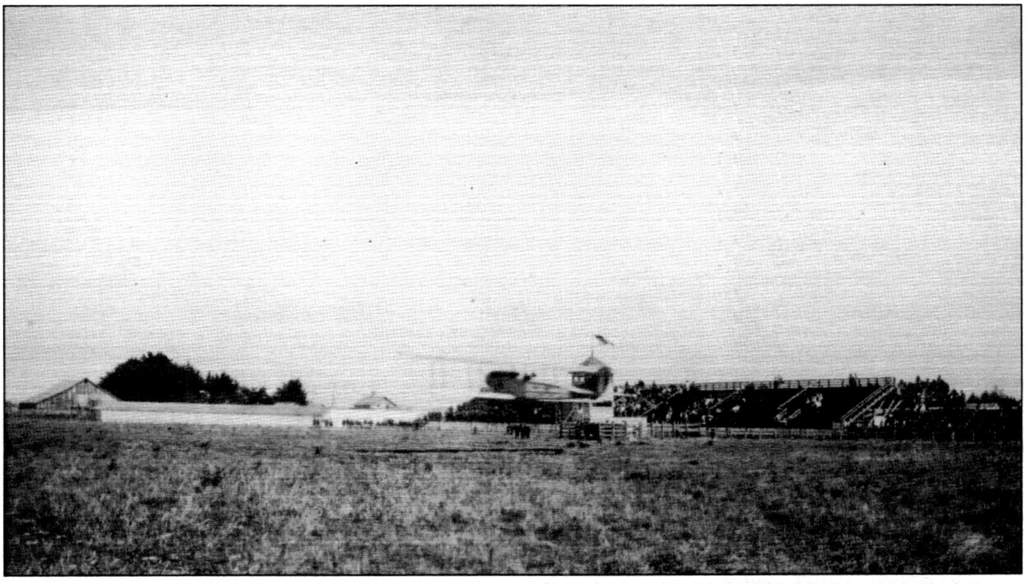

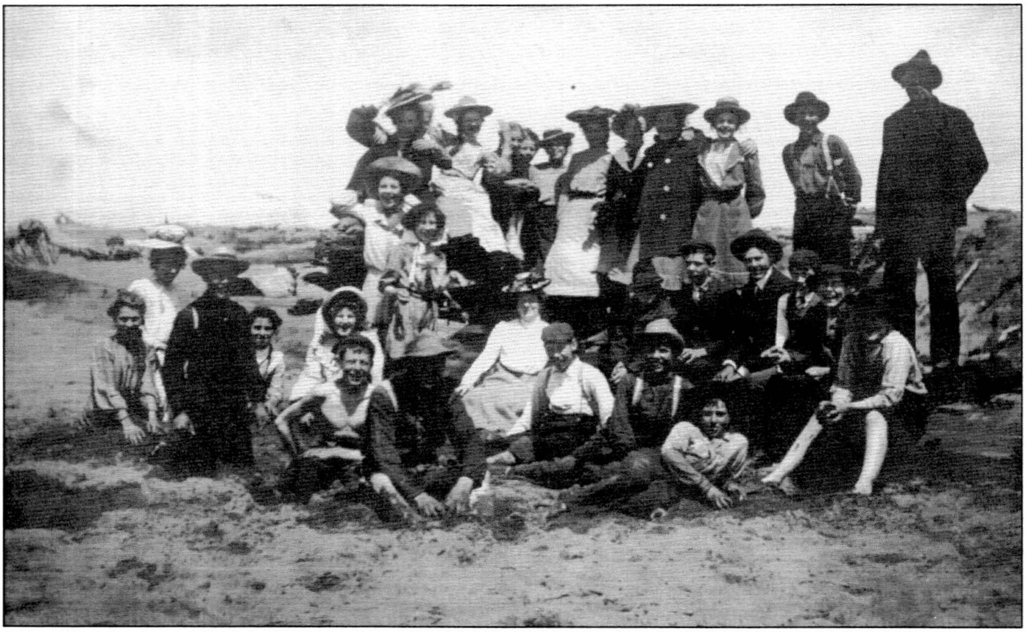

Despite Fortuna's sheltered valley location, which avoids many of Humboldt's worst coastal fogs, the nearest beaches are only about 10 miles away. Mrs. Calderwood's class at Fortuna High took this outing to Table Bluff Beach on May 27, 1904. Calderwood is seated at the center of the picture, and Mr. Heath, who drove the wagon to the picnic, is standing at the right.

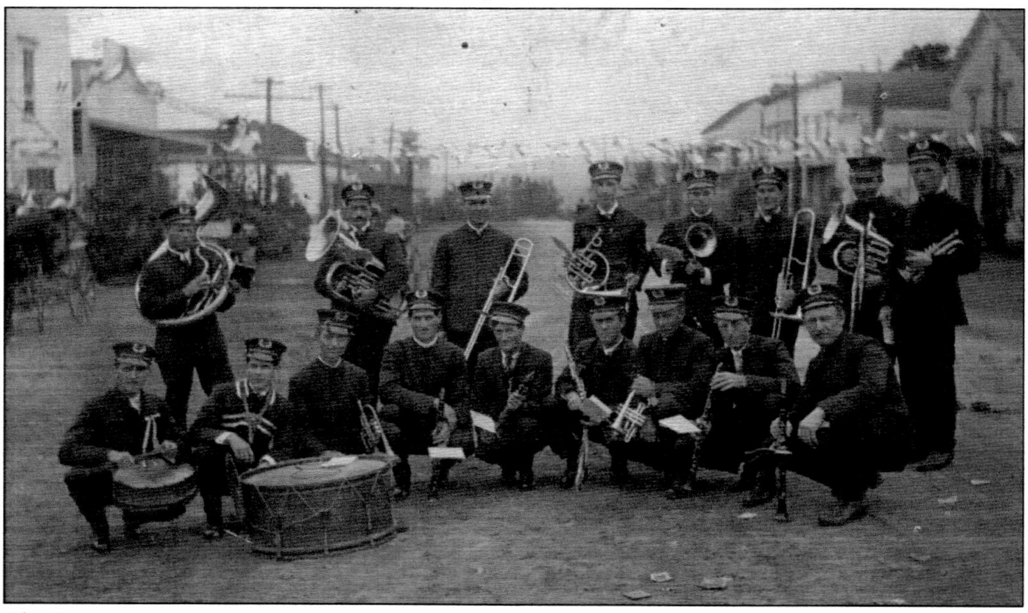

The Fortuna Brass Band posed for this portrait in Rohnerville's main street around 1910. Rohnerville also had its own town band, which played for events like the opening day of the races. On May 30, 1896, the *Eel River Valley Advance* wrote that Fortuna's brass band had "13 pieces" and that it did not "allow itself to be out-played or out-winded by any other aggregation of musical caterers in Humboldt County."

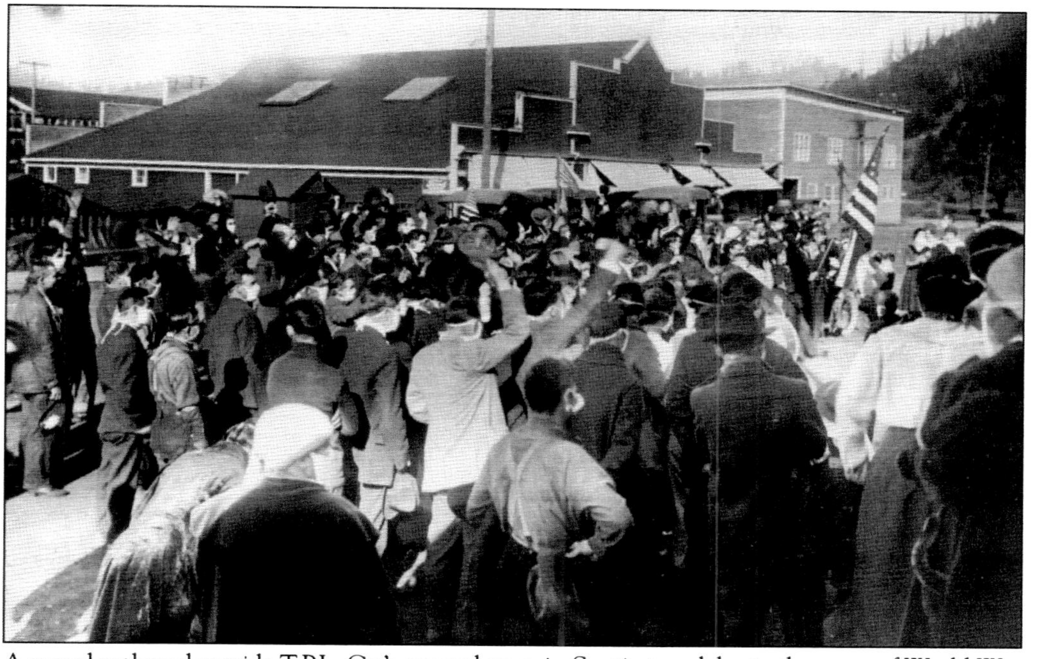

A crowd gathered outside T.P.L. Co.'s general store in Scotia to celebrate the news of World War I's end on November 11, 1918. The masks were an attempt to slow the spread of the Spanish influenza epidemic. Fortuna, Scotia, and the other Eel River Valley towns were badly hit by the disease. The only two Fortuna men to die during their World War I service were felled not in combat but by this illness.

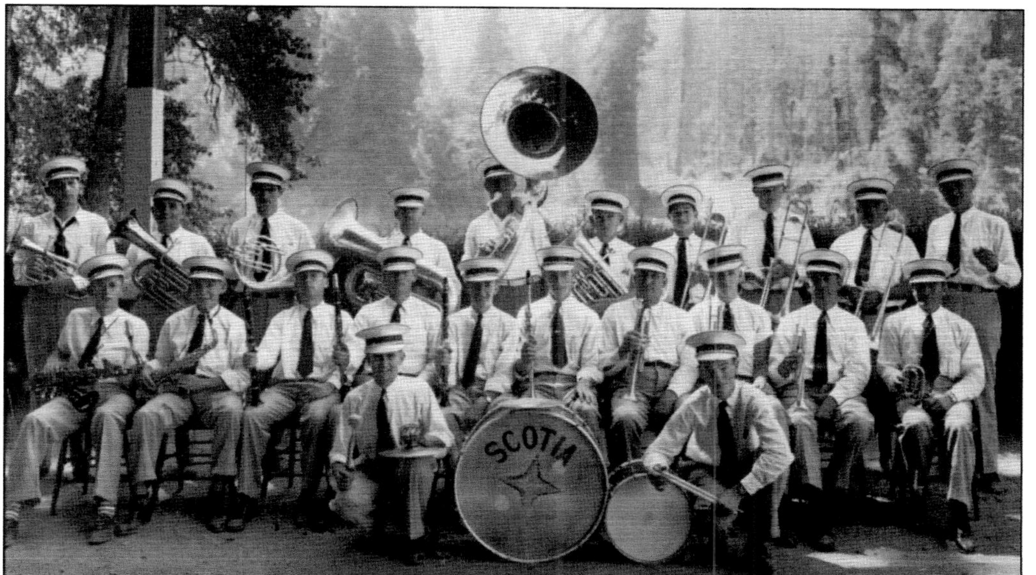

The Scotia Band was formed in 1935 to play concerts at T.P.L. Co.'s Winema Theater. More than 75 years later, the hometown band continues to thrive. This group photograph was taken in 1936. At the center with the tuba is early bandleader Lloyd Anderson, who was the Fortuna Union High School band director for many years and founder of the Fortuna Music Mart.

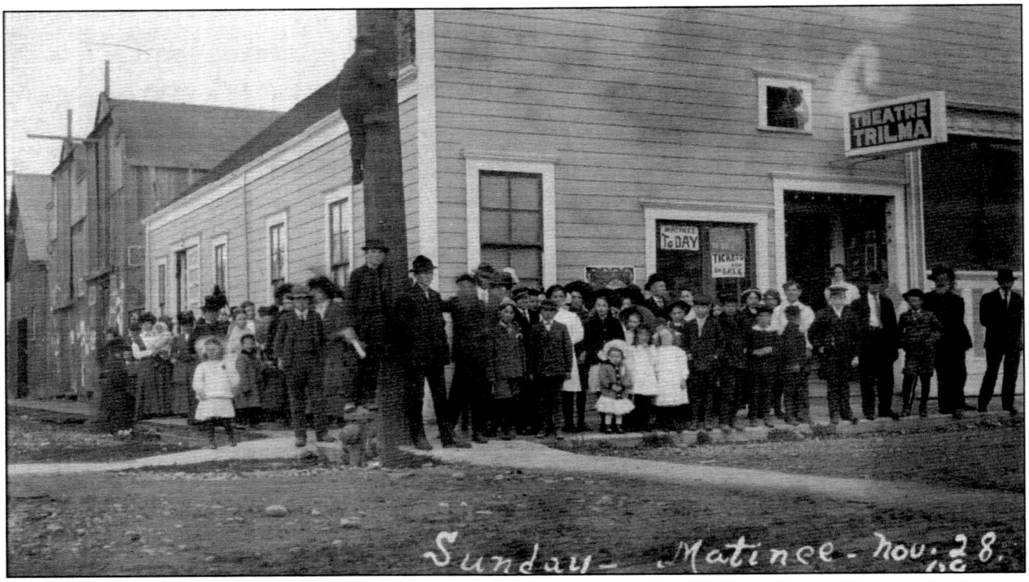

Theatre Trilma at Tenth and Main Streets was in business by 1909 and was Fortuna's cinema until 1920. It was named after a daughter of the theater's owners. In 1913, tickets were 15¢ for adults and 10¢ for children; on Sundays, matinees were 10¢ and 5¢. The *Humboldt Beacon* advised, "When you come to Fortuna Sundays, bring the kiddies—let them enjoy an hour at the Trilma. Remember you were once a kid!"

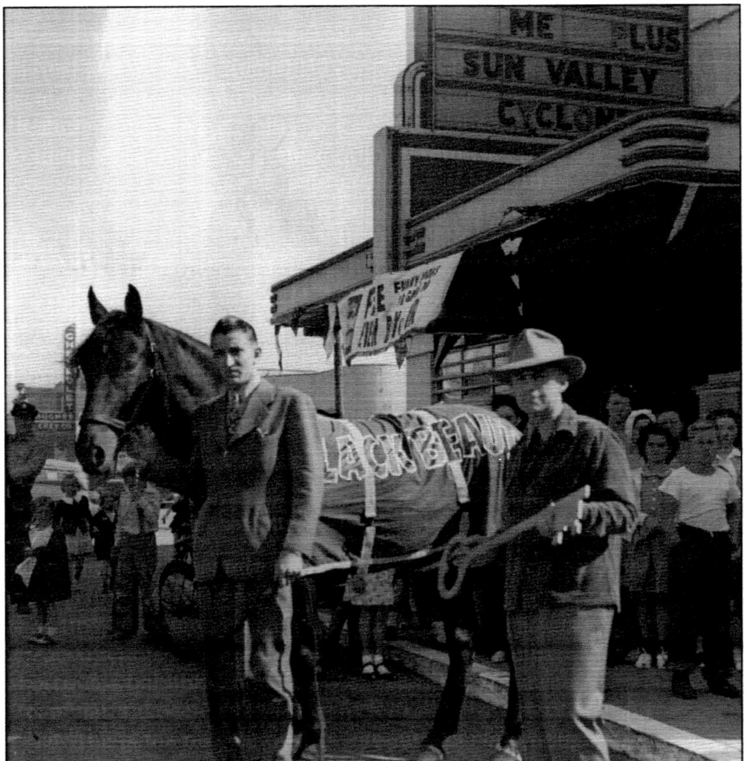

Fortuna Theater manager Ted Roberts and Mayor Clarence Johanson posed with equine star Black Beauty while advertising the 1946 film and also presenting the horse with a ceremonial key to the city. This second Fortuna Theater near Thirteenth and Main Streets was built in 1938, replacing its predecessor, which opened at the same location in 1920. Other events at the cinema under the management of Roberts included fashion shows, a model airplane contest, a Thanksgiving turkey giveaway, and a visit by a traveling hypnotist.

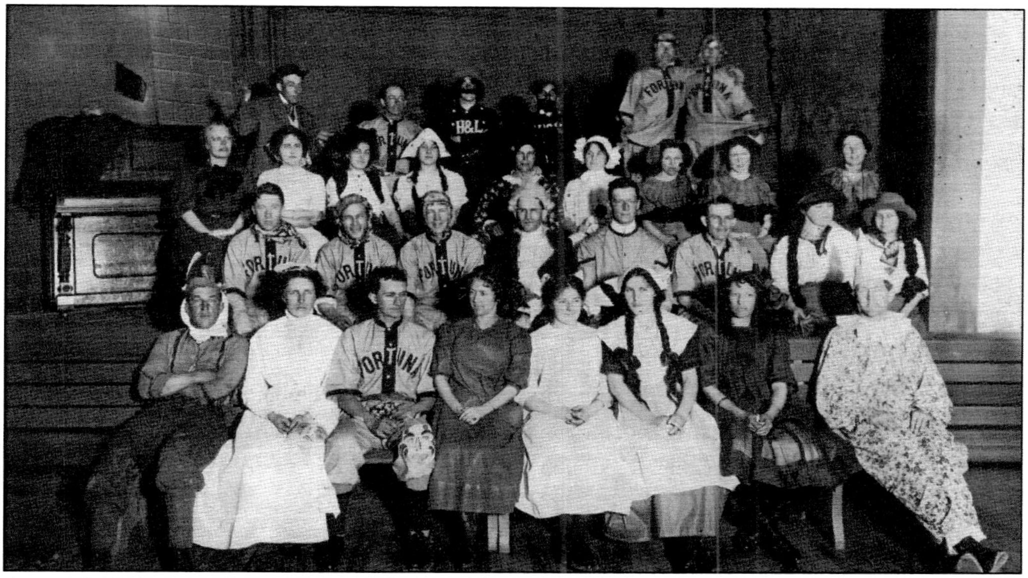

Around 1910, scarcely an issue of the weekly *Humboldt Beacon* went by without announcing masked balls held by one or more clubs. One of The Single Lantern Club's masquerade parties is pictured here. In December 1910, the *Humboldt Beacon* described another event sponsored by this club as including Wallace and Stella McIntyre as Santa Claus and Christmas, Maud Krause as a Snowball, and druggist Reginald Bowman "arrayed in the most extreme style of hobble skirt and a gigantic merry widow hat." (Courtesy of FVFD.)

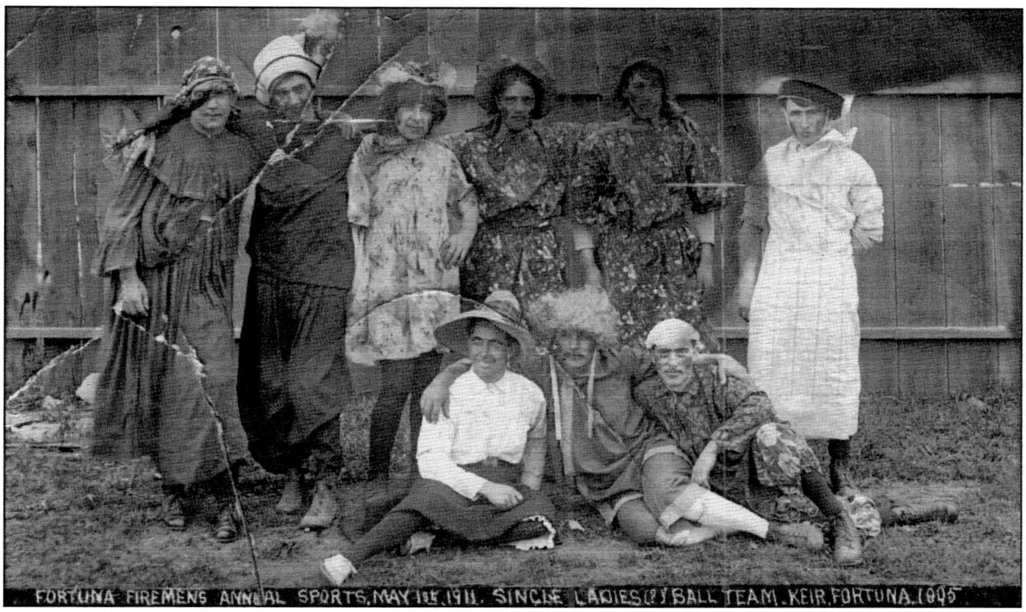

The FVFD's Single Ladies' ball team was a good-natured spoof of Fortuna's real Single Ladies' baseball team, which played against the Married Ladies in 1910 and 1911. The FVFD team, according to the *Humboldt Beacon*, "turned out to be young men dressed to represent young ladies of the town. [Guy] Brown's attempts to play ball, while handicapped with a hobble skirt, were more than laughable. The whole five innings were a scream." (Courtesy of FVFD.)

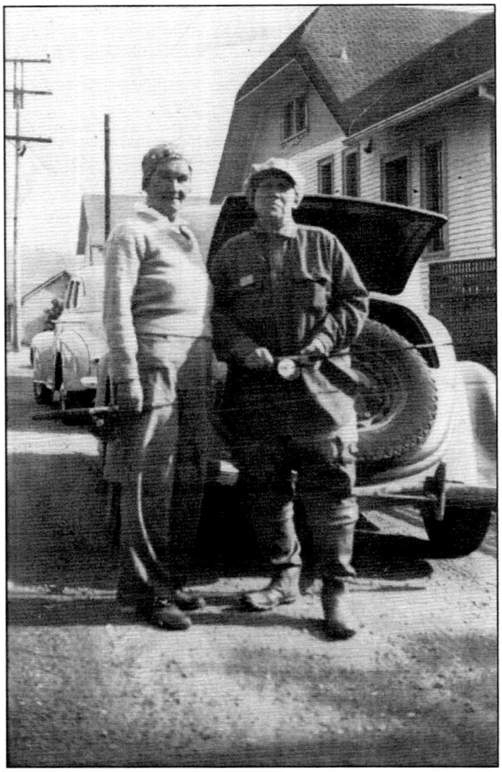

Oma Brown (left) and Nora Wise posed with their fishing gear in November 1941. Eel River fishing has been a favorite recreation for generations of Fortunans and a focus of Humboldt County tourism. An advertisement by the Humboldt Promotion Committee in 1914 promised, "the steelhead of Eel River will give you the greatest sport on the American Continent."

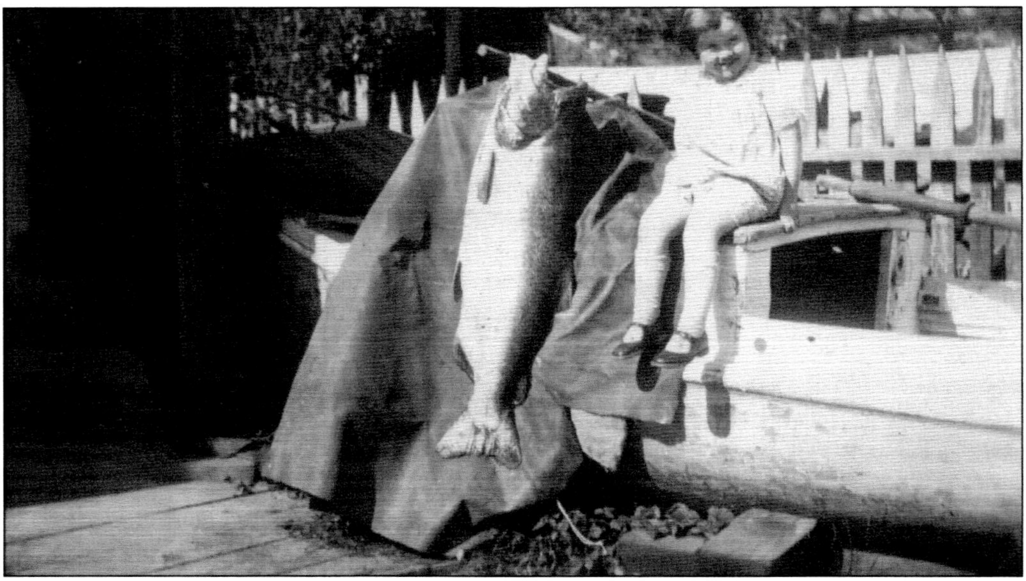

Oma Brown's granddaughter Elsie Mae Adams proudly posed beside part of her grandmother's catch. In the caption for this photograph in her album, she wrote, "I love this picture. Good Eel River salmon, caught by Oma Brown. Boat was a[n] Indian dugout and built at Crab Camp, Loleta." Oma Brown was an active sportswoman for most of her life. In 1910, she was captain of the Married Ladies baseball team.

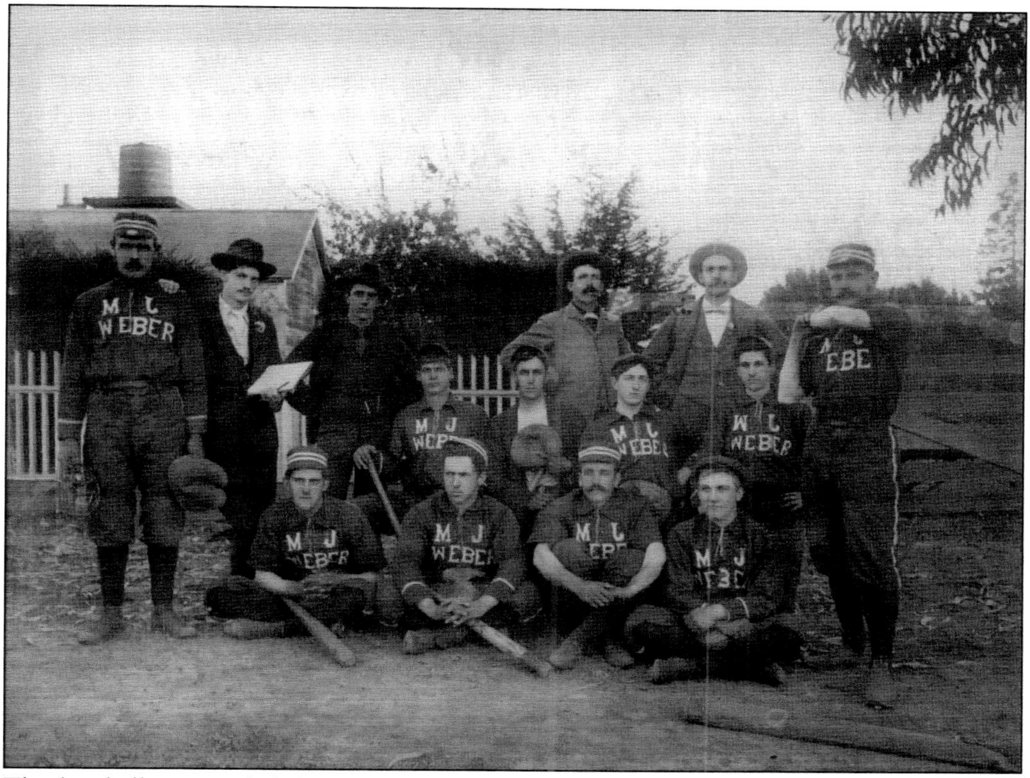

This baseball team included Franklin E. Rohner, seated at left, the youngest son of the pioneer Rohner family. M.J. Weber, the team's sponsor, was a member of another prominent local family. There was a Weber's Saloon in Rohnerville, and Martin N. Weber had been one of Henry's Rohner's partners in the Springville Mill. Young Franklin Rohner also played second cornet in the town band.

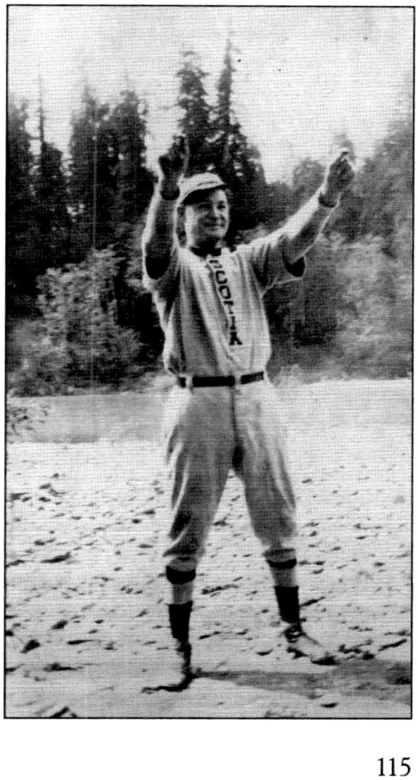

The Humboldt County baseball league included teams from Arcata, Blue Lake, Eureka, Ferndale, Fortuna, and Scotia. A 1910 article in the *Humboldt Beacon* reported that a Fortuna vs. Scotia game in Fortuna would be "called early so that the Scotia team can take the evening train for home" and so that "the game may be over before sun gets far enough in the west to hamper the fielders in their work."

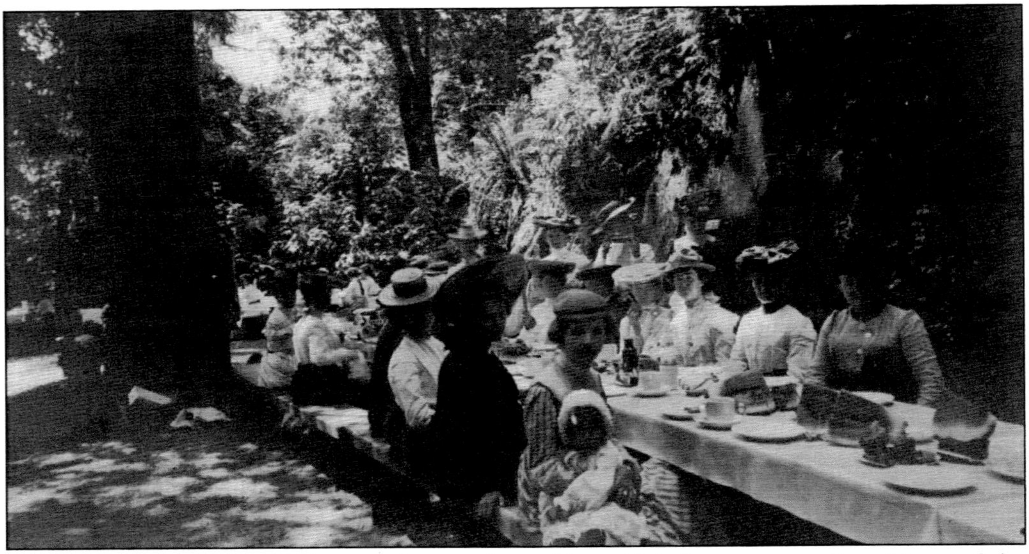

Canyon Park, near Rio Dell, was advertised as a "beautiful pleasure resort" and "one of the prettiest pleasure spots in northern California" when its owner Jacob Jacobsen of Metropolitan put it up for sale in 1913. It was a popular picnic destination for people from local communities. The entrance to the park was through a narrow cleft in the fern-covered rocks. (Courtesy of Clarke Historical Museum.)

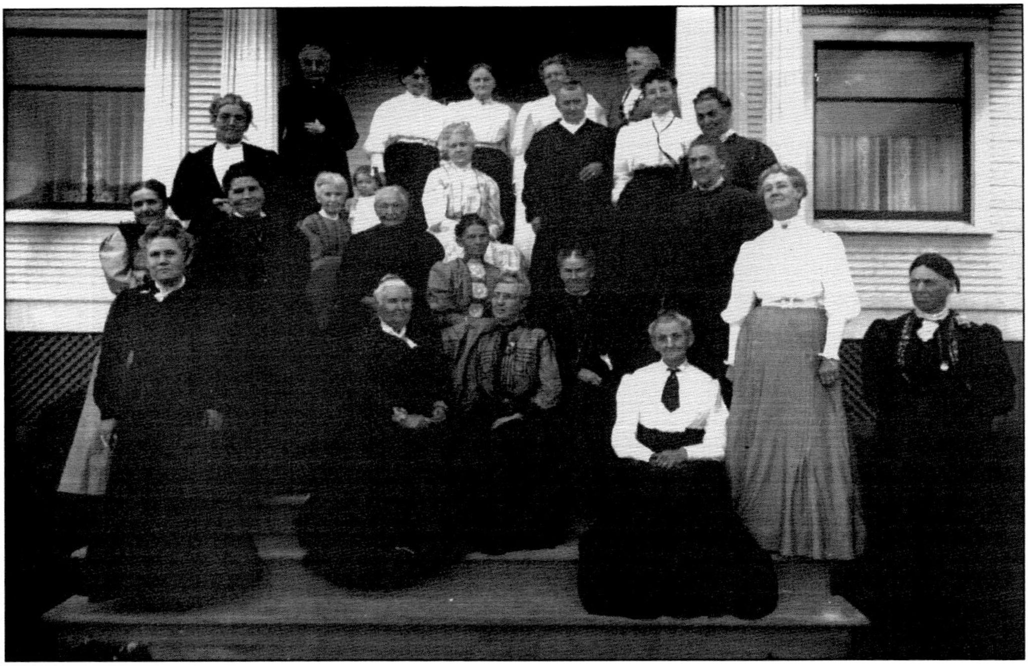

In this photograph are members of one of Fortuna's many early-20th-century women's clubs. These included the Civic Club, the Grandmothers Club (a group of 16 women who, according to the *Humboldt Beacon*, had "experienced the joys of holding in their arms their children's children and answering to the name Grandma"), and the Monday Club, a literary study group formed in 1906. Mary Rohner is seated near the center, wearing a dark dress and long necklace.

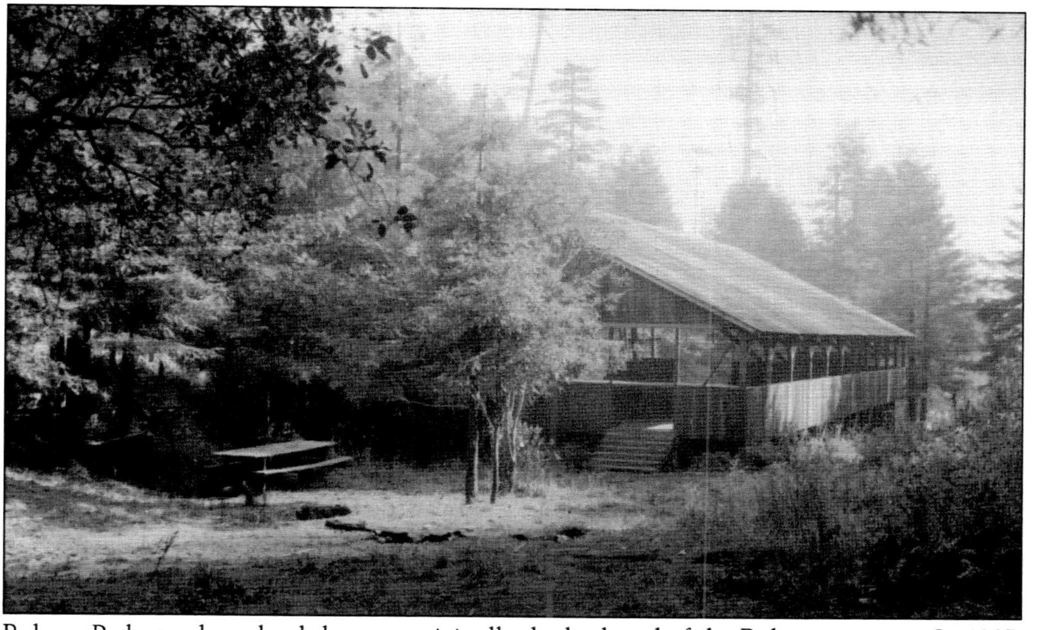

Rohner Park stands on land that was originally the backyard of the Rohner mansion. In 1907, Mary Rohner sold 20 acres to the city for $1,000, and the park expanded over the decades with further sales and gifts by the family. The Rohner Park pavilion, pictured, was the scene of dances, picnics, and other gatherings until it burned in the 1920s.

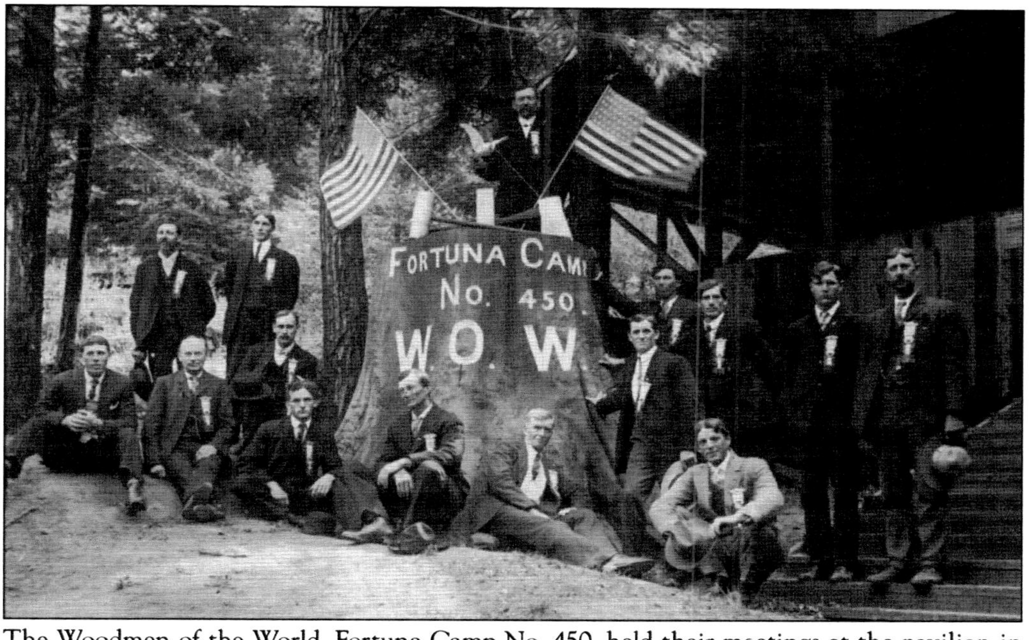

The Woodmen of the World, Fortuna Camp No. 450, held their meetings at the pavilion in Rohner Park. The *Humboldt Beacon* wrote in 1913 that the order was "most peculiarly adapted for the needs of the working man or the man of limited income . . . it provides a life insurance at a low rate, and this helps to protect the home against want when the breadwinner of the family has been removed."

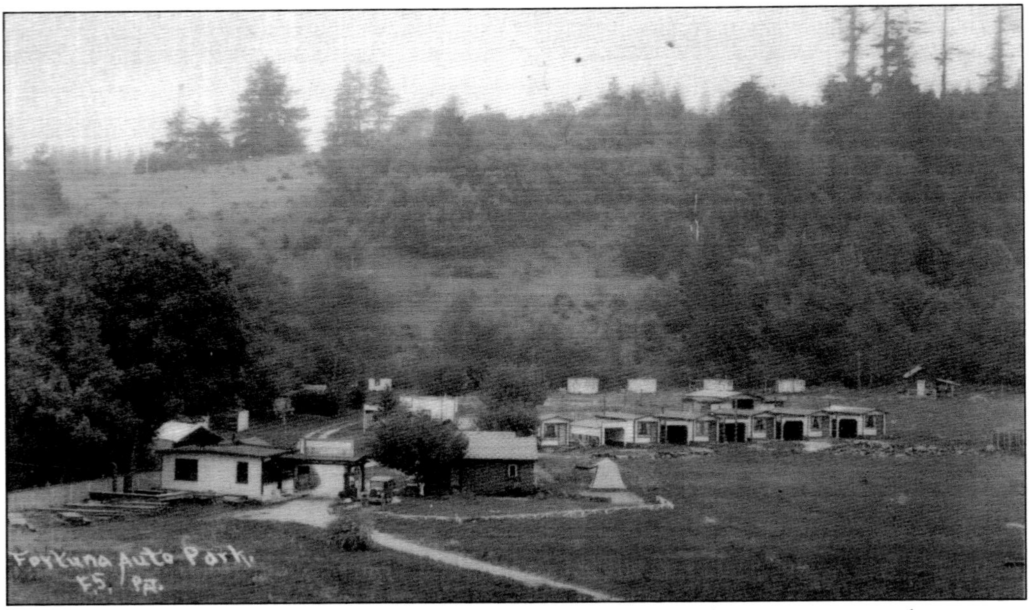

The auto park was the precursor to motels, coming into being in the 1920s to serve the growing numbers of automobile-based tourists. The eight-cabin Fortuna Auto Park was located in Rohner Park in the area that would later become the ball field. Each cabin included an attached car port. A tent in the foreground shows the rise of camping as a recreational hobby.

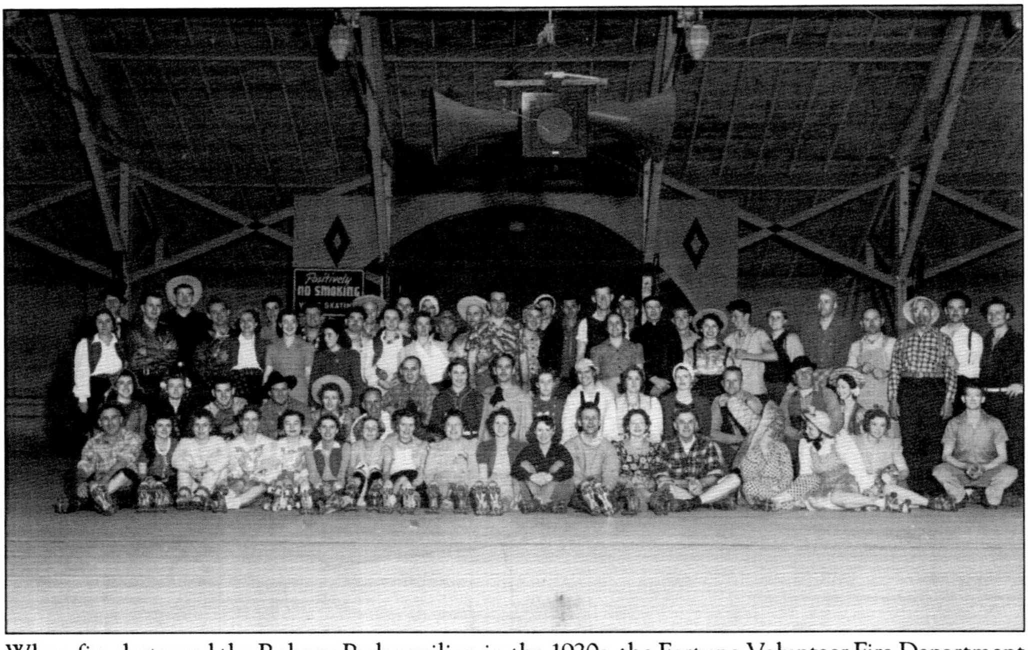

When fire destroyed the Rohner Park pavilion in the 1920s, the Fortuna Volunteer Fire Department formed a committee to raise funds and build a new pavilion. The Great Depression put construction of the Firemen's Pavilion on hold, but it was completed in 1934 with funding by the Works Progress Administration (WPA). The new pavilion's auditorium and ice rink became the venue for community get-togethers, including the skating masquerade party in this 1942 photograph.

WPA officials posed outside the new entrance to the Fortuna Rodeo Grounds in 1940 to mark the completion of upgrades to Rohner Park, which were jointly undertaken by the WPA and the City of Fortuna. In this photograph are, from left to right, William Brown, ? McCarthy, ? Woodruff, and William Lawson. The improvements included new softball and baseball diamonds and bleachers, a new grandstand, and reconstruction of much of the rodeo grounds.

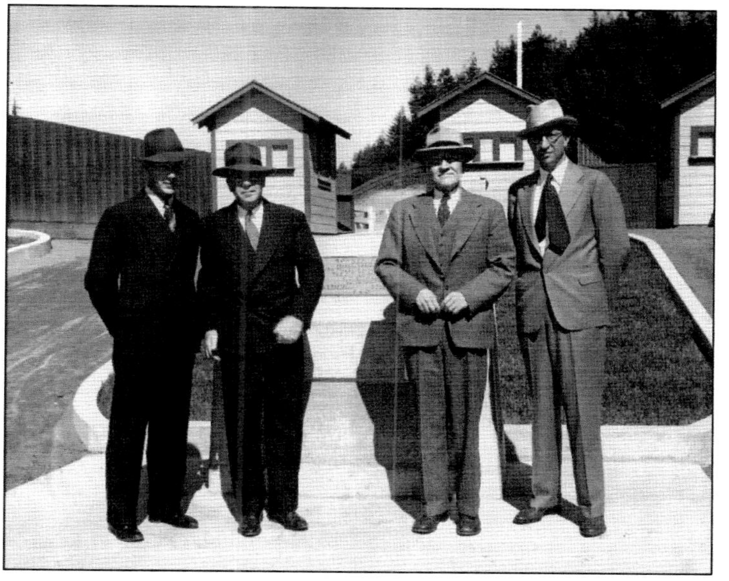

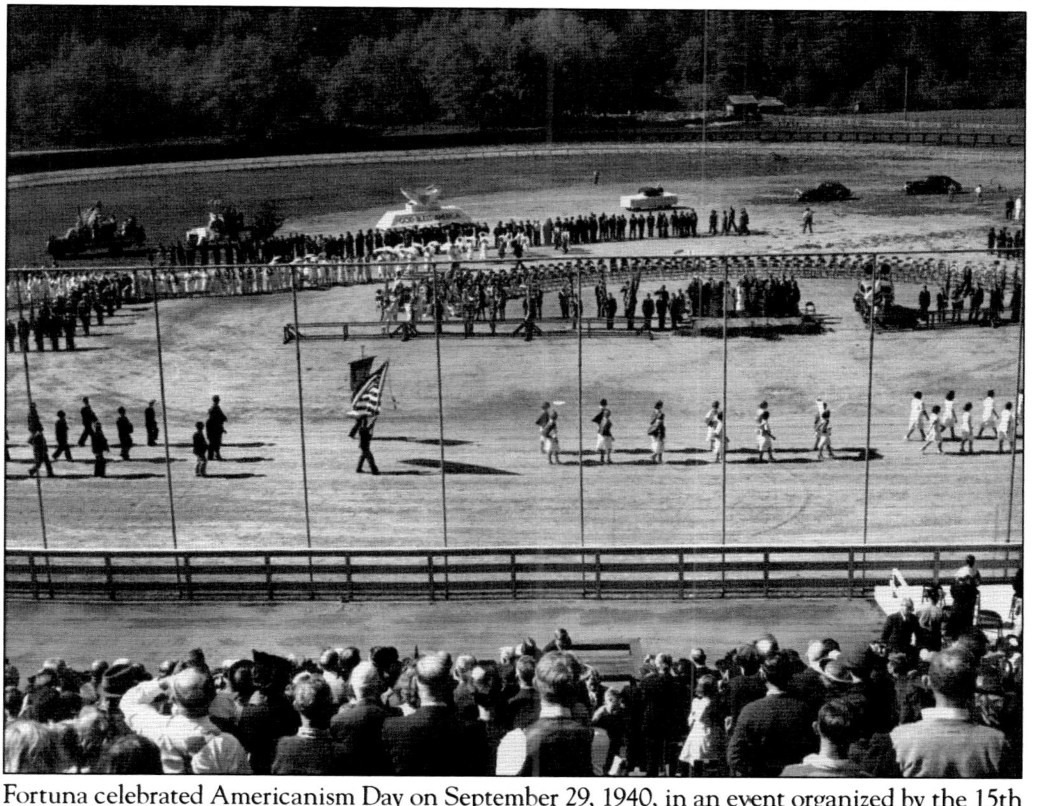

Fortuna celebrated Americanism Day on September 29, 1940, in an event organized by the 15th District of the Veterans of Foreign Wars (VFW). The event, held at the Rodeo Grounds, included speeches by VFW officers, WPA officials, and Father Gaffney of Fortuna's Catholic parish. There were performances by the Fortuna High School band and a cappella choir and the United Bands of Humboldt School Bands.

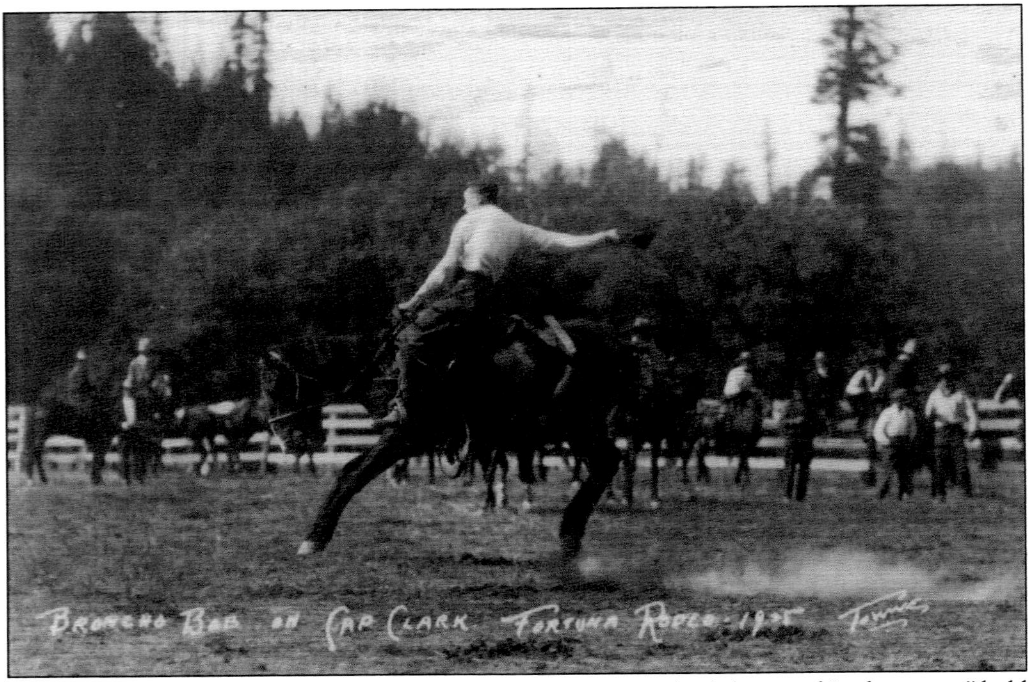

The Fortuna Rodeo traces its beginnings to a picnic, dance, and exhibition of "rodeo stunts" held at Rohner Park by the Humboldt County Cattlemen's Association in 1921. It became an annual event and was only skipped for four years during the Great Depression and the World War II years of 1942 to 1945. It is now a weeklong celebration for the entire community.

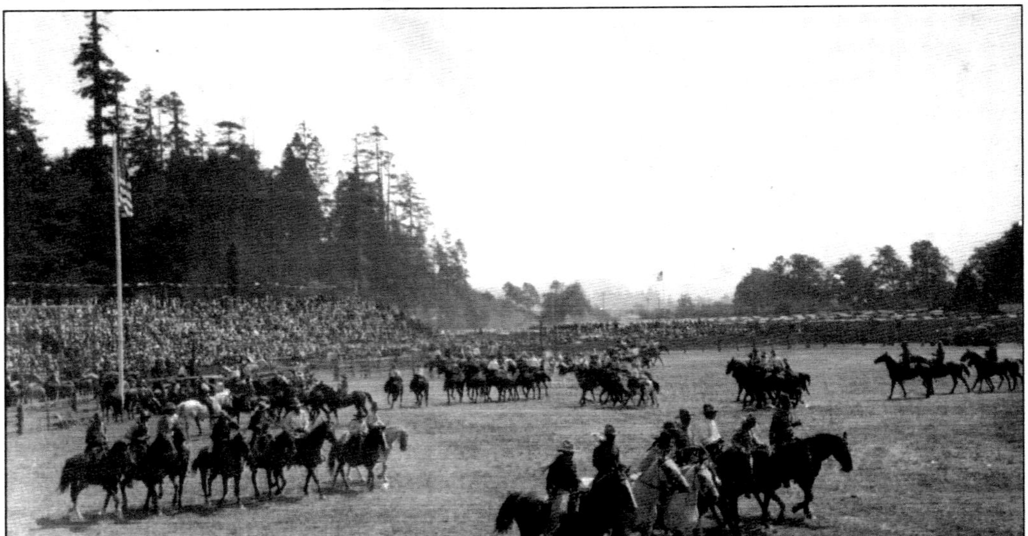

The program for the second annual Fortuna Rodeo in 1922 described the rodeo committee as "the men that put the hum in Humboldt." Among the many rodeo events that year were a Wild West Grand March from Fortuna to Rohner Park, a novelty horse race, a potato race on horses, continuous riding of wild cattle by Northern California cow punchers, a dance and chicken supper, and a musical race.

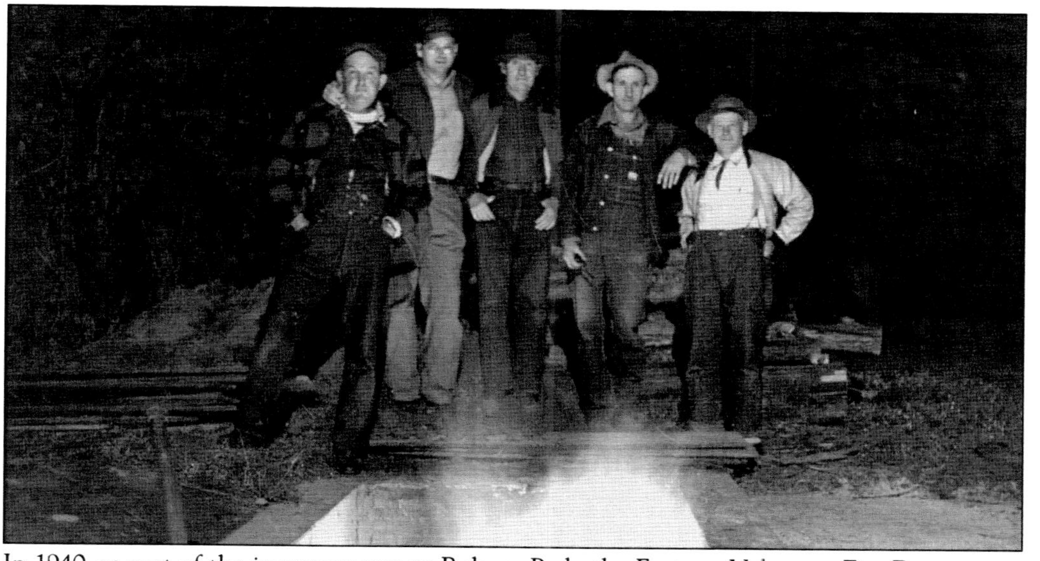

In 1940, as part of the improvements to Rohner Park, the Fortuna Volunteer Fire Department completed a barbecue pit, a cook shack, and an outdoor fireplace. An annual barbecue has become a staple of Fortuna's Rodeo Week. The barbecue pit crew for the 1949 rodeo were, from left to right, Charlie Conant, Delbert Maudlin, George Fields, Del Hansen, and Fred Hart.

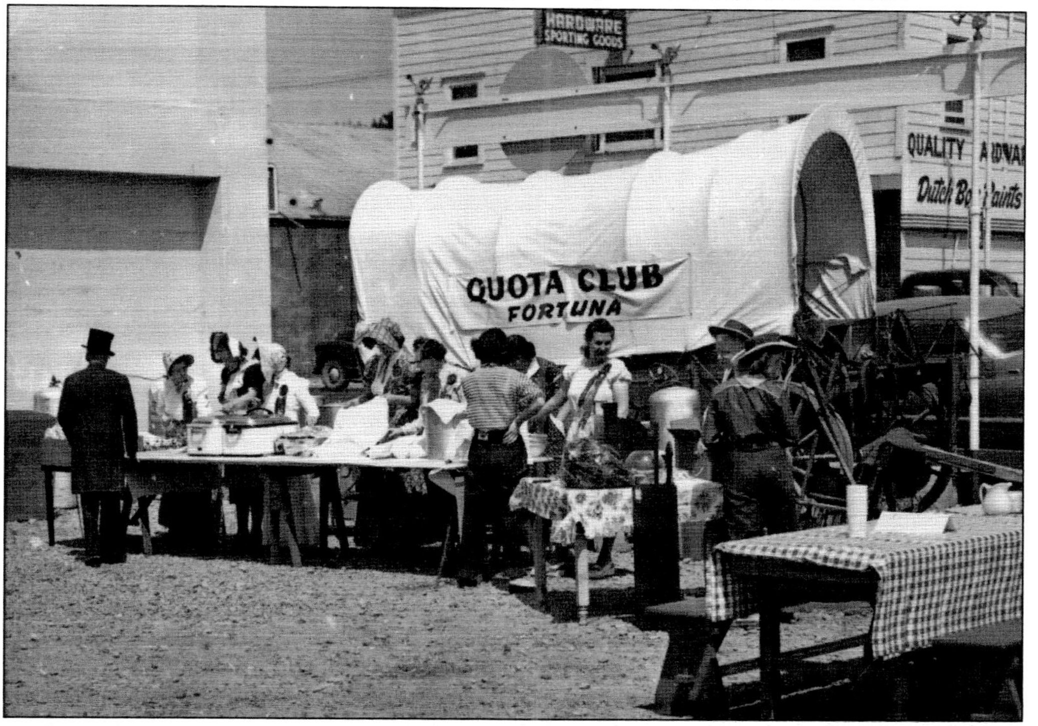

In the early 21st century, Rodeo Week activities include a chili cook-off, cast-iron cook-off, Kiwanis pancake breakfast (the successor to the long-running Fortuna Business and Professional Women's Rodeo Breakfast, which began in 1958), and a deep-pit barbecue on closing day. One such community event is seen in this 1950s shot of a chuckwagon picnic in downtown Fortuna.

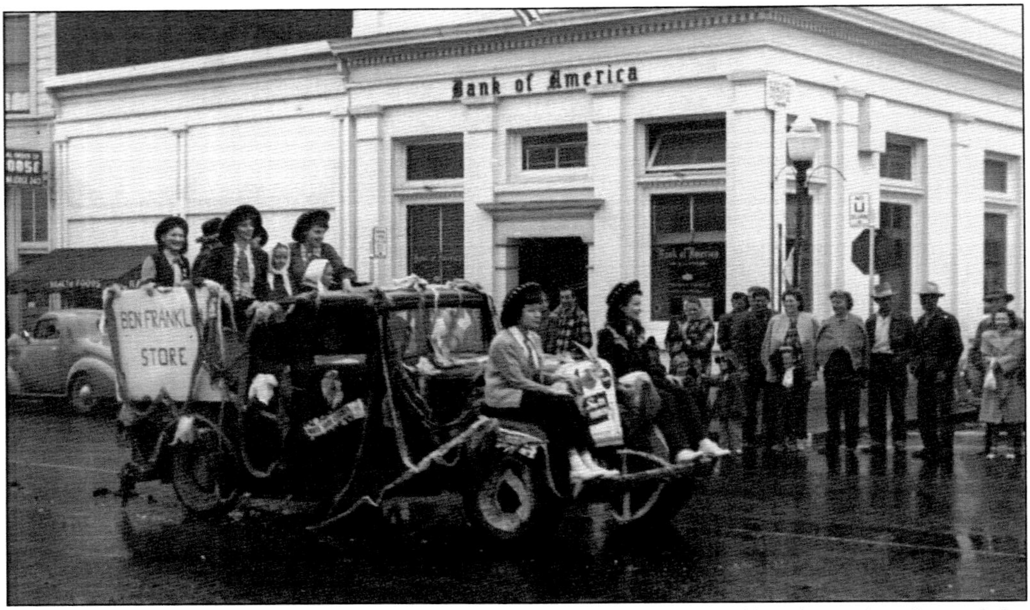

The rodeo parade has become the main summer procession, gradually taking the place of the Fourth of July parade that flourished in the early 20th century. While the weather during Rodeo Week often lives up to the reputation of "sunny Fortuna," this shot of a late-1950s or early-1960s parade on Main Street shows participants and onlookers undeterred by the celebrated Humboldt County rain.

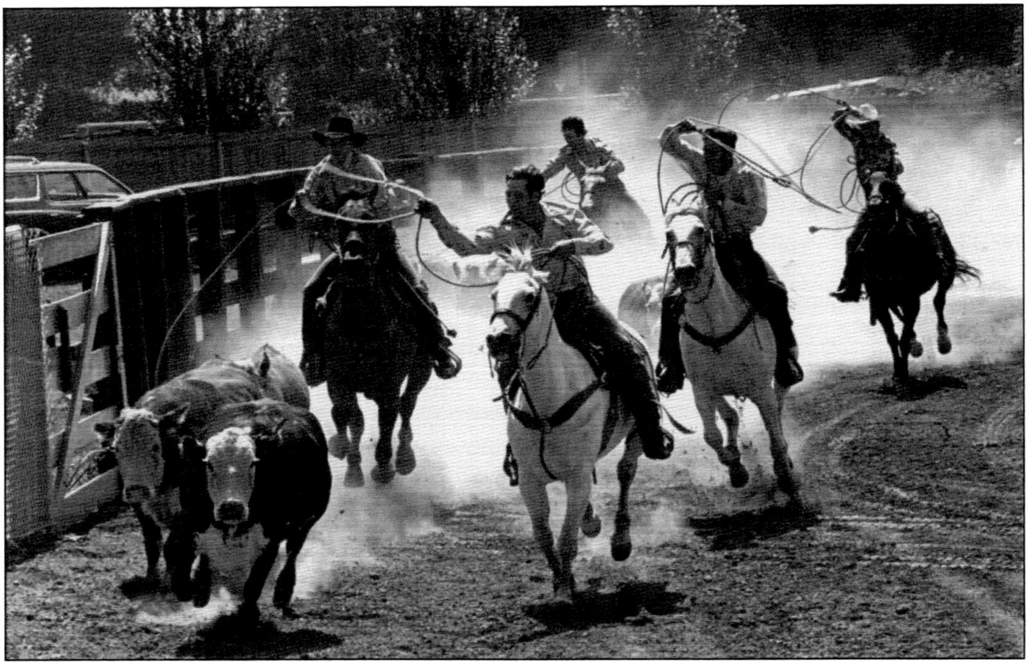

This photograph, taken in the 1970s or 1980s, captures some of the excitement of the event that has been a highlight of Fortuna's summer for nearly a century. In the words of the Fortuna Rodeo Committee in 2010, "The good old days are still happening every year at the Fortuna Rodeo."

Nine

Reflections

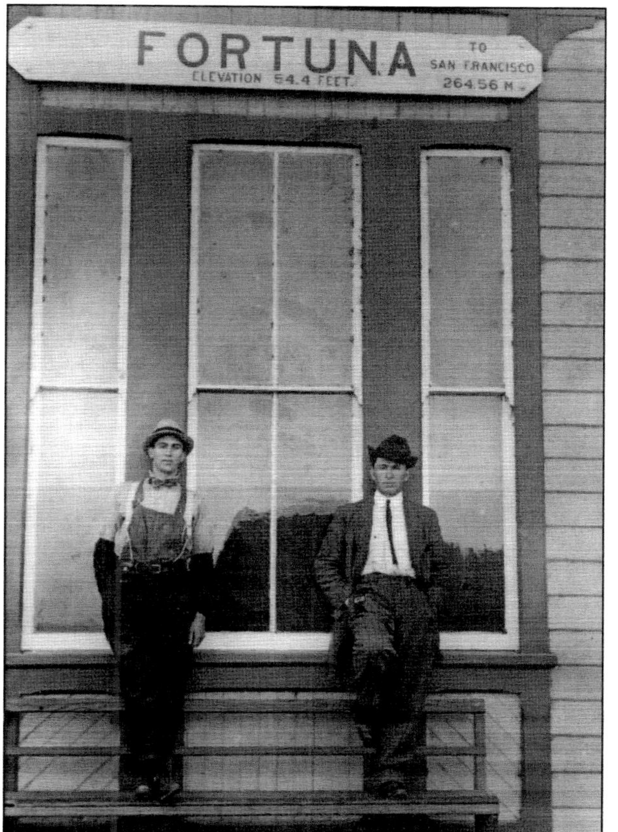

Two unidentified young railroad employees posed for this photograph outside the train depot in the early 20th century. The depot was central to community life. Early resident Paul Mudgett recalled Sunday afternoons when 100 or more people regularly gathered to watch the arrival of the passenger trains that were northbound from Shively and southbound from Eureka.

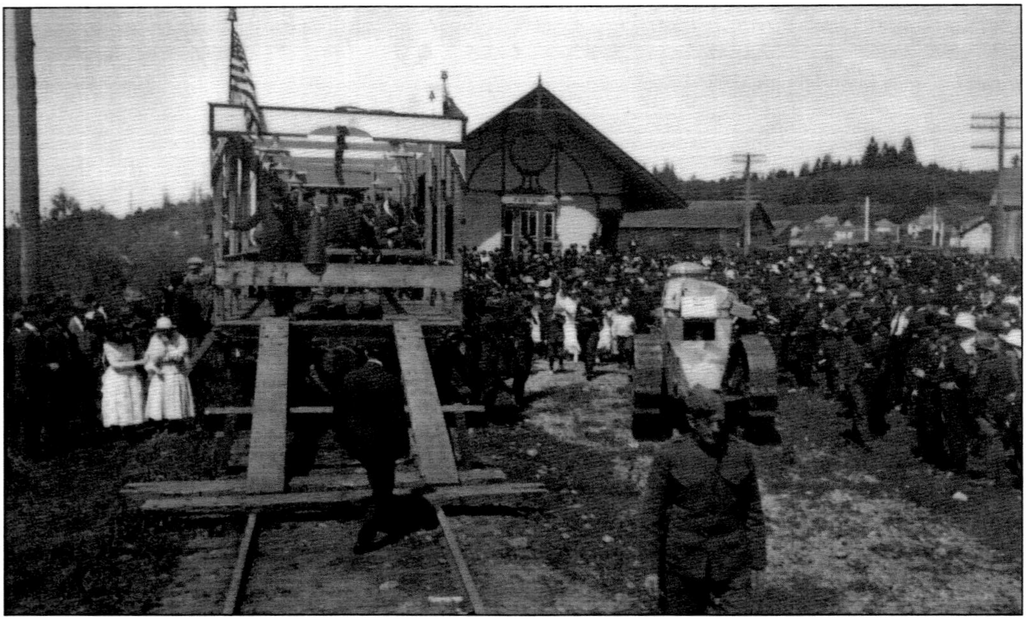

The depot was built in the late 1880s by the Eel River and Eureka Railroad and became part of the Northwestern Pacific system in 1907. The completion of the San Francisco to Eureka rail line in 1914 connected Fortuna to the world. This c. 1918 photograph shows crowds gathered at the depot to view the World War I Liberty Train. It was remembered by area historian Andrew Genzoli as carrying "captured flags, armament, and uniforms."

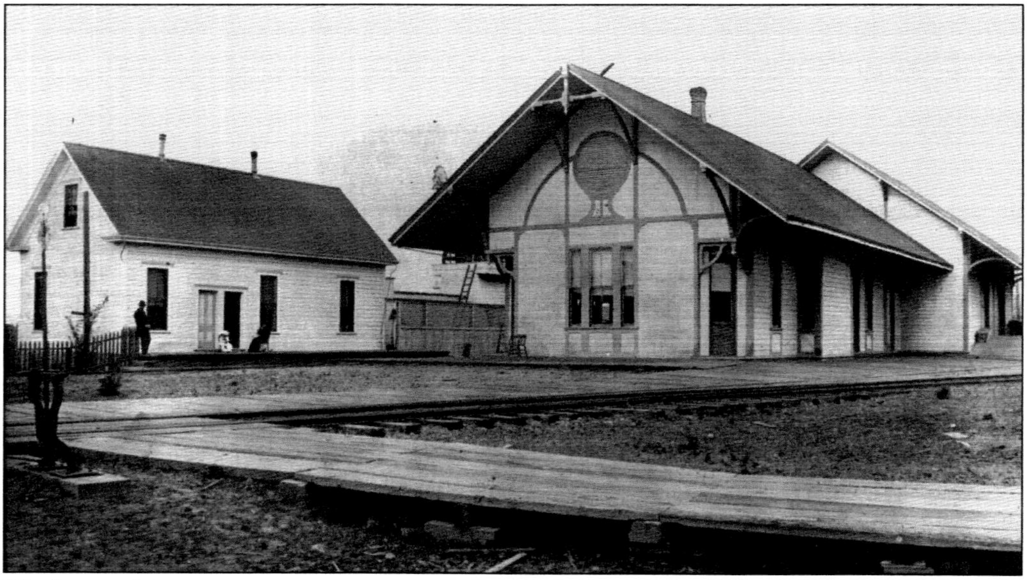

The house of the station agent or stationmaster stood across the track from the depot. The people in this c. 1894 photograph are thought to be A.W. Pratt, an early Fortuna station agent, and his family. The responsibilities of these agents included overseeing telegraph operations, ticket sales, baggage and freight handling, and passing on messages to crews of trains in motion by means of notes attached to train order hoops.

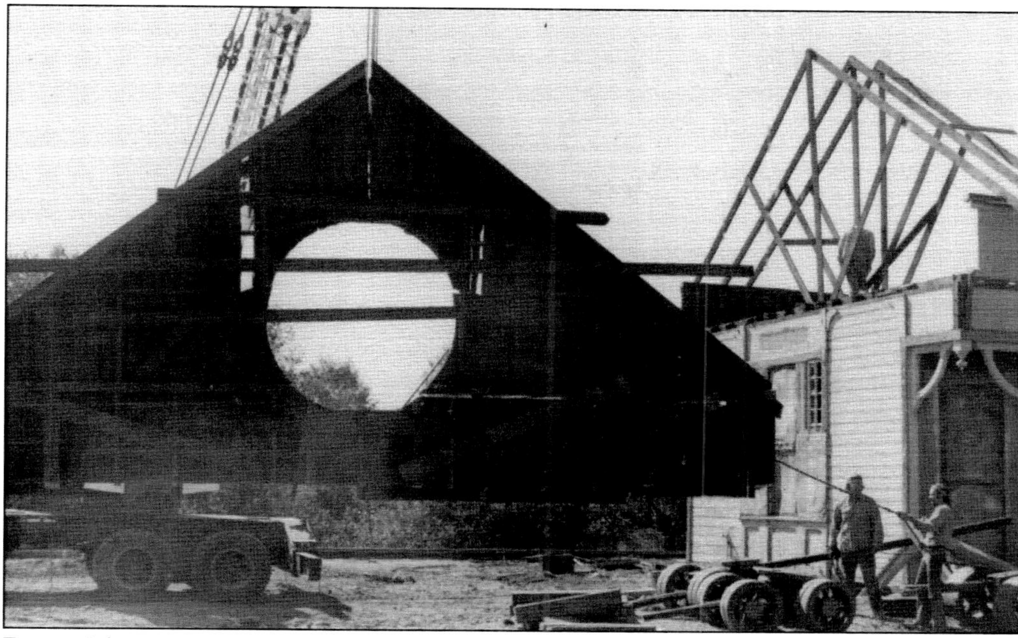

Fortuna's last passenger train service was in 1965. The depot lay dormant for nearly a decade until Fortuna city council member Beth Rundell led a community campaign to refurbish the old depot as a local-history museum. The City of Fortuna purchased the building, and a grant from the Humboldt Area Foundation contributed to its restoration. Here, volunteers and city employees remove the roof in preparation for relocating the depot to its new home.

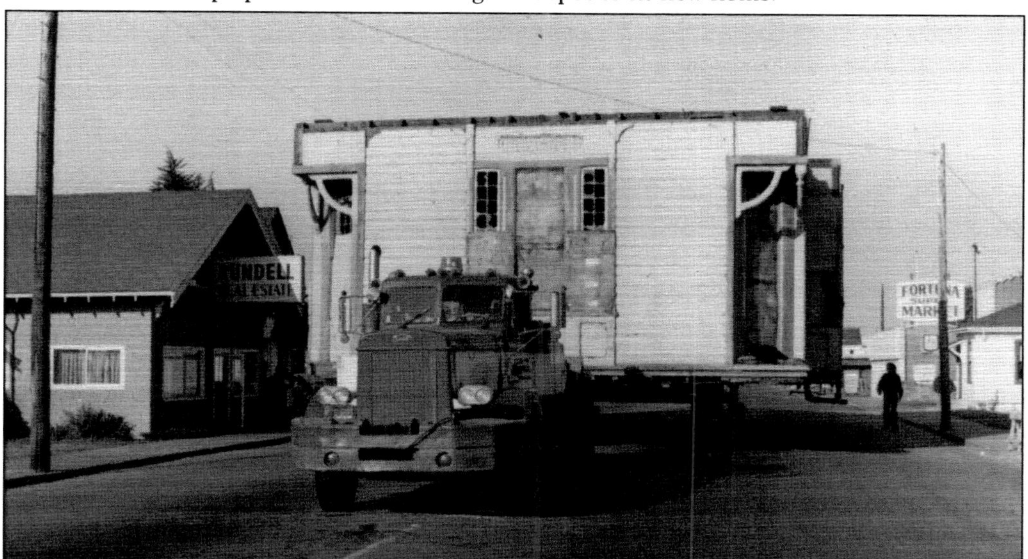

The depot made its way across downtown Fortuna around 11:00 a.m. on Saturday, October 9, 1974. Council member Beth Rundell's real estate office can be seen to the left in this photograph taken while the depot progressed down Main Street. Thousands of volunteer hours later, the Fortuna Depot Museum had its grand opening on July 4, 1976. Fortuna was named an official Bicentennial City, with the creation of the museum as its bicentennial project.

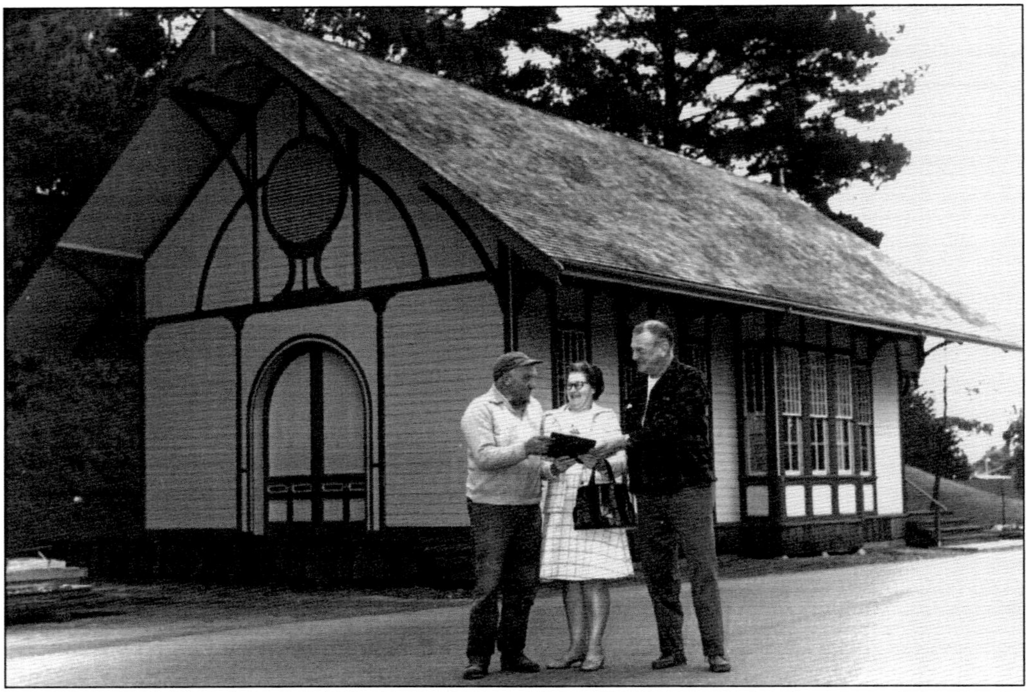

Council member Beth Rundell is shown here with Dudley Maxwell (left), a retired contractor who donated his services as building supervisor, and city carpenter Bob Ross. The image was taken in autumn of 1975 by Rudy Gillard, a local photographer who had been documenting the life of the community and its people for over two decades.

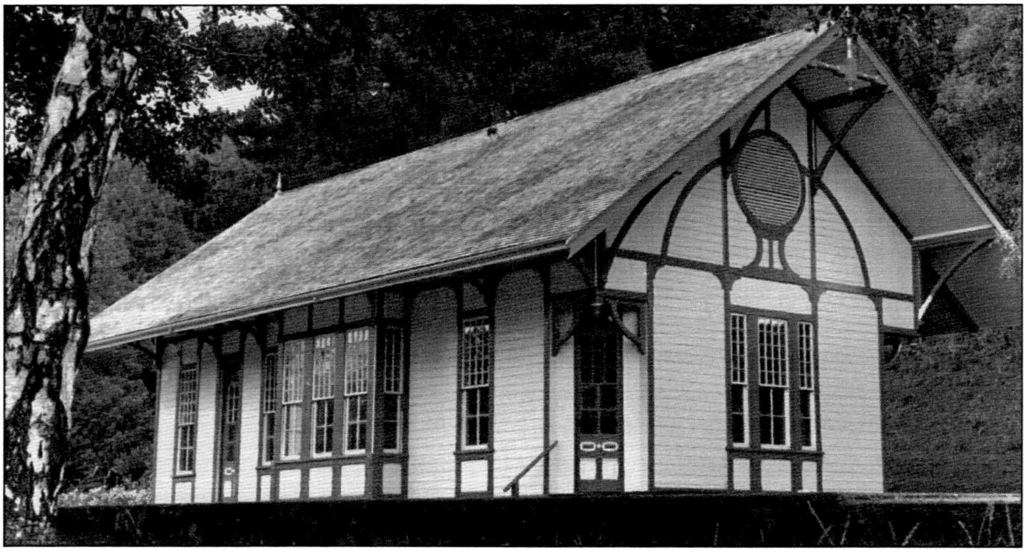

At the museum's grand opening, Andrew Genzoli paid tribute to "the chamber of commerce, to Vice Mayor Beth Rundell, who fired up the efforts to save the depot, to the city council, the Fortuna Historical Commission, to the dozens of citizens who have had a major role in saving this structure, to the many who have donated time, money, and material." He stated, "Fortuna, already famous for its long-lasting cooperative efforts, has shown the way."

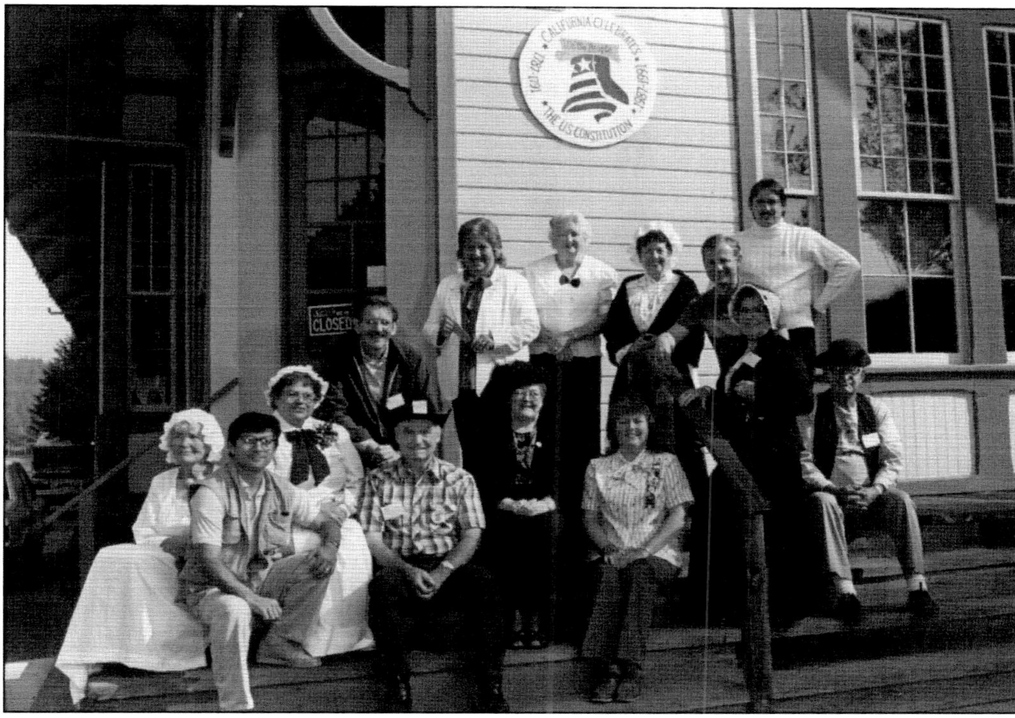

From 1987 through 1991, the Fortuna Historical Commission doubled as the Constitutional Bicentennial Committee, planning the city's celebrations of the US Constitution. Pictured at the Depot Museum are commission members, museum staff, and volunteers. Included in the photograph are Caroline Weed, Fortuna Depot Museum curator from 1986 to 2008, seated third from left; Al Rogers, commission chair and longtime Depot Museum volunteer, on the second step and wearing a dark cowboy hat; and Charlie Conant, commissioner and dedicated museum volunteer, seated at far right.

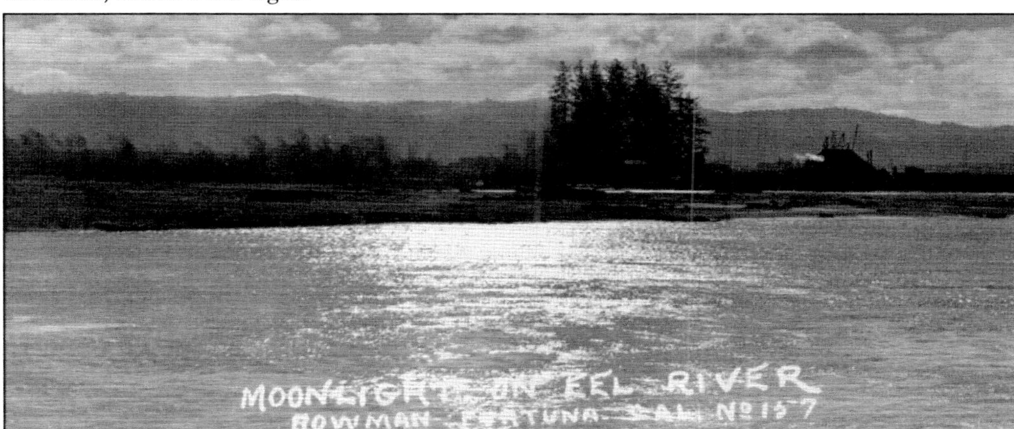

This moonlit reflection on the Eel River, photographed in 1911, captures those elements that have shaped the history of the Eel River Valley. The river—with its floods, the trees, and the rich valley soil that attracted early settlers—are all visible. These elements continue to shape the Eel River Valley and influence those who live here. Valley residents will continue to make history, but the river and the redwoods remain a constant.